Charlie Gehringer

ALSO BY JOHN C. SKIPPER
AND FROM MCFARLAND

A Biographical Dictionary of the Baseball Hall of Fame, 2nd ed. (2008)

Dazzy Vance: A Biography of the Brooklyn Dodger Hall of Famer (2007)

*Wicked Curve: The Life and Troubled Times
of Grover Cleveland Alexander* (2006)

*The Cubs Win the Pennant! Charlie Grimm,
the Billy Goat Curse, and the 1945 World Series Run* (2004)

A Biographical Dictionary of Major League Baseball Managers (2003)

*Take Me Out to the Cubs Game: 35 Former
Ballplayers Speak of Losing at Wrigley* (2000)

Umpires: Classic Baseball Stories from the Men Who Made the Calls (1997)

Inside Pitch: A Closer Look at Classic Baseball Moments (1996)

Charlie Gehringer

A Biography of the Hall of Fame Tigers Second Baseman

JOHN C. SKIPPER

McFarland & Company, Inc., Publishers
Jefferson, North Carolina, and London

LIBRARY OF CONGRESS CATALOGUING-IN-PUBLICATION DATA

Skipper, John C., 1945–
    Charlie Gehringer : a biography of the hall of fame Tigers second baseman / John C. Skipper.
    p.   cm.
    Includes bibliographical references and index.

    ISBN 978-0-7864-3574-6
    softcover : 50# alkaline paper ∞

    1. Gehringer, Charlie, d. 1993. 2. Baseball players—United States—Biography. 3. Detroit Tigers (Baseball team)—History. I. Title.
GV865.G44S45   2008
796.357092—dc22 [B]   2008031306

British Library cataloguing data are available

©2008 John C. Skipper. All rights reserved

No part of this book may be reproduced or transmitted in any form or by any means, electronic or mechanical, including photocopying or recording, or by any information storage and retrieval system, without permission in writing from the publisher.

On the cover: Charlie Gheringer, 1924 (National Baseball Hall of Fame Library, Cooperstown, New York)

Manufactured in the United States of America

McFarland & Company, Inc., Publishers
  Box 611, Jefferson, North Carolina 28640
  www.mcfarlandpub.com

For Michael Grandon

Table of Contents

Introduction   1

1. "You never really leave the game."   5
2. "If that guy is a ballplayer, then so am I."   10
3. "His potential excited me."   19
4. "You can't talk your way into a batting championship."   30
5. "He leads the league in line drives right at somebody."   43
6. "What in the hell is he talking about?"   58
7. "Every time I turn around, the guy's on second base."   72
8. "May you live ten thousand years."   82
9. "The entire town was ga-ga."   91
10. "Too much time to think."   102
11. "The Michigan Mummy."   110
12. "The cry babies."   125
13. "I kept yelling 'home, home, home.'"   136
14. "If my chatter bothers you too much..."   144
15. "He simplified where others dramatized."   149
16. "I didn't know who was and who wasn't."   157
17. "They won't get me in that suit again."   167
18. "The Good Lord needed a second baseman."   174

Chapter Notes   179
Bibliography   191
Index   195

Introduction

Charlie Gehringer used to drive Dan Daniel, the New York sportswriter, nuts. Daniel, whose home terrain was the land of Babe Ruth, Lou Gehrig, Lefty Gomez, John McGraw and Joe McCarthy, and who traveled the country reporting on the exploits of people like Dizzy Dean and Mickey Cochrane and Lefty Grove, was befuddled by the likes of Charles Leonard Gehringer, the farmboy from Fowlerville, Michigan, who grew up to be the greatest second baseman of his generation. He was an outstanding ballplayer, but he was a lousy interview. He didn't make for "good copy" to use the jargon of the newspaper trade. Daniel once lamented that Charlie was "all too drab."

Gehringer was strictly business in nearly everything he did in his adult life. Silent by nature, he did not seek the limelight and was uncomfortable when he was in it. In terms of personality, he was much like Calvin Coolidge, who was president of the United States when Charlie broke in with the Detroit Tigers in 1924 and who was known as "Silent Cal" for good reason. A contemporary of Coolidge's once remarked that he was "distinguished for character more than for heroic achievement." The same could be said for Gehringer, which helps us to understand Daniel's frustration in covering him. Character is honorable but does not often make "good copy."

When Charlie took the playing field, it was like going to the office. He once chided an opposing catcher for talking to him when he was in the batter's box. "I'm working," he said tersely. But he had an infectious sense of humor and often kidded about his shyness. Upon receiving an award at a banquet one night, he got up to the microphone and told the audience he had a reputation of being a man of few words and wasn't going to spoil that reputation. Then he sat down.

Introduction

He took care of business on the ball field by compiling a lifetime batting average of .321, a World Series batting average of .320, and an All-Star Game batting average of .500 for six games in which he played every inning. In 1937, he hit .371 and won the American League's Most Valuable Player Award. Through the end of the 2007 baseball season, he is the last player to have hit 60 doubles in one season. The hitting statistics are easy to document. But those who saw him play also remember him for his fielding. He was not given to making many spectacular plays — or at least they didn't look that way — because he studied opposing hitters, knew their strengths, and had a knack for positioning himself to be where they were most likely going to hit the ball if they hit it in his direction. Because of his fluid fielding, he became known as "The Mechanical Man" — hardly a nickname as dramatic as "The Sultan of Swat" or "The Yankee Clipper," or as fun as "Dizzy" or "Dazzy" or "Daffy," but appropriate nonetheless.

Charlie took care of business off the field as well. After his father died in 1924, he took it upon himself to care for his diabetic mother, purchasing a home where the two of them lived. He shied away from serious relationships with prospective wives because he didn't think it would be fair to either his wife or his mother to have to share his attention. His mother died in 1946. Three years later, Charlie got married at the age of 46. He and his beloved Jo had been married for almost 44 years when Charlie died in 1993.

Another way Charlie Gehringer took care of business off the field was in how he prepared for the day when he would no longer be able to compete as a ballplayer. Long before he retired, he entered a business partnership with Ray Forsyth, a friend and Detroit area auto dealer. The two men started an auto accessories sales business that flourished for years and made both men wealthy and well respected for their success in the business world.

This is the story of a man who was quietly efficient in most everything he did, a man who decided early on that he didn't want to slop hogs for the rest of his life and thought he'd try to make a go of it as a professional athlete. His baseball career allowed him to cross paths with many greats of the game, from Cobb to Kaline, and propelled him into baseball's Hall of Fame in Cooperstown. Charlie missed his Hall of Fame induction ceremony because he had a higher priority, which you will read about in this book.

Introduction

Finally, to say only that Charlie Gehringer was "strictly business" misses an important facet of the man's personality. It is more accurate to say that he was unswervingly devoted to the causes he championed and, put in that light, he was anything but drab. Like Coolidge, he is remembered for character more than heroic achievement, and that's the way he would have wanted it.

CHAPTER 1

"You never really leave the game."

During March 1983, a month in which an earthquake killed scores in the Philippines, Americans were talking about the new concept of desktop home computers, North Carolina State University was on its way to winning the NCAA basketball championship, and *Harper's Magazine* was featuring many letters to the editor in response to its article on sex and the Democrats. Spring training was under way in preparation for another Major League baseball season. President Ronald Reagan was proposing a "Star Wars" missile defense system in outer space at about the same time that residents of New York and New Jersey were reporting seeing a UFO that was triangular, with holes like you'd see in Swiss cheese and flashing lights easily visible in the night sky.

Detroit was chilly, like it always is at that time of year. A man approaching his 80th birthday came out of a hotel restaurant. There are no photographs of him as he emerged, but his reputation is such that one can surmise he was wearing a suit and tie with neatly pressed pants, the suitcoat buttoned and the tie secured with a perfect Windsor knot. There was a military straightness to the way he carried himself, looking much too tall, sturdy and straight for a man his age, the kind of man who would be deemed elderly only by someone who paid attention solely to the person's date of birth. His gray eyes were liquid as if always in a gaze that was at once arresting, the look of a man either deep in thought or suspicious of something, and yet at other times seemed wistful, kind and unthreatening. Either way, this was a man who took it all in.

He was not an unpleasant man, nor was he solemn. He was as meticulous as a watchmaker and had made a lifetime of seeing that everything was always in place, from the neatly combed and parted hair, now gray, on the top of his head to dotting the i's and crossing the t's on the hundreds of contracts he had drawn up or signed over the past 60 years. His given name was Charles, but in his signature, he shortened it to "Chas." for he didn't believe in wasting time or energy.

As he left the restaurant, walking at his usual brisk pace, a man and a woman who appeared to be in their 60s approached him. The man was wide-eyed as he got the older man's attention. "You're Charlie Gehringer, aren't you?" The older man, not ever given to speaking more than he had to, gave only a polite nod. "My gosh, you were my favorite ballplayer. Nice to see you looking so well."

Indeed, Charlie Gehringer did look well. Onlookers would hardly notice the occasional slight hitch in his gait, the result of an arthritic hip. He was most probably amused by the reaction of the man and woman he had just encountered, for he had not worn a baseball uniform in 40 years. In fact, he had just been interviewed by Frederick C. Klein of *The Wall Street Journal*, not for anything he had done in baseball but for the example he set as a successful auto accessories executive after his playing career was over.

The newspaper article also featured Dr. Charles Huggins, a Nobel Prize–winning cancer researcher; Royal Little, a retired corporate executive; Gloria Swanson, an actress from yesteryear; and Sam Ervin, the country lawyer still practicing, who, as a U.S. senator 10 years earlier, chaired the Judiciary Committee that voted to impeach President Richard Nixon. "All five are at least well-off financially and their fame assures them of the kind of attention and respect accorded to few contemporaries," wrote Klein. He noted that each was blessed with good genes and good luck, "but their determination to be purposely active" was what set them apart from others their age. It was pretty good company for Charlie Gehringer — a man who chose baseball as a career more than 60 years earlier over his mother's strong objections, so that he would not spend the rest of his life slopping hogs and doing laborious farm work like his father had.

Gehringer was amused by the couple in the hotel. "I retired from baseball 40 years ago," he said. "But to some people, I'll always be a ballplayer. Under those circumstances, you never really leave the game," he said.[1]

Charlie signed with the Detroit Tigers in 1924 and played under the watchful eye of Ty Cobb, the Tigers' great hitting but mean-spirited manager. "Cobb was a hateful guy. I think he wanted it that way; felt it made him a better player. I never heard him say a good word about anybody," said Gehringer. Later, Gehringer played for Mickey Cochrane, who was nearly as intense as Cobb in his desire to win but had a much better rapport with his players. In between, his managers were George Moriarity and Bucky Harris, who were nondescript compared to Cobb and Cochrane.[2]

Gehringer played for the Tigers for parts of 19 seasons and was considered by contemporaries to be the best second baseman of his generation and maybe as good or better than Nap Lajoie, who played in the American League in its infancy. Gehringer had a lifetime batting average of .320, a World Series batting average of .321, an All-Star Game batting average of .500, and was the starting second baseman in the first six All-Star Games, playing every inning.

He was among the top five in batting in the American League five times and won the batting title in 1937 with a .371 average. He was in the top five in runs scored nine times and led the league twice. He was in the top five in hits seven times and led the league twice. He was in the top five in doubles six times and led the league twice. He was in the top five in triples four times and led the league twice. He played in 150 or more games nine years and led the league in games played four times. He is tied for fourth all-time in number of seasons with 200 hits or more (7) and tied for fourth all-time in number of seasons with more than 40 doubles (7). He played in more than 500 consecutive games twice in his career, one span that started in 1927 and stretched into 1931 and the next starting later in 1931 and ending in 1935. In nine seasons he played in at least 98 percent of the Tigers' games. He had hitting streaks of 21 and 20 games in his career.

Gehringer had many great days at the plate. On Aug. 5, 1929, he hit three triples in one game against the Washington Senators. Nine days later, on "Charlie Gehringer Day" in Detroit, he got four hits — three singles and a home run — and stole home in a game against the Yankees. On May 27, 1939, he became the first player ever to hit for the cycle in natural progression — single, double, triple then home run — in one game.

The batting statistics rank him as a great ballplayer, and he was elected to the Hall of Fame in 1949, just six years after he quit playing. But many who saw him play say he was an even better fielder than a hitter. His fielding wasn't flashy because he knew opposing hitters and their habits so well that he positioned himself for each batter to be in the best place for a ball hit in his direction. In that way, he made routine plays out of what would have been difficult ones for most second basemen.

His teammate, pitcher Elden Auker, put it this way: "He had an uncanny knack for positioning for hitters, and the hands of a magician. No such thing as a bad-hop grounder in the vicinity of Gehringer. His hands would adjust so quickly, so smoothly, the bad hop was barely visible to the audience. It was just another out."[3]

George Lerchen grew up watching Tiger games at Briggs Stadium and eventually played with the Tigers for one season. He too marveled at Gehringer in the field. "He made plays at second base you wouldn't believe. You'd say to yourself: Where did he come from?"[4]

There aren't many film clips of Charlie Gehringer making spectacular plays, but the statistics paint a vivid picture of what he accomplished. He is second all-time in career assists by a second baseman (7,068). Only Eddie Collins had more. He is sixth all-time in career putouts and seventh all-time in career double plays.[5]

Charlie didn't showboat nor did he brag. He knew that few ballplayers are in the limelight because of their fielding. "Hitting is the thing that people remember most vividly," he once said. "You can make the greatest fielding play in the world and they probably won't remember it the next day. Particularly in the infield."[6]

He went through his entire career as one of baseball's most eligible bachelors. Teammates say he went to mass at the Catholic church just about every morning, accompanying his mother when the Tigers were home. After his father died in 1924, the loyalty and responsibility Gehringer felt to take care of his mother, a diabetic, was one of the things that curtailed his social life. That, and his preference to be the quietest person in any room he happened to be in.

The stories of his thrifty use of words are almost as legendary as his feats on the baseball diamond. He played football as well as baseball at the University of Michigan. One day his baseball coach ran into him at football practice. "Now, don't get too excited out there," he said. Young Charlie looked at him with chagrin and simply replied, "I won't."

When Gehringer had retired from baseball, a writer asked him to expound on the importance of good fielding in baseball games. The writer knew better than to think he was going to hear a Gettysburg Address. Gehringer simply said, "Infielders don't win games. They save them."[7]

1. "You never really leave the game."

This is the story of Charles Leonard Gehringer, in some ways the Theodore Roosevelt of baseball because, indeed, he spoke softly but carried a big stick — and glove. He left baseball when he realized his skills had begun to diminish and then spent 25 years as a successful businessman. He did not marry until his baseball career was over but was as committed to his beloved "Jo" for 44 years as he had been to anything or anybody before he met her. Theirs was a love story that never diminished. Summing up his life's work in that interview with Klein 40 years after his baseball career was over, Charlie said, "Us ballplayers do things backwards from most people, you know. First we play, then we retire and go to work."[8]

CHAPTER 2

"If that guy is a ballplayer, then so am I."

Fowlerville, Michigan, is so small that even most mapmakers ignore it. To the townspeople, about 1,000 of them, it has a clear, distinct identity. To others, the best way to describe Fowlerville is to say how close it is to other places — 25 miles from Lansing, 32 from Ann Arbor, 57 from Detroit. "Fowlerville is such a small town that its 'suburbs' consist of farm houses, fields, cows, horses, chickens and pigs," said one writer passing through town.[1]

Originally named Cedar, the town was first settled by Ralph Fowler in 1836. By 1838, it was large enough to have its own post office. Eleven years later, a man named Amos Adams platted the town and renamed it Fowlerville, after its first settler. By 1871, it was organized as a village.

It was in this rural community that Lenard Gehringer and his wife, Therese, both German immigrants, settled after their marriage near the end of the 19th century. The Gehringers were farmers and proud of the life they had in their new country and their ability to have a home, raise a family, and earn a livelihood by tilling the soil, planting crops, feeding livestock, and milking cows.[2]

Not far away, the industrial revolution was in full force. Detroit was emerging as the "Motor City," the automobile capital of the world. Eventually it would have the Packard plant on Grand Boulevard, the Hudson plant on East Jefferson (bankrolled by J.L. Hudson, the wealthy department store magnate), and the Hupmobile plant on Bellevue, all forerunners to Ford, Chevrolet, Buick, Oldsmobile, Pontiac, Cadillac, and all the rest.

2. "If that guy is a ballplayer then so am I."

In Fowlerville, about an hour away if you used any of those vehicles, day-to-day life was much simpler and quieter. It was the kind of life that Lenard and Therese Gehringer envisioned turning over to their children someday. Charles Leonard Gehringer, the fourth of five children, was born on May 11, 1903.

The Gehringers began their farm life by working several acres of another man's land in Livingston County, northwest of Detroit, and splitting the earnings 50–50 with the owner. When Charlie was in high school, his parents purchased their own 230-acre dairy and grain farm just outside of Fowlerville. "We raised corn, oats, wheat, barley — everything," said Gehringer. And of course there were cows to milk early in the morning. "My brother, being five years older, ran all the machinery so my mother and sisters and I had to do the tedious jobs," he said, things like weeding, shocking up the wheat, digging potatoes, milking cows — most anything that needed to be done by hand. The family had a hired hand who helped with the chores, but one of Charlie's lasting memories of him was the day he introduced him to chewing tobacco. "He used to catch me when I was a kid and plug my mouth full of it, trying to get me to chew," said Gehringer. "Almost choked me to death. As soon as I would get up off the ground I would spit it out."[3]

Much to the chagrin of his parents, Charlie didn't care much for farming. But the chores he did helped him develop strong arms and legs, and he took a liking to athletics. As a youngster, Charlie started following baseball through the newspapers and kept a scrapbook that he filled with clippings about Detroit Tiger games and players such as Ty Cobb, Harry Heilmann, and Bobby Veach. Charlie and his brother Al converted a pasture near the family's barn into a make-shift baseball field. They mowed it, filled used grain sacks with sand for bases, and invited the neighbor kids over to play. There were no organized teams; the kids just chose up sides and played ball. The next day, it might be the same youngsters playing but the teams would be different, and that is the way it would go throughout the summer. Charlie wasn't big, but he was strong and could hold his own playing with boys often older than he was.

At Fowlerville High School, Charlie played football, basketball and baseball. Many thought he had a promising future in basketball. In 1920, Fowlerville finished second in the state high school basketball tournament, losing in overtime to Holly, a small town near Flint. On his baseball team, young Gehringer was a pitcher who lost only one game in his high school career, a 2–1 decision to Detroit Northern. Later, he tried pitching in professional baseball but soon learned there was a big difference between what he was used to and the pros. "They started knocking me around pretty good and I said, 'well, there must be a difference.'" So he gave up pitching and became an infielder. But wherever Charlie played, he could hit. It seemed that from the first time he picked up a bat in his father's farmyard through the day he called it quits after 19 seasons with the Detroit Tigers, Charlie knew what to do with a bat in his hand.

Gehringer broke his mother's heart when he went off to college at the nearby University of Michigan in Ann Arbor in the fall of 1922 with his eye on a career in sports instead of farming. Wanting to be in sports and perhaps coach some day, he loaded up on physical education classes as best he could and played football, basketball and baseball — what was expected of future gym teachers and coaches. Ironically, he lettered in basketball but not in baseball.[4]

During this time Ray Fisher, the baseball coach, happened upon Gehringer at football practice and told him not to get too serious about football. Years later, in recalling the incident, Charlie said he never intended to get heavily involved in football. Fowlerville High School didn't have a football team, so Gehringer had no experience in the game. He only went out for football at Michigan because, as a P.E. major, it was expected of him.[5]

In the summer, Gehringer played baseball, first in the barn yards, then at county fair grounds, and eventually for an independent team out of Angola, Indiana. One of his teammates there was Benny Frey, who later played for the Cincinnati Reds.

The word was starting to spread about Charlie Gehringer, the ballplayer. There are several versions to the story of how he was discovered by the Tigers, but all of them involve Tiger outfielder Bobby Veach and Floyd Smith, Veach's hunting friend who lived near Fowlerville and had seen Gehringer play. One popular version is that Veach heard about Charlie and decided to see him play while he was on a hunting trip near Fowlerville. Another version is that Veach set up the tryout just going on word of mouth without ever seeing Gehringer play. However, this is unlikely. Veach was a veteran ballplayer who spent 11 years in the Tiger organization and was no slouch. He hit over .300 eight times, drove in

2. "If that guy is a ballplayer then so am I."

100 runs or more six times, led the American League in RBIs twice and tied for the lead another time but always seemed to play in the shadow of Cobb, Wahoo Sam Crawford, and Harry Heilmann. Veach was a baseball man through and through and almost certainly would not have recommended someone without seeing him play. For one thing, no player would want to incur the wrath of Ty Cobb if the prospect turned out to be a busher.[6]

Gehringer's version of the story was that a Tiger fan from Fowlerville (probably Smith) was a hunting friend of Veach's and asked if Veach could arrange a tryout for Charlie in Detroit. Veach agreed and the tryout was set up.[7]

There was just one sticking point. Lenard and Therese Gehringer were still holding out hope that Charlie would return to the farm. And Charlie, who had a profound respect for his parents, wanted their blessing. His father was the first to give in, realizing Charlie had a right to lead his own life. For Therese, the decision was much more difficult for she wanted what was best for her son and didn't think that included professional baseball. But she too gave reluctant approval. So in 1923 Charlie, 20 years old, shy and wide-eyed at what lay ahead of him, left Fowlerville and headed for the big city of Detroit, carrying with him barely more than the clothes on his back and some pocket money.

Gehringer went to Navin Field in Detroit, named after Tiger owner Frank Navin, and went through workouts under the watchful eye of player-manager Ty Cobb, the not-too-long-ago object of adoration for young Charlie's scrapbooks. By this time, Charlie had abandoned his desire to pitch. His brief experience in independent leagues convinced him he didn't have the right stuff for that, so in college he played third base, and he went to the Tiger tryouts as a third baseman — and a hitter.

The Tigers finished second in the American League in 1923 with an 83–71 record but were 16 games behind the front-running New York Yankees. Detroit had pretty much a no-name pitching staff except for George "Hooks" Dauss, who was 21–13. Dauss pitched 15 years in the major leagues and is the answer to a popular trivia question in Detroit because he still holds the Tiger record for most wins with 222. Other pitchers included Bert Cole, who was 13–5, the best year of his six-year career, but he never won more than seven in any other year. Sylvester Johnson was 12–7 in a year when he managed to remain pretty much injury-free. He played for

19 years with four teams and suffered the misfortune of having balls hit right at him throughout his career. He was struck with line drives that broke his cheekbone, ribs, three fingers on three different occasions, and his big toe. Herman Pillette tied for second-most wins among Tiger starters in 1923 with 14, but lost 19. In his four-season career, Pillette won 34 games, 33 of which came in two years—19 in 1922 and 14 in 1923. Ken Holloway also won 14, losing only 6, the best season of a nine-year career that saw him win 64 games.

Clearly, the Tigers stayed in ballgames because they could hit. Harry Heilmann led the league with a .403 average, one of four batting championships he won with averages surpassing .390. His lifetime batting average was .342. Cobb, Gehringer's manager and mentor, hit .340. The two future Hall of Famers formed a formidable duo in the heart of the Tiger batting order. The third outfielder, Veach, the man who "discovered" Charlie Gehringer, was no patsy at the plate, hitting .321. Shortstop Topper Rigney hit .315, and catcher Johnny Basler just missed the .300 mark, finishing with .298. At second base was Del Pratt, a 10-year veteran who was a good hitter, a slick fielder, and a feisty competitor.

The Tigers hovered at about the .500 level for ⅔ of the season but then put together several short winning streaks of two, three, and four games and started climbing up the standings. They ended the year with a five-game winning streak, but by that time, the Yankees had long since clinched the American League championship.

This was the environment the 20-year-old farm kid from Fowlerville found when he went to Detroit for the tryout. But Gehringer was too young and too dream-filled to be scared. For some youngsters, their future is ahead of them, out there somewhere, but in the fall of 1923, Charlie Gehringer's future was all around him as he stood on the diamond at Navin Field.

Charlie took the field and did what came naturally. He hit line drives, some with power and, playing third base, fielded ground balls with ease. Cobb was so impressed with him that he climbed the stadium stairs in his spikes to find Frank Navin. He wanted the owner to get a look at the young prospect. Gehringer signed a contract that included a bonus of $300. Charlie said later he would have signed for nothing. He had two big challenges ahead of him. He had to prove himself as a professional ballplayer—and he had to tell his mother.

2. "If that guy is a ballplayer then so am I."

The Tigers had thoughts about keeping Gehringer with the big league club, and they might have done it except for some problems with one of their minor league teams. The London-Ontario team in Canada got off to a rough start and needed some punch in its lineup. Manager Jack Beatty asked traveling secretary Bill Rhodes to go to Detroit to see if Cobb and the Tigers had anyone they could spare. Cobb agreed to "loan" them Gehringer and shortstop Frank Naleway, partly because he wanted Gehringer to get the feel of playing second base, where Cobb envisioned him fitting into the Tiger scheme.[8]

Gehringer joined the minor league ballclub at Bay City, Michigan. In the fourth inning, in his second at-bat, he got his first hit in professional baseball — a triple off John Wilson — and it produced his first RBI. A man named Eiffert, whose first name has been lost, had singled and scored on the Gehringer triple. Charlie finished the day 1-for-4 and had three putouts and four assists in a flawless game at second base. Bay City overcame a 4–1 deficit, scoring two in the sixth, one in the eighth, and one in the ninth to secure the victory.

The next day was the home opener for London, also against Bay City. London won 8–7. Charlie had two hits in three at-bats, both singles, and scored two runs. He also committed his first error in pro ball. On May 14 at Flint, he hit a single, double and triple in five at-bats. He was having a little difficulty adjusting to the roughness of minor league infields and committed his second error of the season. But clearly, he was proving that he belonged in professional baseball and that sooner or later Cobb would collect on his "loan" and bring his budding young second baseman back to Detroit.[9]

Gehringer's First Professional Game

London	AB	R	H	Bay City	AB	R	H
Sandquist 3b	2	1	0	Hegedorn ss	4	1	1
Naleway ss	4	1	1	Hughes rf	4	0	0
Parker lf	4	0	1	Connolly 3b	4	1	1
Nason cf	1	1	0	Hauger lf	4	1	0
Beatty 1b	3	0	1	Tomer 1b	4	0	1
Eiffert c	3	1	2	Harris lf	3	0	1
Germain rf	4	0	1	Pryrock 2b	4	0	2
Gehringer 2b	4	0	1	Boelzie c	4	1	2

CHARLIE GEHRINGER

London	AB	R	H		Bay City	AB	R	H
Fields p	4	0	0		Wilson p	3	1	2
					Lahsie p	1	0	0
Totals	29	4	7		Totals	35	5	10

```
London     0 0 1 2 1 0 0 0 0 — 4   7  3
Bay City   0 0 1 0 0 2 0 1 1 — 5  10  0
```

Doubles — Wilson, Connolly, Hauger. Triple — Gehringer. Sacrifices — Hegedorn, Lahaie, Harris, Hughes, Naleway, Nason. Stolen bases — Tomer, Hegedorn, Naleway. Double plays — Pryrock to Hegedorn. Struck out — By Wilson 3; By Lahaie 4; By Fields 1; Bases on balls — Off Wilson 4; Off Fields 1; Time — 1:51; Umpires — Harper and Ward.

Even as a young player, Charlie was strictly business, even in posing for a picture with a bat in his hand ca. 1924 (photograph courtesy of the National Baseball Hall of Fame).

While Gehringer was playing in Canada, tragedy struck back home. His father, Lenard Gehringer, died in Fowlerville. The German immigrant farmer, who had trouble understanding the importance of playing ball but nonetheless supported his son in what he wanted to do, was now gone. He never knew that his son would make it to the major leagues and one day be inducted into baseball's Hall of Fame. Charlie took three days off to attend his father's funeral. On his next paycheck, he discovered he had been docked three days' pay. He earned $3,500 for playing ball for London. The minor league club paid part of it; Frank Navin paid the remainder. They saved a lit-

2. "If that guy is a ballplayer then so am I."

tle cash by not paying Charlie while he was at his dad's funeral, a circumstance that the young, hungry ballplayer thought was "pretty chintzy."[10]

Joe E. Brown, who would later become a famous comedian in movies, radio and television, was also a fledgling infielder on that London team. Many years later, after Gehringer was an established star and Brown had abandoned his baseball career, the comic, with tongue in cheek, took some credit for Charlie's success. He said Gehringer was shy and kept pretty much to himself and didn't have the nerve to ask for more playing time so he could show what he could do. "He is just about to give up and go home when he notices me working around second base and taking batting practice," said Brown. He said Charlie watched him for a half-hour and came to a career-altering conclusion. He figured "If that guy is a ballplayer, then so am I," said Brown. With confidence up once again, Gehringer went on to have a tremendous year with London.[11]

Gehringer hit .292 for London and was called back up to the Tigers in September and did all right for himself—but not right away. He made his major league debut September 22. Recalling his first big league game years later, Gehringer said, "I had a tough day. I booted two or three balls and didn't get any hits. On my last trip to the plate, I thought I had one. I smashed the ball to leftfield but somebody jumped up in front of the scoreboard and made a great catch." He appeared in four more games and more than made up for his bad first game. Charlie got up 13 times overall and had six hits, all singles, for a .462 average. He also had an RBI and a stolen base.[12]

He must have gone to spring training in 1925 with hopes or at least thoughts of making the team. But Cobb had plans of grooming Gehringer to someday replace the aging Del Pratt at second base, and Pratt had one more good year left in him. He had played for the Yankees and Boston before coming over to Detroit after the 1922 season. The former running back at the University of Alabama was hard-nosed and always ready for a fight if the situation called for it—just the kind of player that manager Cobb could relate to—and it didn't hurt that Pratt was regarded as one of the best defensive second basemen in the league. He led the American League in total chances five times. The Tigers had a capable backup for him in Fred Haney who was experienced at playing both third base and second base. All of this spelled another year in the minors for young Gehringer, who was sent to Toronto.

Charlie responded by having a good year. Playing a full season, he hit .325 with 206 hits, 25 home runs, and 108 runs batted in. Once again, the Tigers brought him up in September, but this time, he didn't fare too well. He got into eight games but had only 3 hits in 18 at-bats with no extra base hits or runs batted in. Still, with the season he had in Toronto and the retirement of Del Pratt at the end of the 1925 season, Gehringer had high hopes that 1926 would be the year he would stick with the Major League club.

CHAPTER 3

"His potential excited me."

Ty Cobb was a man almost everybody respected but nobody liked. His accomplishments were undeniable. As an outfielder for 24 years, all but two with the Tigers, Cobb held more than 90 all-time records by the time he retired. His lifetime batting average of .366 is still the highest. He hit over .400 three times and won 12 batting titles. In 1915, he stole 96 bases, a record that held up for 47 years until Maury Wills of the Los Angeles Dodgers stole 102, the first of many players who would eventually top the 100 mark. Cobb's 892 career stolen bases were the highest until Lou Brock and then Rickey Henderson both surpassed him long after he retired. His career hit total of 4,192 and career triple total of 295 are second highest all-time.

Despite all of his feats as a ballplayer, Cobb is equally remembered for his meanness. The story that he once killed a heckler under the stands after a ballgame has been cast into doubt in recent years, but Cobb never disputed the story and was well known for the brawls he started or more than willingly joined. At Navin Field, visiting teams had to make their way through the Tiger dugout to get from their clubhouse to the playing field. Cobb made a habit of sitting in the dugout, sharpening his spikes, as opposing players passed him. "I always had to be right in any argument I was in. I always had to be first," he said. And he expected the same attitude out of his players.[1]

Gehringer said nobody liked Cobb as a manager, primarily because he had trouble relating to players who didn't have the same talent level as he did in his prime. Bill Moore came up with the Tigers in 1925 and pitched in only one game — one inning, in fact. He walked three batters and threw ball one to the fourth hitter. Cobb didn't even come out to get him, said Moore. He just hollered for me to get out of there. "I never had any use for the man," he said.

Moore recalled seeing the Tigers playing an exhibition game against the Georgia Tech college team. On one play, Cobb headed for second base with a full head of steam and his spikes high, at about eye level of the second baseman. The infielder grabbed the ball, reached down, and tagged Cobb on the chest for the out. Cobb got up, picked up a handful of dirt, and threw it in the face of the surprised college player. That was Cobb. It didn't matter whom the Tigers were playing.

One time, Cobb hoped to get Bobby Veach out of a slump and talked Harry Heilmann into needling him continually to get his dander up and his competitive juices flowing. Veach responded by developing an intense dislike for Heilmann. At the end of the season, Cobb went home to Georgia without explaining his little ploy. Veach had little to do with Heilmann — and Heilmann, whom Cobb had befriended and mentored, lost any respect he had for his manager.

Cobb was held in low regard throughout the league, a reputation he worked hard to earn and seemed to relish. He was extremely jealous of Babe Ruth, who had become the darling of baseball because of his home run power. When the Tigers played the Yankees, whenever Cobb got where Ruth could overhear him, Cobb referred to him as "Nigger" and said things like, "Do you smell something funny around here? I think it's a polecat."[2]

This was the atmosphere in which Gehringer found himself when he joined the ballclub for the 1926 season, which turned out to be Cobb's last as manager. He rented a bungalow from a family originally from Fowlerville at 12th and Pingree Street for $10 a week plus meals. He got along well with Cobb at first, with the manager working with him on his hitting — even letting him use his bat, sitting with him on the long train rides and just generally looking after his young ballplayer. Cobb did everything but play him.

Young Gehringer was baffled by his manager's sudden mood changes. Most of the other players were used to it. An incident early in 1926 may have led to Charlie riding the pines for a while. It occurred as the Tigers headed up north from spring training. During an exhibition game with one of the town teams in a southern city, Cobb became upset with his ballclub because of their lethargic play. As they came off the field, he seemed to single out Gehringer and said, "C'mon, let's make some noise

3. "His potential excited me."

Ty Cobb was Gehringer's first manager in the major leagues in 1924. Charlie described him as a man almost everyone respected but also hated (photograph courtesy of the National Baseball Hall of Fame).

out there." Charlie, who wasn't given to saying much to anybody, responded, "I'm making as much noise as anyone else." Cobb gave him an icy stare.

Pratt was gone, but the Tigers had acquired veteran Frank O'Rourke who was their regular second baseman in 1925 and opened the season at second in 1926. So Gehringer, happy to be with the big club rather than in the minors, bided his time on the bench. He got his break in a way he never would have expected. "Some of us get our starts in strange ways," said Gehringer. "I was sitting on the Detroit bench, wondering if I would ever get a break." The break came when O'Rourke, who was 35 at the time and who was to spend 70 years in baseball, was stricken with a case of the measles. How many times does that ever happen, Gehringer mused years later, reflecting on his career. "Well, Frank got sick, I went to second, and I stayed there for quite a while," he said.[3]

The measles did more than sideline the affable O'Rourke. It ultimately cost him his job with the Tigers. In January 1927, he was traded to the St. Louis Browns, where he played five seasons before retiring. Ironically, O'Rourke was a native of Ontario, Canada, where Gehringer enjoyed a minor league season that propelled him into the majors.[4]

Charlie got his chance with the Tigers just a year after another temporary illness changed the course of two careers. In 1925, Wally Pipp, the Yankee first baseman, asked to be taken out of the lineup because of a headache. He was replaced by Lou Gehrig, who remained there for 2,130 games, and Pipp was shipped off to Cincinnati.

On April 28, 1926, Gehringer started at second base for the Tigers and stayed there for the next 17 years. The Tigers had opened the season on a hopeful note, winning three in a row after losing on opening day. But then they lost five in a row and were struggling to get back to .500. At the end of the day on April 28, after losing to Chicago 9–5, Detroit had a 5–8 record and was already five games behind the league-leading Yankees.

Before the season started, Cobb had decided to concentrate on managing and to use himself sparingly, primarily as a pinch hitter. But the Tigers always seemed to do better when he was in the lineup, even though he was older, slower, and heavier than he had been in his prime. In 1925, when Cobb was in the starting lineup, the Tigers were 58–46. Without him, they were 23–27. So on April 27, a day before Gehringer replaced O'Rourke at second base, Cobb wrote his own name on the lineup card—and hit a single, double, triple and drove in four runs as the Tigers beat the White Sox 8–7. The Georgia Peach still had it. He just didn't have it as often as he once did.

The Tigers were depending on their hitting because the pitching staff was in a state of flux. Hooks Dauss and Ken Holloway, starters in years past, were now seeing a lot of bullpen duty. The starters were Earl Whitehill, on his way to a successful big league career, Ed Wells, one of the few players who said he always got along well with Cobb, Sam Gibson, and Lil Stoner.

"It's a funny thing," said Wells. "The opposition hated Cobb. He was a hustler and he'd spike you to get that base." Wells, who pitched for Cobb for seven years, said he knew that many of his teammates—Heilmann, Dauss, Holloway—didn't like the manager. Some despised him. "But me and Cobb always got along great. I thought a lot of him and he thought a lot of me," he said.[5]

Whitehill had become the ace of the Tiger staff, which put him in a better standing than others to challenge Cobb's authority. The lefthander was temperamental on the mound and would chastise teammates for not hustling, umpires for making bad calls, and Cobb for running in from centerfield to talk to him about how to pitch to certain batters. "The Earl" felt like he was in control when he was on the mound, and he wanted control. Whitehill pitched 17 years in the major leagues, the first 10 with the Tigers. He won 218 games, and his 4.36 earned run average remains the highest of any pitcher with 200 wins or more.

3. "His potential excited me."

Gibson, a sidearming right-hander, was a legend in the Pacific Coast League where he had seven 20-game seasons and won 307 games. In the majors, he lasted four years but managed to win 12 games for Cobb's Tigers in 1926.

Ulysses Simpson Grant Stoner, nicknamed "Lil"— short for Ulysses — hailed from Bowie, Texas, and was as big a hero in the Texas League as Gibson was in the Pacific Coast League. Stoner won 27 games in Texas in 1923, including a no-hitter, an 18-strikeout performance, and a 13-inning shutout. He came up with the Tigers in 1924 and had marginal success in a six-year career. As a fourth starter for Cobb in 1926, he won seven games.

Clearly, the fate of the Tigers rested on the bats of three terrific outfielders: Heilmann, Heinie Manush — both of whom were later elected to the Hall of Fame — and fun-loving Bob "Fats" Fothergill. Heilmann was a good hitter who became a great hitter under the guidance of Cobb and also because baseball entered into the "live ball" era which saw Heilmann's statistics skyrocket. Henry Everett "Heinie" Manush came up with the Tigers in 1924, won the batting title for Cobb with a .378 average in 1926, and later starred for the Washington Senators. Cobb tabbed him as his replacement as the starting centerfielder for the Tigers, and Manush did not disappoint. Fothergill, at 5 foot 10, 230 pounds, took a lot of ribbing around the league about his size. But he could hit. In a 12-year Major League career, his lifetime average was .325, and he still holds the record of being the only player with more than 200 pinch-hit at-bats to hit over .300. Fothergill was deceptively fast and agile for a man his size. In a game against the Athletics in which the Tigers were getting drubbed, Fothergill hit a meaningless home run in the ninth inning. As he rounded third base and headed for home, he did a complete flip and landed on his feet on home plate.[6]

The Tigers lost to Cleveland 3–1 on opening day in 1926 but won their next three games. They had trouble finding consistency and lost five in a row the next week and finished the month with a 6–9 record. On May 5, their bats came alive as they pounded five Chicago pitchers in a 14–7 win highlighted by Red Wingo's grand-slam home run. Wingo, an outfielder, hit .370 for the 1925 Tigers but was overshadowed by Heilmann and Manush, his Hall of Fame outfield teammates. When Wingo "slumped" to .282 in 1926, he lost his starting job to Fothergill.

Three days after pummeling the White Sox, Detroit hitters scorched the Yankees for 14 runs, overcoming New York's seven-run second inning. This game, coupled with a Washington win, put the Senators in first place ahead of the Yankees. While that was occurring in the American League, Grover Cleveland Alexander of the Chicago Cubs was beating the New York Giants 6–4. It was Alexander's last win as a Cub. Chicago manager Joe McCarthy, in his first year as a big league manager, grew tired of putting up with Alexander, one of the game's greatest pitchers, but a man whose alcoholism tainted his career and his life. McCarthy suspended Alexander and not long after that shipped him to the St. Louis Cardinals.[7]

On May 10, the Yankees went back into first place by beating the Tigers 13–9. Babe Ruth and Lou Gehrig hit back-to-back home runs off of Sam Gibson. Detroit put together some modest two and three-game winning streaks and climbed over the .500 mark, winning 17 games in May and finishing the month with a 23–21 record.

Meanwhile, Gehringer was holding his own, not hitting with power but with consistency — and was already establishing himself as top-notch defensive second baseman. He was also establishing a routine off the field of a man who went to Mass in the morning, to the ballpark in the afternoon, and home after work (or to the hotel if the Tigers were on the road). Detroit put together a seven-game winning streak in June, the Tigers' longest streak of the year, but were 7–13 the rest of the month, so they didn't make much of a move up in the American League standings. As play began on July 1, Detroit was 37–34, 11½ game behind the first-place Senators.

The Tigers continued to win just about as many as they lost during July, but they did it in bunches. They had a five-game winning streak but also a six-game losing streak. On July 15, Gehringer cracked his first major league home run off Urban Shocker as Detroit, behind Sam Jones, beat the Yankees 7–2. Six days later Heinie Manush hit a double, triple, and three-run homer against Washington, but the Senators still managed to eke out a 7–6 win to salvage a split in a doubleheader. Walter Johnson was the winning pitcher. The next day in the National League, Cincinnati set a record that has never been broken or equaled when the Reds hit four triples in an inning. They came in an 11-run second inning as the Reds beat the Braves 11–2.

On July 23, the Tigers beat Washington 9–6, but the big news out of that game was that it took 2 hours and 46 minutes to complete — an

3. "His potential excited me."

unheard of amount time for a nine-inning game in those days. Part of the reason for the length of the game involved two arguments that Cobb instigated — one over a balk call, the other due to his attempts to have a heckler removed from the grandstand. While there is no recorded word-for-word account of the discussion with the umpires about the heckler, it is within reason to think that Cobb complaining about someone with a sharp tongue was tantamount to the pot calling the kettle black. All the ranting and raving didn't have much effect on Detroit's impact in the pennant race. The win over the Senators put them at 49–46, in sixth place, 11 games behind the New York Yankees.

While Detroit meandered its way through the 1926 season, other teams and players were making some noise. On Aug. 21, Ted Lyons of the White Sox tossed a no-hitter against Boston, throwing only 81 pitches in a game that lasted one hour and seven minutes. Lyons' string of 32 straight scoreless innings included a shutout of the Tigers in his start before the no-hitter. On Aug. 28, Babe Ruth hit his 40th home run — eclipsing the totals of many other teams — but Bob Fothergill of the Tigers went 5-for-5, and Detroit beat the Yankees 8–4. The Tigers had a pretty good run in August and going into play on Sept. 1 had climbed to six games above .500 at 67–61. But their pitching couldn't hold enough opposing batters at bay, so Detroit struggled in September and limped off to a 12–14 finish, a 79–75 record for the year. It was a sixth place finish though the Tigers ended up just 12 games behind the pennant-winning Yankees.

The hard-hitting outfield did its part. Manush won the batting title with a .378 mark. Heilmann and Fothergill each hit .367. Cobb, playing sparingly, still managed to hit .339. Detroit had four pitchers who were fairly dependable — Whitehill, who posted a 16–13 record; Gibson, who was 12–9; Wells at 12–10; and Dauss, now used primarily in relief, was 12–6. The rest of the staff was 27–37.

Gehringer had a decent year, hitting .277, owing much of his regular playing time to O'Rourke's measles. Cobb said he never doubted Charlie's potential but wanted to ease him along so as not to put too much pressure on him. "I worked with his stance and how to hold his arms and hands because his potential excited me," said Cobb. He also gave the youngster tips on the stock market — buy Coca Cola and General Motors, he told him — advice that Charlie listened to but could hardly act on. "I was making $4,000 a year. I had to live," he said.[8]

Cobb, who everyone agreed was one of the greatest ballplayers of all time, Babe Ruth notwithstanding, knew he was on shaky ground as the Tiger manager. His temper tantrums were not confined to the field. He had many explosions with team owner Frank Navin because he thought Navin was penny-pinching and unwilling to get him the ballplayers he needed. This was complicated by the fact that Cobb was impatient with the players he was given because most of them didn't measure up to his standards for performance and passion. Under Cobb's direction, the Tigers had finished sixth, third, second, third, fourth, and sixth. Their 79 wins in 1926 were the lowest since Cobb's second year at the helm. By his own admission he was tired and thought the strain of both playing and managing was getting to him. Gehringer, Heilmann, Whitehill, and others would attest to that. On November 3, he submitted his resignation as manager but wanted to continue as a player.

Cobb's resignation caused Charlie Gehringer's career to take another unusual turn, but not before a drama unfolded that involved two of baseball's greatest stars. An old pitcher who thought Cobb had humiliated him saw a chance to get back at him.

Cobb's resignation was not surprising, but when Tris Speaker quit as manager of the Cleveland Indians on November 29, the baseball world seemed to be off its axis. Speaker, another of the game's greatest hitters, had just completed a season in which his Indians gave chase to the New York Yankees and finished in second place, just three games behind the champions. From all appearances, the Indians' fortunes as well as their manager's were on the rise.

Why would two of baseball's greatest stars quit their managerial jobs within a month of one another? The link between the two was a retired pitcher named Hubert Benjamin "Dutch" Leonard, regarded as one of the Boston Red Sox's greatest pitchers. His 1.01 earned run average with the Red Sox in 1914 is still the lowest for any starting pitcher in baseball history. Leonard also threw two no-hitters and had wins in two World Series with the Red Sox. The Dutchman finished out his career with the Detroit Tigers and had developed a reputation as kind of a whiner who would rather not pitch against the league's best opponents, an attitude that surely did not sit well with his manager. Leonard's last year in the majors was in 1925, and during the season he complained to Cobb of soreness in his arm from being overworked. Cobb's response was to keep him in the rotation

3. "His potential excited me."

and allow him to take the brunt of a 12–4 pasting by the Philadelphia Athletics on July 14 at Navin Field. When the Tigers went on a road trip, a bitter Leonard refused to go. Subsequently, when he was put on waivers and nobody picked him up, he was convinced that Cobb — and probably Cobb's friend Tris Speaker — put the word out to blackball him.

In May 1926, Leonard informed American League president Ban Johnson that he had letters and other evidence proving that Cobb and Speaker bet on a game between the Tigers and Indians on September 25, 1919. Leonard had pitched and beaten the Indians the previous day and claimed that after the game, he met with Speaker, Cobb, and Cleveland player Joe Wood. Speaker's Indians had already clinched second place, but the Tigers were still fighting for third place. According to Leonard, Speaker told Cobb he didn't have to worry about tomorrow's game, not suggesting to "fix" the game, but merely pointing out that the Tigers were scheduled to pitch Bernie Boland, who seemed always to beat the Indians. As the men talked, said Leonard, they decided to put some money on the game. He said Cobb agreed to put up $2,000, Leonard $1,500, and Wood and Speaker $1,000 each. Leonard said Cobb arranged for the Tigers' clubhouse man, Fred West, to place the bets for them. At it turned out, said Leonard, the Detroit bookmakers wouldn't accept bets that high, putting a $600 limit on them. Detroit won the game 9–5. Speaker legged out two triples — peculiar behavior for someone who supposedly bet on the opponent to win.

Leonard had in his possession letters Cobb wrote to him, including one from October 23, 1919, which contained vague language and yet was enough to implicate the Detroit manager. Cobb wrote such things as "Wood and myself were considerably disappointed in our business proposition." He said it was "quite a responsibility and that he would never do it again." Later, Cobb maintained he never received any money — and Wood agreed.

Johnson told Frank Navin about the allegations, and he and the Detroit owner met with Leonard in the summer of 1926. Their purpose was to buy him off, hoping to stop him from selling his story and proof to a newspaper or magazine. They arranged for the American League to pay Leonard $20,000, the amount he claimed he lost when the Tigers released him. In return, he surrendered Cobb's letter. They felt they had squelched the matter, but there was one other loose end. Both thought it was necessary to inform other American League club owners about it, which they did at a secret meeting in Chicago on September 9. The club owners convinced Johnson and Navin that they must report their findings to baseball's commissioner, the hardline, no-nonsense judge Kenesaw Mountain Landis. He was the man hired by owners to help clean up baseball after the infamous "Black Sox" scandal of, coincidentally, 1919, when eight members of the Chicago White Sox were accused of conspiring with gamblers to fix the World Series against Cincinnati. The players were exonerated in court, but that didn't matter to Landis. He banned them from professional baseball for life.

Now Landis was handed evidence that two of the game's greatest players may have been involved in betting on baseball. In the meantime, Johnson met with both Cobb and Speaker just after the season was over to tell them what he knew. They both denied any wrongdoing. No matter, said Johnson. They would have to resign as managers of their respective teams. Then both teams gave them their unconditional releases as players.[9]

But that wasn't the end of it. Landis conducted his own investigation. He went to Leonard's home in California and took testimony from him. His story didn't change from the one he had told Johnson in May. When Landis contacted Cobb and Speaker, they jumped at the chance to tell their side of the story and said they would come to Chicago to talk to him. But they demanded that Leonard be there too so they could face their accuser. Leonard declined to leave California.[10]

When they met at Landis' office in the People's Bank building on Chicago's lakefront, Cobb admitted to being an intermediary between Wood and Leonard but claimed that he never placed any bets. He said there was no meeting under the stands on September 24 as Leonard had alleged. Speaker told Landis he knew nothing about any of this until he was informed of Leonard's allegations. If there was a meeting after the game on September 24, he wasn't aware of it and certainly did not take part in it. Nor did he bet on the game. He pointed out to Landis that he hit two triples in the game he was accused of fixing. Wood, who had been the baseball coach at Yale University for the past several years, vouched for Cobb's and Speaker's versions of what happened.

On January 27, Landis issued a ruling in which he exonerated both Cobb and Speaker of any wrongdoing, saying point blank there was no

3. "His potential excited me."

evidence to indicate they had fixed any baseball games. Cobb signed with Connie Mack's Philadelphia A's for the 1927 season, and Speaker hooked on with the Washington Senators. In 1928, Speaker joined the A's, so he and Cobb were teammates for one season.

For Charlie Gehringer and his teammates, the investigation of Cobb was just another sideshow that they had become accustomed to with their manager. Their attention shifted to the new man at the helm, George Moriarty, an American League infielder for 13 years, including seven with the Tigers, but who had been an umpire in the league for the past several years.[11]

Meanwhile, young Charlie Gehringer received a vote of confidence from the *New York Times*. On October 21, it reported, "Gehringer has just finished his first season in the American League. He closed a gap in the Detroit infield.... What is more, Gehringer is likely to occupy that position for many seasons. In addition to his other assets, Gehringer carries youth on his side."[12]

Navin and many of the Tigers felt that some new life might be just what the ballclub needed to once again become a pennant contender. But when new management comes in, changes are inevitable — and one change in particular startled young Charlie Gehringer. The Tigers made a trade — and acquired a new second baseman.

Gehringer had his share of run-ins with Cobb, but they understood each other, and Charlie had felt secure as the Detroit second baseman. Now he might have to prove himself all over again.

CHAPTER 4

"You can't talk your way into a batting championship."

The transition process hit full force on January 15, 1927, while Judge Landis was still investigating the allegations against Cobb and Speaker, when the Tigers made what on the surface looked like a minor deal. They traded Lefty Stewart, Frank O'Rourke, Billy Mullen, and Otto Miller to the St. Louis Browns in exchange for Pinky Hargrave, Bobby LaMotte, and Marty McManus. It involved a lot of players but no really big names.

Stewart was a left-handed pitcher who appeared in five games for the Tigers in 1921 and had been in the minor leagues ever since. O'Rourke was the veteran second baseman who had lost his job to Gehringer the year before when he came down with the measles. Mullen and Miller were utility infielders who had been used sparingly. Detroit acquired Hargrave, a catcher who spent 10 years in the major leagues, mostly as a backup; LaMotte, an infielder who never got into a single game with the Tigers; and McManus, who had played every infield position for the Browns for the past six years, hit .333 in 1924, and led the American League in doubles with 44 in 1925.

Clearly, the key to the trade seemed to be swapping veteran infielders O'Rourke and McManus — but why? Gehringer found out when he went to spring training in 1927. Moriarty told him to start working out at third base. McManus was to be the club's regular second baseman. Charlie was to be Jackie Warner's backup at third. The managerial change and the trade with the Browns appeared to have a profound impact on Gehringer's baseball future. Once again, he was a utility player and would once again have to prove to a manager what he could do.

4. "You can't talk your way into a batting championship."

"When we came up north to start the 1927 season, I was still the utility infielder," said Gehringer, who had hoped those days were behind him. But the fates of the baseball world smiled down on him once again. Similar to what occurred the year before when Frank O'Rourke got the measles, Gehringer got his chance when McManus took ill and was out of the lineup for a few days. Charlie took his place at second base, and this time he stayed there for 16 years. He said, "Marty became ill and I went to second base. I didn't miss a game until my arm went bad in St. Louis four years later."[1]

Gehringer was developing habits at bat and in the field that became trademarks of his career. He rarely swung at the first pitch, preferring to take a look at what the pitcher had to offer. He was to become one of the best two-strike hitters of all-time. Charlie said some batters go up to the plate thinking they have three swings, so they might as well hack away. Gehringer's philosophy, he said, was to be selective because you only have so many chances. "You just can't go up there like you're taking batting practice. It's not that easy. You've got to get your pitch — or try to — and do something with it."

In the field and in the dugout, Gehringer was too busy concentrating to talk with teammates or razz other players. "I wasn't a big noise maker in the infield which a lot of managers think you've got to be or you're not showing an interest. But I don't think it contributes much," said Charlie. "You can't talk your way into a batting championship."[2]

Gehringer didn't win a batting championship in 1927, but it was a milestone year for him. He established himself as a solid, steady, everyday ballplayer who was a tough out and an outstanding fielder. Though it took him three years to break into the starting lineup for good, it would be five years and a string of more than 500 games before he missed another game. He also produced a 21-game hitting streak which remained the longest of his career, even though his greatest success as a hitter came in later years.

But 1927 was the year of the Yankees — the "Bronx Bombers" led by Babe Ruth and Lou Gehrig but with a supporting cast that included Earle Combs, Bob Meusel, Tony Lazzeri, and Mark Koenig and a pitching staff that included Waite Hoyt, Urban Shocker, and Herb Pennock.

The season started on an unusual note. The Washington Senators, in Walter Johnson's last year on the mound, won their first three games before Detroit had even taken the field. Then, on April 15, in Detroit's opener, the Tigers and Browns played to a 2–2 tie in a game called because of darkness. So the Tigers found themselves a game and a half out of first place with an 0–0 record. On April 17, the Tigers got their first win, a 5–1 decision over Cleveland with Sam Gibson picking up the win. But the Yankees, flexing their muscles early, scored 52 runs in their first five games and already had a two-game lead over the undefeated Tigers. Detroit was 6–6 by the end of April, still two games behind the Yankees, who had cooled off a little and were 9–5.

One of the unexpected surprises for the Tigers was the extraordinary hitting of Bob "Fats" Fothergill, the big, round outfielder who entered May with a 12-game hitting streak. Meanwhile, the Senators thought they might have discovered their next mound ace — someone to follow in the footsteps of Walter Johnson — in young Hod Lisenbee. On May 1, Lisenbee shut out the Red Sox 6–0 in his first major league start. By the end of the year, he would have four shutouts and an 18–9 record. But he developed arm trouble and never won another big league game.

On May 8, Marty McManus, healthy again but now playing third base, singled home two runs in the bottom of the ninth as Detroit beat Boston 3–2. A casualty in the game was Fothergill's hitting streak, which was stopped at 18. The Tigers were playing great defense. On May 31, first baseman Johnny Neun caught a line drive off the bat of Cleveland's Homer Summa, tagged base runner Charlie Jamieson at first, and then ran to second base in time to tag Glenn Myatt, who had taken off with the pitch and was scrambling back to second. Neun had pulled off one of baseball's most unusual feats — an unassisted triple play — and remarkably, it was the second one in two days in the major leagues. The day before, Cubs shortstop Jimmy Cooney pulled it off by catching a line drive and then tagging a runner going from second to third and another runner coming into second. Heroics aside, the Tigers struggled and entered June with an 18–22 record, in seventh place, nine games behind New York. The Yankees had already won twice as many as they had lost and gave every indication of running away with the American League championship, now owning a 28–14 record.

Gehringer, now firmly entrenched as the Tiger second baseman, was hitting over .300 and establishing a characteristic that would stay with him for the rest of his career: he was one of the league's most difficult hitters to strike out. This facet of his game was made even more amazing by the

4. "You can't talk your way into a batting championship."

fact that he almost always took the first pitch — so was often behind in the count.

Wes Ferrell, a seven-time 20-game winner in the major leagues, said Charlie was the toughest batter he ever faced. "He'd never offer to hit the first pitch," said Ferrell. "You could just lob it in there, throw it right down the middle of the plate, and he'd just stand there. Sometimes he'd spot you two strikes. You say to yourself, 'as good a pitcher as I am, I'm gonna get him.' But you couldn't do it. He'd hit that ball."[3] Del Baker, one of Gehringer's later managers, said of him, "I honestly believe that Charlie could spot a pitcher two strikes all season and still hit within 15 points of his regular average." As usual, Gehringer didn't have a lengthy explanation. "I like to look around up there," he said.[4]

But, like most everything else he did, Charlie had a plan, a reason for doing whatever he did in the batter's box. And he said there were exceptions to taking the first pitch. Knuckleballers and spitball pitchers could drive a batter crazy if he had two strikes on him, because the hitter had to guard against the floaters and sinkers, thus becoming defensive instead of offensive in the batter's box. Gehringer said those kinds of pitchers liked to get ahead in the count so they often threw fastballs on their first pitch. So he was ready to pull the trigger because he knew it might be the last fastball he'd see in that at-bat. "But against the average pitcher, I thought I was a better hitter with two strikes," he said. Charlie said many times a batter can go up to the plate, get careless, and swing at anything because he figures he'll have a few more chances in that at-bat. "With two strikes, you concentrate more, you cut down on your swing, and put the ball in play," he said.[5]

The 1927 season was shaping up to be a milestone year in baseball, and Detroit was either a bystander or an unwilling victim. On July 8, the Tigers split a double header with the Yankees, winning 11–8 and then losing 10–8. In the second game, Babe Ruth hit an inside-the-park three-run homer, his 27th of the year and the only homer he hit that year that didn't leave the park. The next day, the Tigers pitching collapsed again with Ruth hitting two home runs and two doubles as the Bronx Bombers clobbered Detroit 19–7. Nine days later, the Tigers managed to beat the Philadelphia A's 5–3 with Gibson besting Lefty Grove — but Ty Cobb, playing against his old teammates, got his 4,000th major league hit.

In August, the Tigers showed some signs of life. They had propped themselves up comfortably above the .500 mark at 55–48 and were in third place. But they were 19 games behind the Yankees and 12 in back of the second place Senators. On August 10, they beat the St. Louis Browns 2–1 and then swept the Browns in the next four games of that series. Then the Tigers took on the Red Sox and swept that four-game series. In the space of a week, Detroit had won nine in a row. Next, they went up against the Washington Senators in a battle for second place. On Aug. 20, they beat Washington 5–0 in the first game of a doubleheader. The second game was called because of darkness with the score tied 6–6, leaving the winning streak still intact. The next day, they beat the Senators 11–4, and the following day, they swept a doubleheader 4–2 and 7–3 and now had sole possession of second place, three games ahead of the Senators but 12 behind the Yankees. In the double header nightcap, McManus and Heilmann hit back-to-back home runs off Walter Johnson, the only time in his career that occurred.

Any hope Detroit had of inching closer to the Yankees vanished quickly when the Tigers followed their 13-game winning streak with an eight-game losing streak, including getting swept in a three-game series with New York. By the end of the season, Detroit had slipped back to fourth place at 82–71, 29 games behind the Yankees and also behind Connie Mack's A's and the Senators. However, Detroit's hitting had come through as expected in the first year without Cobb. Heilmann won the batting title with a .398 average and also drove in 120 runs. Fothergill, the round man with the big bat, hit .359 with 114 RBIs, and Manush hit .298 with 90 runs batted in. Gehringer had a solid season, finishing at .317 with 61 runs batted in. Plus, hitting ahead of Heilmann, Fothergill, and Manush gave him the opportunity to score 110 runs, fourth best in the American League.

The Tigers' downfall was their pitching, which just wasn't good enough to compete over the long haul with the likes of Pennock and Hoyt with the Yankees, Grove with the A's, and Johnson with the Senators. Earl Whitehill, who would be the Tigers' ace for the next several years, finished with a 16–14 record while leading the league in walks (105) and balks (2). Rip Collins at 13–7 was the only other starter above .500. Gibson's final record was 11–12, and Stoner was 10–13. In other words, Whitehill and Collins were a combined 29–21. The rest of the staff was 53–50.

Detroit's problems notwithstanding, not many teams in the history

4. "You can't talk your way into a batting championship."

of baseball would have beaten the 1927 Yankees. They won 110, lost 44, and hit .307 as a team. Babe Ruth, Lou Gehrig, and Tony Lazzeri finished one, two, and three in home runs with 60, 47, and 18, respectively. Four Yankees drove in more than 100 runs — Gehrig 175, Ruth 164, Bob Meusel 103, and Lazzeri 102. Three of their starters hit over .350 — Gehrig .373, Ruth .356, and Earle Combs, also .356 — and two others hit over .300 — Meusel at .337 and Lazzeri at .309. A Yankee led the American League in every offensive category except for one — getting hit by pitches. The Browns' Frank O'Rourke, a former Tiger, held that distinction with 12. Gehrig led the league with 52 doubles, and Combs was tops in triples with 23. The Yankees combined that offense with a pitching staff that included four men who won at least 18 games. Waite Hoyt was 22–7 with an earned run average of 2.63. Wilcy Moore was 19–7 with a 2.28 ERA. Herb Pennock finished at 19–8 and a 3.00 ERA. Urban Shocker, the pitcher who gave up Charlie Gehringer's first major league home run the year before, was 18–6 with a 2.84 ERA.

Charlie spent the off-season working as a sales clerk at the big J.L. Hudson department store in downtown Detroit. It was an unusual job for someone as shy as he was, but he enjoyed meeting the people, and besides, it gave him something to do. Still caring for and living with his mother, Charlie would go to mass with her each morning, then take the Trumbull Street streetcar downtown to Hudson's on Woodward Avenue. In its day Hudson's was the tallest department store in the country (27 stories) and second largest in square footage. Only Macy's in New York was bigger. So Hudson's was a place where Charlie could make a living in the off-season, as all ballplayers had to in those days, yet most of the time he could be just another face in the crowd, which suited him just fine.[6]

The fall and winter of 1927–28 brought many changes in major league baseball. On October 14, Walter Johnson announced his retirement as a pitcher with the Washington Senators, ending his career with 417 wins, including 110 shutouts. On October 17, Ban Johnson, the man who organized the American League in 1901 but had difficulty adjusting to the dictums of commissioner Kenesaw Mountain Landis, retired. On October 22, Ross Youngs, a popular outfielder for the New York Giants, died of Bright's disease at age 30. And on November 28, legendary umpire Billy Evans resigned to become business manager of the Cleveland Indians.[7]

The managerial merry-go-round was in full tilt. On October 13, Dave

Bancroft resigned as manager of the Boston Braves and signed on with the Brooklyn Robins to resume his Hall of Fame playing career. On November 7, Bill McKechnie replaced Bob O'Farrell as manager of the St. Louis Cardinals, and Burt Shotton took over the top job with the Philadelphia Phillies, inheriting a team that finished eighth with Stuffy McInnis at the helm. In yet another managerial shift, the Cleveland Indians hired Roger Peckinpaugh on December 16, replacing Jack McCallister.

Perhaps the biggest news of the winter came with the trades of three great ballplayers. On November 28, the Pittsburgh Pirates traded KiKi Cuyler to the Chicago Cubs for second baseman Sparky Adams and outfielder Pete Scott. Cuyler was an outstanding outfielder with the National League champion Pirates but feuded with manager Donie Bush, who benched him in August and did not play him at all in the World Series against the Yankees. Cuyler went on to have several great years with the Chicago Cubs.[8]

On January 10, 1928, the New York Giants traded temperamental second baseman Rogers Hornsby to the Boston Braves. Hornsby, who hit .424 just four years earlier, didn't draw much interest in the trade market. All the Giants got in return were journeyman catcher Shanty Hogan and outfielder Jimmy Welch. Before the season was over, Hornsby would be managing the Braves.

The trade that directly impacted the Tigers came about two months after the 1927 season ended, when Heinie Manush, a good hitting outfielder who had trouble getting along with manager Moriarty, was traded with regular first baseman Lu Blue to the St. Louis Browns for Chick Galloway, Elam Vangilder, and Harry Rice. Blue had been the Tigers' first baseman for seven years but was considered expendable as Detroit hoped to groom rookie Bill Sweeney to be their first baseman of the future. Sweeney lasted parts of three seasons before departing. Rice was an outfielder who could also play third base, was a consistent .300 hitter, and, in the opinion of the Tiger brass, was easier to handle than Manush. Galloway was a veteran who had played nine years with the Philadelphia A's. He was sold to the St. Louis Browns and then traded to Detroit on the same day. Vangilder was a pitcher the Tigers hoped would bolster their starting rotation. He was pretty much a .500 pitcher with the Browns over nine seasons but was dependable; he had the team record for most games, 323, when he was dealt to the Tigers.

4. "You can't talk your way into a batting championship."

So the Tigers who took the field in 1928 had a different look than the team of the previous year. Sweeney was at first base instead of Blue. Rice joined Heilmann and Fothergill in the outfield, and Pinky Hargrave was now the regular catcher instead of Johnny Woodall. Whitehill and Gibson were still the mainstays of the pitching staff, joined by Vangilder, Vic Sorrell, and Ownie Carroll. Sorrell was a better than average pitcher who reached only modest success in the big leagues, partly because he played on mediocre teams like the Tigers, where he was a rookie in 1928. Carroll was a college sensation, winning 50 and losing only 2 at Holy Cross and had his best year in the majors with the Tigers in 1928, winning 16 games. The Tigers put so much faith in Carroll that on April 28, they sold another of their young pitchers, Carl Hubbell, to Beaumont in the Texas League. Hubbell would re-emerge in the big leagues and have a Hall of Fame career with the New York Giants.

The strength of the Tigers defense was up the middle with shortstop Jack Tavener and Charlie Gehringer. Tavener was only 5 feet, 5 inches tall and weighed 138 pounds, making him just about the smallest player in baseball. He was an adequate hitter, but his value to the Tigers was his speed on the bases and his sparkling defense. Tavener and Gehringer made up a formidable defensive duo up the middle for Detroit.

It didn't take long for Moriarty and the Tigers to see that 1928 could be a long season. On April 19, Detroit beat the Browns 9–8 in a game in which the pitchers combined to walk 16 batters in a span of five innings. The winning margin was provided by a home run by rookie Paul Easterling, his second in two days. On April 20, Easterling connected again as the Tigers beat the Browns 3–0. (He didn't hit another homer all year.)

By July, Detroit was in last place, but on July 25 they surprised the Yankees by sweeping a doubleheader, 3–2 and 10–7. In the second game, Tavener stole second, third, and home. The next day the two teams played in another doubleheader. In the opener, Vic Sorrell and Waite Hoyt dueled to a 1–1 tie after 11 innings. The Yankees then scored 11 in the 12th to win 12–1. Detroit salvaged the nightcap 13–10 with the aid of a Heilmann grand slam.

In August, Tiger management indicated the high value they placed on Gehringer by refusing to trade him on two separate occasions. The pursuer was Clark Griffith, owner of the Washington Senators. He offered Detroit Stanley "Bucky" Harris, a veteran infielder and the Senators player-manager straight up for Gehringer. Navin said no. Later, Griffith sweetened the deal, offering Harris and Ossie Bluege for Gehringer. Again, Navin said no. He knew the Tigers weren't going anywhere in 1928 but also knew that he wasn't going to renew Moriarty's contract as manager. The acquisition of Harris would have solved some problems for Detroit, but Navin and the Detroit brass thought the departure of Gehringer would create a bigger problem and wanted no part of it.

The Tigers managed to climb into sixth place in September. On September 24, they beat the hapless Boston Red Sox 8–0 before only 404 customers at Navin Field. Al Wingo, John Stone, and Gehringer performed the rare feat of hitting consecutive triples in the seventh inning. For Charlie, it was his 16th three-bagger of the year.

The Tigers didn't have enough offensively or on the mound to be a legitimate contender in 1928. They buried themselves in sixth place, winning only 68 games while losing 86 as they finished 33 games behind the front-running Yankees. Nothing seemed to go right. Heilmann "slumped" to a .328 batting average. Sweeney was adequate in the field but provided little pop at the plate. Rice had a decent year replacing Manush in the outfield, hitting .302 with 81 runs batted in, but Manush hit .378 for the Browns with 13 home runs and 108 runs batted in. Carroll and Vangilder were the only Detroit pitchers with winning records. Carroll led the staff with a 16–12 mark. Vangilder, the man who made a habit of being just about a .500 pitcher, was 11–10. The rest of the staff was 41–63.[9]

Despite the team's struggles, Gehringer had a good year. Steady as always at second base, he improved his numbers at the plate, hitting .320 with 193 hits, 29 doubles, 16 triples, 6 home runs, and 74 runs batted in. He played in every game (154), a feat that he would accomplish for the next three years. Two other hallmarks that would become a natural part of Charlie's game were his ability to put the ball in play when he was batting and turning the double play when he was fielding. Despite his penchant for taking pitches, often putting himself in the hole, he struck out only 22 times in 603 official at-bats. In the field, he participated in 101 double plays, most of them with Tavener.

On October 17, Moriarty complied with management wishes and resigned, then soon after signed on to resume his umpiring career. Two days later, the Tigers hired Bucky Harris to be their new manager. Har-

4. "You can't talk your way into a batting championship."

ris was considered the "boy wonder" when, at age 27, he had taken over as manager of the Washington Senators in 1924 and led them to their one and only World Series championship in a thrilling seven-game series against the Giants. In 1925, the Senators won the American League pennant again. But by 1928, they had fallen below .500, and Griffith thought Harris was expendable. Perhaps his .204 batting average was a factor. Griffith realized in August that he wasn't going to get Gehringer for Harris, so in October, he settled for Tiger veteran third baseman Jackie Warner.

On the day he was hired, Harris, a second baseman, made it clear that Charlie Gehringer would not have to fight to keep his job or wait for someone to get sick in order to play in 1929. "I will be in uniform daily but I will not play except in emergencies," he told the press.[10]

The Tigers also announced the signing of Roy Johnson, a 24-year-old outfielder for the San Francisco Seals in the Pacific Coast League who had hit .359 in 1928. With Heilmann and Rice coming back, McManus establishing himself at third base — and staying healthy, and Whitehill, Carroll, and Sorrell anchoring the pitching staff, the Tigers were optimistic that they'd be on the rise in 1929. Their hopes grew higher when on December 11, they pulled off a trade with Cleveland, acquiring veteran pitcher George Uhle for Ken Holloway and Jackie Tavener. Uhle was 22–16 for the Indians in 1922, 26–16 in 1923, and 27–11 in 1926 but hadn't won 20 games since then. Uhle was not only credited with throwing a slider but also with naming it. In addition to what he could do on the mound, Uhle had the ability to help himself in ballgames because of his hitting prowess. In 1923, he got 52 hits, a record for pitchers that still stands, and he hit .361. Perhaps, it was thought, he could help lead the Tigers out of the second division doldrums.

But it wasn't to be. Gehringer liked his new manager personally but thought he might be a little too gentle to be the leader and disciplinarian of 25 ballplayers. "Bucky was a little too nice," said Charlie. "You've got to be tough in a way because you've got all kinds of guys to handle. But I never heard Bucky Harris second-guess anyone."[11]

Just before the season started, the *New York Times* speculated that Harris might insert himself at second base and move Charlie over to shortstop, but noted that the new manager would certainly keep Gehringer, "one of the regular regulars," in the lineup every day. As it turned out, Bucky kept the promise he made on the day he was hired — that Gehringer would be his second baseman — and for yet another season, Charlie played in every game.

Harris decided to roll the dice and start two rookies — Johnson, the Pacific Coast League star who joined Rice and Heilmann in the outfield; and Dale Alexander, a good hitting first baseman but a struggling fielder. McManus, the man whose illness opened the door for Gehringer at second base, was now a fixture at third base.

The Tigers opened their 1929 season with a 5–4 loss to Cleveland, the first of many extra-inning thrillers during the season. Earl Averill of the Indians hit a home run off of Whitehill in his first major league at-bat. Gehringer also homered, the first time in his major league career that he hit a home run on opening day. On April 21, Alexander hit the first of 25 home runs he would hit that year, and Whitehill also homered to help his own cause in a 16–9 victory over the Browns.

On May 5, Gehringer got another homer and two other hits as Detroit beat Boston 10–2 at Navin Field. McManus also homered for the Tigers. Ten days later, Detroit beat the up-and-coming Philadelphia A's 6–5 on a bizarre play in the ninth inning. With Harry Heilmann on first, Alexander hit a double to deep centerfield. Heilmann tried to score standing up, but as he raced toward the plate, Philadelphia catcher Mickey Cochrane got the throw and took a swipe at Heilmann running by. The swipe hit the runner so hard that it rendered him unconscious. As Heilmann crumbled to the ground, home plate umpire George Hildebrand signaled that he was out. But Cochrane had dropped the ball as he tagged him. Seeing that, Hildebrand reversed his call, giving the Tigers the win. The game would not have reached that point had the A's not scored in the top of the ninth with the help of a rare Charlie Gehringer error.

On May 21, Johnny Mostil of the White Sox broke his leg while trying to steal home. The injury ended his career. Chicago, behind Ted Lyons, prevailed in the game, 10–3. Three days later, the White Sox and Tigers played a 21-inning marathon, finally won by Detroit, 6–5. Charlie got the game-winning RBI with a sacrifice fly in the top of the 21st. Not worried about pitch counts or surrendering the ball to middle relief specialists, Ted Lyons and George Uhle battled it out on the mound. Uhle went 20 innings before yielding to Vic Sorrell, who got the last three outs. Lyons went all the way for the loss. Two days later, Red Faber, the famed Chicago spitballer, tossed a one-hitter for the White Sox as they beat the Tigers 2–0.

4. "You can't talk your way into a batting championship."

Gehringer had his team's only hit, a single in the fourth inning. On May 29, Uhle notched his ninth straight win, a 7–6 decision over the St. Louis Browns.[12]

Going into June, the Tigers were 24–21, in fourth place, 8.5 games behind the Philadelphia A's who were temporarily replacing the New York Yankees as the dominant team in the American League with stars such as Jimmy Foxx, Mickey Cochrane, and Lefty Grove. On June 3, the A's took 13 innings to down the Tigers 3–2, breaking Uhle's nine-game winning streak. On July 12, Detroit scored four runs in the ninth inning in a wild, come-from-behind victory over the Red Sox. Gehringer "drove in" the winning run when he was hit by a pitch with the bases loaded in the ninth inning. Twelve days later, Charlie hit two triples, and Harry Rice hit two homers, but Detroit still fell to New York 7–5 at Yankee Stadium.

By August, the Tigers had slipped back into their customary second-division standing, but Gehringer remained hot. On August 5, the Senators clobbered Detroit 21–5, but Charlie tied a major league record by hitting three triples in the game. He was an established star now as well as a fan favorite. On August 14, the Tigers honored him with a "Charlie Gehringer Day" at Navin Field. He got four hits—three singles and a home run—and stole home as the Tigers beat the Yankees 17–13. He was busy in the field, too, handling 10 chances without an error.

The Tigers and White Sox, who always seemed to hit well in games against each other, split a double header at Navin Field on September 2, Detroit winning the opener 10–8 and dropping the nightcap to Ted Lyons 8–2. Charlie was 4-for-4 in the first game and touched Lyons for a homer in the second game. On September 24, Gehringer had his third multiple-triple game in a month, hammering two three-baggers and a home run in a 9–4 victory over the Browns.

At the end of the season, the A's were on top, and the Tigers were in their familiar spot of sixth place. With their 70–84 record, they had amassed just two more wins than they had in 1928.

Gehringer had the greatest year of his career, and, for the fifth straight season, he increased his totals from the year before in home runs, runs batted in, and batting average. He went to the plate 634 times and, despite his penchant for taking pitches and working the count so that he was often behind with two strikes, he only struck out 19 times all year. He led the league in games played (155), plate appearances (715), runs scored (131), hits (215), doubles (45), triples (19), and stolen bases (27). He hit .339 and had 13 home runs.

The Tigers knew when they obtained Uhle that his 20-win seasons were probably behind him, but he led the staff with 15 wins, while losing 11. Whitehill and Sorrell were each 14–15 while Ownie Carroll slumped badly to 9–17. The two prized rookies had come through. Alexander hit .343 with 25 home runs and 137 runs batted in. Johnson finished at .314 with 10 homers and 69 RBIs. Once again, Heilmann delivered, hitting .344 with 15 home runs and 120 runs batted in. One statistic more than anything else told the story of the Tigers in 1929: they led the American League in runs scored — and in runs allowed.[13]

The end of the 1929 season also marked the end of an era in Detroit baseball. Harry Heilmann, suffering from arthritis and unhappy with the managing of Bucky Harris, was placed on waivers and sold to Cincinnati on October 14. He had played for the Tigers for 15 seasons and was one of the few players who blossomed under the scrutiny of Ty Cobb. Heilmann had been a good hitter but became a great one when Cobb took over as manager in 1921. Between 1921 and 1927, Heilmann hit over .390 four times — .394 in 1921, .403 in 1923, .393 in 1925, and .398 in 1927. In 1928 and 1929, he had "tailed off" to .328 and .344.

As the 1930 season approached, the Tigers needed pitching help, hitters to help fill the void left by Heilmann's departure, and another good year from Charlie Gehringer.

CHAPTER 5

"He leads the league in line drives right at somebody."

Charlie Gehringer hadn't changed much over the years. Now an established star in the major leagues, he still went to mass every morning, accompanied by his mother when he was home. He sometimes drove, sometimes took the trolley to the ballpark, and was content to be quietly efficient.

A book of famous baseball quotations facetiously attributed this one to Charlie: "_____." Another favorite line about Gehringer has been attributed to several teammates and players over the years. "He says hello at spring training, good-bye at the end of the season — and hits .320 in between."[1]

Joe Falls, sportswriter and columnist for the *Detroit Free Press* and *Detroit News*, said he once accepted an invitation to play golf with Gehringer because, "You never pass up a chance to hear Charlie Gehringer speak, even if all he says is, 'Fore.'" Falls knew that Charlie always signed his name as "Chas." but said he was surprised when he called on Gehringer at his home and saw the nameplate on the front door. There it was in shiny brass: "Chas. Gehringer."[2]

Some people found his quiet nature as a detriment. Dan Daniel, the New York sportswriter who had a decidedly Bronx bias, criticized Charlie's personality frequently. "For his skill and rating, Gehringer is an all-too-drab ballplayer," he once wrote.[3] Yet Chick Feldman, a sportswriter covering the Tigers in spring training many years after Gehringer retired, saw him eating alone in a hotel coffee shop in Lakeland, Florida, when Tiger manager Billy Martin came in and sat down alone at a nearby table, not seeing or not recognizing Gehringer. Charlie never said a word, said

Charlie Gehringer

Name: **GEHRINGER** (LAST NAME) **CHARLES** (FIRST NAME) **LEONARD** (MIDDLE NAME) _____ (NICKNAME)

Exact Place of birth: **FOWLERVILLE MICHIGAN** (If born on farm, please name nearest village)

Date of birth: **MAY** (MONTH) **11** (DAY) **1903** (YEAR)

Permanent address: **32301 WAHSER RD** (STREET) **BIRMINGHAM** (TOWN OR CITY) **MICHIGAN** (STATE)

Current occupation: **MANUFACTURER'S REPRESENATIVE** (Please describe exact duties)
GEHRINGER + FORSYTH (Name of firm)

How did you bat? (L, R or B) **LEFT** How did you throw? (L or R) **RIGHT**

What is your height? **5-11½** What was your playing weight? **185**

Nationality (American, but of what descent?) **GERMAN**

Elementary School attended **GRADE SCHOOL**, Years completed **8**

High school attended **FOWLERVILLE MICH**, Years completed **4**

College attended **UNIVERSITY OF MICH**, Years completed **1**

Degrees granted _____

Wife's maiden name in full **JOSEPHINE STILLEN** (Please list all marriages) Date of marriage **JUNE 18 1949**

Were you ever in the armed forces? **YES** What branch of service? **NAVY**
When? **1942 - 1945**

What was your first year of professional baseball? **1924**

What was your last year of professional baseball? **1942**

If you had it all to do over, would you play professional baseball? **I PROBABLY WOULD**

Chas. L. Gehringer (SIGNATURE)

Charlie Gehringer almost always signed his name as "Chas," including on a biographical card he filled out for his file in the National Baseball Hall of Fame in Cooperstown, New York. He was elected to the Hall in 1949 (courtesy of the National Baseball Hall of Fame).

5. "He leads the league in line drives right at somebody."

Feldman, probably opting to give the manager the same kind of "quiet time" that Charlie relished so much.

Falls said Charlie was once honored by the hometown folks of Fowlerville and was given a set of golf clubs as a gift. The clubs were traditional ones made for right-handers, but Charlie golfed like he batted — left-handed. He never told the gift-givers about their mistake. In fact, Falls said, Charlie learned to play golf right-handed. He was also honored by a civic group at the Book Cadillac Hotel in Detroit, an event in which speaker after speaker heaped praise upon him. When it was Charlie's turn to speak, he got up to the microphone and said, "I'm known around baseball for saying little and I'm not going to spoil my reputation." He then sat down.[4]

Charlie graciously accepted good-natured kidding about his shyness. But as a ballplayer, he always maintained that you don't hit with your mouth. And his hitting just seemed to keep getting better.

Year	G	AB	R	H	D	T	HR	RBI	AVE.
1924	5	13	2	6	0	0	0	1	.462
1925	8	18	3	3	0	0	0	0	.167
1926	123	459	62	127	19	17	1	48	.277
1927	133	508	110	161	29	11	4	61	.317
1928	154	603	108	193	29	16	6	74	.320
1929	155	634	131	215	45	19	13	106	.339

In the five-year span from 1925 to 1929, Charlie improved each year in home runs, runs batted in, and batting average, the three Triple Crown categories. The only other player in baseball history to accomplish that was Rogers Hornsby. Bucky Harris said Gehringer's numbers could have been even higher. "I've never seen one man hit in so much hard luck consistently," he said. "Year after year, he leads the league in line drives right at somebody. No wonder he looks so sad."[5]

The Tigers had a relatively new look by mid-season 1930. Alexander and Johnson had earned their right to stay in the lineup with Gehringer and McManus, but Harris inserted a rookie and got a couple of veterans in a trade with the Yankees, hoping the championship experience would rub off. On May 30, Detroit traded outfielder Rice, starting pitcher Ownie Carroll, and a seldom-used utility infielder Yats Wuestling to the Yankees for veteran pitcher Waite Hoyt and shortstop Mark Koenig. Hoyt broke in with Boston but had nine seasons with the Yankees during their glory years and won 157 games for them. The Yankees may have thought the big right-hander was on the downside of his career, but Hoyt lasted 10 more years in the big leagues. Koenig broke in with the Yankees and had played with them for five years and was one of the unsung heroes of the 1927 ballclub because of his steady, if not flashy play.

For the second straight year, Harris put a rookie in the outfield, Elias "Liz" Funk. Another outfielder, John Stone, had played sparingly in 1928 and 1929 for the Tigers. With Heilmann gone, Alexander, in his second full season, was the veteran in the outfield and was counted on to supply some pop at the plate like he had the year before. Two pitchers who would gain fame with later Tiger ballclubs were Elon "Chief" Hogsett, a half-Cherokee Indian who became an outstanding relief pitcher, and Thomas Jefferson Davis Bridges, better known as simply Tommy Bridges. He was a southern boy with a great curve ball who would pitch for four Tiger World Series teams before his career was over.

But none of that was happening in 1930. Connie Mack's Philadelphia A's had replaced the Yankees as the top team in the American League with hitters Eddie Collins and Jimmy Foxx and pitcher Robert "Lefty" Grove, who Gehringer said was the toughest hurler he ever faced.

Charlie often talked about the game when he faced Grove for the first time. Detroit hitters on the bench had been talking about how Grove was never wild inside so there was no fear of getting hit by one of his pitches. Gehringer got in the batter's box, leaned in, and Grove's first pitch, a fastball, hit him on the elbow. Charlie felt like he had been shot. His arm swelled up so fast he couldn't get his sleeve over it. "By the time I got to first base, I had tears in my eyes. I had to quit," he said. "I came back to the bench and said, 'Well boys, he's wild inside.'"[6]

The 1930 season started out on a good note as the Tigers beat the Browns 6–3 behind Uhle and then came back the next day with Earl Whitehill throwing a gem for a 6–1 win over St. Louis. The Bengals then got knocked around as Cleveland hung the Tigers with their first loss, 7–1. But Chief Hogsett got the victory the next day as Detroit beat Cleveland 6–4. The Tigers had won three out of their first four games and things were looking up, but not for long. The Tigers lost their next seven and hit such a tailspin that by May 12, they were 8–19, had lost 18 of their last 23 games, and were in last place, 10 games behind Philadelphia. They

5. "He leads the league in line drives right at somebody."

were sixth in the league in runs scored and had given up more runs than anyone else in the league, a deadly combination.

With the help of timely hitting by Gehringer, another good offensive year from Alexander, and usually reliable starting pitching from Uhle and Whitehill, the Tigers made attempts at getting back to .500, and were 56–57 on Aug. 10 after beating the Red Sox 4–2, but they lost three in a row after that and never got any closer to breaking even.

Charlie hit .330 for the year with 16 homers and 98 runs batted in. In the Tigers' July 4th double header sweep of the Indians, Gehringer's 12th-inning two-run homer won the second game after Cleveland had pushed across a run in the top of the 12th. On July 22, Detroit beat Philadelphia 7–6 on the strength of a double and triple by Gehringer. On August 5, he hit a two-run homer and then a grand slam home run in the 12th inning as the Tigers beat the White Sox 7–6.

Gehringer played in every Tiger game for the third consecutive year and had more than 200 hits (201) for the second straight year. He led the American League in games played (154), was third in runs scored (144), third in doubles (47), fifth in triples (15), second in stolen bases (19), and third in the league in getting hit by pitches (7). He also had the dubious distinction of being caught stealing more than any other base runner in the American League (15).

Whitehill had a good year on the mound, at one point winning nine in a row and finishing at 17–13. Sorrell was 16–11, and Uhle was 12–12. Hoyt, the old Yankee, was 9–8 as was Chief Hogsett. Alexander had another good year with the bat, hitting .326 with 20 homers and 135 runs batted in. McManus hit .320 with nine homers and 89 RBIs. Stone, pressed into a starting role at the beginning of the year, responded with a .311 batting average but did not provide much power. He had but three home runs and 56 runs batted in. Between July 12 and August 9, Stone had a 27-game hitting streak. The odd man out in the Tigers' revamped outfield was big, burly Bob Fothergill, who contributed a grand slam home run in Detroit's 12–10 win over the Browns on May 17 but was sold to the White Sox two months later. In one of the season's more unusual pitching displays, young Tommy Bridges, getting a start on August 25, walked 12 batters but still got the win when the Tigers beat St. Louis, 7–5.

If 1930 was a disappointment, 1931 was a disaster for the Tigers. Alexander, the young outfielder who provided so much punch in the middle of the lineup in his first two seasons, hit only three home runs all year. Gehringer hit only four, and John Stone led the team with 10. Alexander led the team in runs batted in with 87, and Stone contributed 76. No one else had more than 55. With that kind of anemic hitting, the pitching had to be spectacular. Instead, it was only good occasionally. Whitehill and Sorrell each won 13, while losing 16 and 14 respectively. Uhle was 11–12, Hogsett was 3–9, and Bridges, who would have some great seasons in the years to come, paid his dues in his first full season, finishing at 8–16.

Gehringer had an "off year" for him, hitting just .311. On May 8, a nagging sore arm reached the point where he could not play, ending his consecutive game streak at 604. He played in only 101 games all year. When he came back, he started another streak, which lasted another 500 games. By now his peers recognized him as the premier defensive second baseman in the major leagues. In his typical work ethic, Charlie studied hitters with the same focus and attention pitchers employ to know the batters they're facing and batters use to anticipate what pitch is coming. Gehringer wasn't flashy in the field. He just always seemed to be in the right place at the right time. But he would smile when people complimented him on his fielding, saying that good fielding was the best way to get up to bat again.

Gehringer was called "The Mechanical Man" because of the seemingly easy way he went about everything he did, including fielding ground balls, catching popups, and converting double plays. But ballplayers don't make headlines with their fielding. "That's the mechanical part that you just take for granted," he said. "I never had a manager who asked me about my fielding; why I had a better year fielding this year or that; but they'd all ask you how many runs you brought in or how many you scored or how often you got on base."[7]

Charlie said the secret to playing second base was throwing the ball quickly from any angle and straddling the bag so you could touch it with either foot, depending on which way you had to lean to take the throw. With a runner on first, the key is to get rid of the ball before you get hit. "You're a pigeon out there," said Charlie. If you get rid of the ball before you get hit, the runner can flip you upside down and it doesn't matter. "That happened to me a hundred times," he said.

One of the problems for the Tigers in 1931 was not enough good fielding — or good hitting or good pitching. The result was a seventh-place

5. "He leads the league in line drives right at somebody."

finish. They won only 61 games and lost 93, finishing 47 games behind the Philadelphia A's, the dominant team in the American League. It was Detroit's worst finish since 1920, Hughie Jennings' last year as manager, when they also had a 61–93 record and also finished seventh in the eight-team league.

The Tigers had gotten off to a good start in 1931 and were 16–13 on May 16, a month into the season. Then the roof caved in. They lost eight in a row, won two, then lost another eight in a row. In the month between May 16 and June 15, Detroit won five and lost 22, and for all practical purposes, their quest for first-division status (being among the top four teams) was gone.

The Tigers' problem was they couldn't avoid long losing streaks. In the course of the season, they had the two eight-game losing streaks, one of seven games, two of six, one of five, and two of four in a row. When they weren't mired in losing streaks, their record was 61–45.

Another indication of the Tigers' troubles was that shortstop Mark Koenig was brought in as a relief pitcher three different times during the season when Detroit had either exhausted its bullpen or the game was so out of reach that Harris didn't want to waste another bullpen arm. That season Koenig pitched seven total innings in three games, giving up five runs (all earned), with eleven walks, one wild pitch, and only three strikeouts for a 6.43 ERA.

The Tigers made some moves in 1932 to shake up the lineup and hopefully advance in the standings. On April 21, they released Koenig, confident that they had the shortstop for their future in Billy Rogell, a switch hitter who was quick on the bases and in the field. Rogell had played parts of three seasons with the Red Sox before joining the Tigers in 1930. He was Koenig's backup in 1931. Gehringer liked playing with Rogell; actually he was just glad the Tigers had settled on one shortstop. "Before that, I had played with something like 22 different shortstops. I don't think any one stayed a year (after Jackie Tavener was traded)."[8]

Detroit added some flair to the lineup by putting Gerald "Gee" Walker into the outfield. Walker and his brother Hub, also an outfielder, were rookies in 1931. Hub didn't last long, but "Gee" with a good bat, speed, and glove quickly became a fan favorite. Walker's only apparent flaw was often a costly one. He had a tendency to be inattentive to game situations. In one game, he was thrown out trying to steal second — while the batter was being given an intentional walk. In another game, when the Tigers batted around, Walker made two of the three outs in the inning by being picked off base twice. That is still a major league record.

In later years, Gehringer used Walker as an example when he defended his own quiet nature as opposed to the crowd-pleasing antics of other ballplayers. Charlie conceded that Walker was a valuable teammate but said Gee had cost the Tigers some games because of the reckless way he often played.

On June 13, the Tigers proved their confidence in Walker when they traded Roy Johnson, the rookie slugger of just two years before, and the other highly touted rookie from that same year, first baseman Dale Alexander, to the Boston Red Sox for outfielder Earl Webb, who had hit a record-setting 67 doubles for the Red Sox in 1931. Fittingly, on June 15, in his first game with the Tigers, Webb hit two doubles and had two stolen bases as Detroit beat the Washington Senators 7–6.

Detroit was much improved in 1932, finishing fifth. Their record of 76–75 marked the Tigers' first winning season since 1927. Whitehill led the staff once again with a 16–12 record, Sorrell was 14–14, and Hogsett was 11–9. Emerging as one of the up-and-comers among American League pitchers was Tommy Bridges, who won 14 and lost 12. The year before Bridges had walked 12 batters in one game, but on August 5, 1932, he brushed with baseball immortality when he retired the first 26 Washington Senators in order. Dave Harris then got a bloop single to prevent the perfect game, but Bridges retired the next batter and settled for a 13–0 one-hit shutout.

Gehringer returned to form by playing in every game and driving in 107 runs. He hit 19 home runs, and his 44 doubles were second in the league, but his batting average slipped to .298, the first time he was under .300 since his rookie season. Gehringer said a couple of early season home runs led to the lower batting average. "I thought I was Babe Ruth," he said, and began swinging for the fences instead of just trying to spray the ball all over the field.

John Stone's numbers were nearly identical to Charlie's: .297 with 17 home runs and 108 RBIs. Walker was the only regular to hit over .300, finishing at .323 with eight home runs and 78 runs batted in. Webb hit .287, also with eight home runs and 78 runs batted in — and 28 doubles.

The Tigers were starting to make their move. They won 15 more

5. "He leads the league in line drives right at somebody."

games in 1932 than they did in 1931, and something new was on the horizon. Detroit had a chance to start building from within their own system instead of depending on making trades and relying on players past their prime. The Beaumont Exporters, the Tiger affiliate in the Texas League, won the league championship behind the pitching of a tall, lean pitcher named Lynwood "Schoolboy" Rowe, who won 19, lost 7, and had an earned run average of 2.24. Outfielder Pete Fox hit .357 with 19 home runs, and Hank Greenberg, a first baseman-outfielder of Jewish descent, won the Most Valuable Player award after hitting .290 with 39 home runs and 131 runs batted in. All three were in the major leagues in 1933.

The Tigers thought they had their third base puzzle solved with the development of another farmhand, Marv Owen, who seemed ready for full-time big league service. Marty McManus had been a fixture there for several years but was traded to the Red Sox in August 1931 for Muddy Ruel, a veteran catcher with a rather storied past catching for the Yankees and Senators. He was behind the plate on August 16, 1920, when Yankee pitcher Carl Mays beaned Cleveland shortstop Ray Chapman, who crumbled at the plate and later died from his head injury. In 1924, Ruel was the Senators catcher when Walter Johnson won his first World Series game. For the Tigers, Ruel filled in for Ray Hayworth from time to time but was given his unconditional release at the end of the season. However, baseball being the unpredictable game that it always is, while Ruel wasn't of much use to the Tigers, trading McManus opened the door a year later for Owen, who became part of one of the most potent infields in baseball history.

On December 14, 1932, Detroit signaled that the Tigers were ready to start a new era. They traded their left-handed ace Earl Whitehill to the Washington Senators for two pitchers: Frederick "Firpo" Marberry and Carl Fischer. It was a trade that stunned Tiger fans. Whitehill, a colorful, temperamental but steady performer had won 133 games in 10 years with Detroit. Marberry was a dependable starter at this stage in his career but is best known as being baseball's first true relief pitcher with the Senators, where he came out of the bullpen regularly for several years.[9] In addition to the revamped pitching staff of Marberry, Bridges, Sorrell, Rowe, Uhle, and Fischer, the Tigers fielded a 1933 lineup that had Hayworth behind the plate; an infield of Greenberg, Gehringer, Rogell and Owen; and Stone, Gee Walker and Fox in the outfield.

Before the season was over, Uhle would play for three different teams as the Tigers put their focus on younger pitchers. But he was around long enough to experience one memorable night with Gehringer, Johnny Grabowski, and Joe Dugan, a Tiger coach. The four men went out for a beer after a ballgame in Chicago and, while sitting in the bar, someone mentioned the gangster Al Capone. The bar owner, overhearing the ballplayers' conversation, asked if they would like to meet him. They all said yes. The bar owner told them to come back the next night, which they did. He drove them to the Lexington Hotel, Capone's Chicago headquarters. The men were searched as they approached the elevator, searched when they got off the elevator several floors up, and searched again as they were led to a room down the hall. They went through two sets of doors and into a large room where they were directed to sit against a wall. Across the room, "Scarface" Al Capone, the king of the underworld, sat behind a desk. On the wall behind him were portraits of George Washington and Abraham Lincoln.

Capone talked baseball with the players and showed some knowledge of the game. They bantered for a few minutes as Charlie and his companions watched and listened, almost frozen in their seats and speaking only when it was clear that it was their turn to talk. After a few minutes, Capone rose and said he had to leave. He was going out to dinner and taking a bunch of showgirls with him. He invited Charlie and the others to accompany him, but they declined, having had enough excitement for one night. They were escorted back to the elevator, out of the hotel, and driven back to the bar, each having a night to remember.[10]

Detroit started the 1933 season with two losses to Cleveland, 4–1 in 13 innings on opening day and 7–4 the next day. On April 15, Rowe made his major league debut. He got his nickname because as a kid, he played sandlot ball with much older players, and they gave him the moniker that stayed with him the rest of his life. Schoolboy was a big right-hander from Arkansas who had three speeds to his fastball — fast, faster, and "what-was-that?" He nailed down the Tigers' first win of the year by shutting out the White Sox 3–0. Detroit hovered around the .500 mark for much of the early season, putting together a four-game winning streak in April but not being able to muster a sustained pattern of winning. On May 4, Yankee Lefty Gomez took a no-hitter into the ninth inning, but Gehringer broke it up with a home run. New York won 5–2.

5. "He leads the league in line drives right at somebody."

Two days later, Greenberg hit his first major league home run against Washington, but the Senators, behind the pitching of Earl Whitehill, won the game 6–2. On May 24, Bridges, who by now had learned to control his devastating curve ball, threw the second one-hitter of his young career as Detroit beat Washington 3–1. The month of May ended on a tragic note for a former Tiger. Dale Alexander, the first baseman who showed so much power in his first two seasons, then won the batting title with a .372 average after he was traded to Boston in 1932, twisted his knee while sliding into home plate in a game against the A's on May 30. The injury ended his career.[11]

As June rolled around, the Tigers found themselves in a familiar place—fifth, nine games behind the New York Yankees and seven games below .500 at 16–23. The Tigers had the nucleus of a good ballclub. Gehringer was back on the beam after having an off-year (for him) in 1932. He was hitting well over .300, was on a pace to hit about 50 doubles, and was playing his usual stellar defense at second base. Greenberg was emerging as one of the American League's top sluggers, and Bridges, Rowe, and Marberry were the best 1-2-3 punch that a Tiger pitching staff had offered in many years. There were still some pieces missing to the puzzle, but the team had not progressed much under the leadership of Bucky Harris. As the season wore on, it became apparent that his days were probably numbered as the Tiger manager. "The fact that he was so easy to play for probably didn't help his managing," said Gehringer. "But you'd never want to play for a nicer guy."[12]

On July 6, Major League Baseball took a break from regular competition and presented the first All-Star Game, featuring the best players from each league playing against each other. The game was the brainchild of Arch Ward, sports editor of the *Chicago Tribune*, who thought it would be a terrific addition to Chicago's "Century of Progress" exposition going on at the same time.

The players were selected by vote of the fans and by managers John McGraw of the National League and Connie Mack of the American League. More than 49,000 people jammed Comiskey Park on Chicago's south side to witness this extraordinary event. Wild Bill Hallahan was the National League's starting pitcher while Lefty Gomez of the Yankees took the mound for the American League. At second base for the American League was Charlie Gehringer, who by now had earned the reputation as being the best second baseman in all of baseball. This would be the first of six consecutive All-Star starts for Charlie, who played every inning of every game.

In the third inning, Gehringer drew a walk from Hallahan, the first walk in All-Star Game history. Babe Ruth then hit a booming home run into the right field stands to the uproarious cheers of the crowd and the respect of even the man who gave up the gopher ball. "We wanted to see the Babe," said Hallahan. "Sure he was old and had a big waistline but that didn't make any difference. We were on the same field as Babe Ruth."

Frankie Frisch homered for the National League but Ruth's blast proved to be the difference in the ballgame as the American League won, 4–2. Gomez was the winning pitcher, and Hallahan picked up the loss.

July 6, 1933

National	AB	R	H	RBI	American	AB	R	H	RBI
Martin 3b	4	0	0	1	Chapman lf-rf	5	0	1	0
Frisch 2b	4	1	2	1	Gehringer 2b	3	1	0	0
Klein rf	4	0	1	0	Ruth rf	4	1	2	2
P. Waner rf	0	0	0	0	West cf	0	0	0	0
Hafey lf	4	0	1	0	Gehrig 1b	2	0	0	0
Terry 1b	4	0	2	0	Simmons cf-lf	4	0	1	0
Berger cf	4	0	0	0	Dykes 3b	3	1	2	0
Bartell ss	2	0	0	0	Cronin ss	3	1	1	0
(c) Traynor ph	1	0	1	0	R. Ferrell c	3	0	0	0
Hubbell p	0	0	0	0	Gomez p	1	0	1	1
(e) Cu'nello ph	1	0	0	0	Crowder p	1	0	0	0
Wilson c	1	0	0	0	(b) Averill ph	1	0	1	1
(a) O'Doul ph	1	0	0	0	Grove p	1	0	0	0
Hartnett c	1	0	0	0					
Hallahan p	1	0	0	0					
Warneke p	1	1	1	0					
(d) English ph	1	0	0	0					
Totals	34	2	8	2	**Totals**	31	4	9	4

```
National    0 0 0 0 0 2 0 0 0—2 8 0
American    0 1 2 0 0 1 0 0 x—4 9 1
```

(a) Grounded out for Wilson in 6th
(b) Singled for Crowder in 6th
(c) Doubled for Bartell in 7th
(d) Flied out for Warneke in 7th
(e) Struck out for Hubbell in 9th

5. "He leads the league in line drives right at somebody."

Double — Traynor. Triple — Warneke. Home runs — Ruth, Frisch. Stolen base — Gehringer. Sacrifice — Ferrell. Error — Gehrig. Double plays — Bartell-Frisch-Terry; Dykes-Gehrig.

	IP	H	R	ER	BB	SO
Hallahan	2	2	3	3	5	1
Warneke	4	6	1	1	0	2
Hubbell	2	1	0	0	1	1
Gomez	3	2	0	0	0	1
Crowder	3	3	2	2	0	0

Winning pitcher: Gomez. Losing pitcher: Hallahan

When the regular season resumed, the Tigers meandered along but managed to provide some thrills before the season was over. On August 22, they beat the Senators 10–8 behind two Greenberg home runs, ending Washington's 13-game winning streak. On September 24, Detroit beat the St. Louis Browns 7–0 on a two-hitter, with Bridges taking a no-hitter into the ninth inning for the third time of the season and the fourth time in his career. The other three times resulted in one-hitters. After the game, Harris announced his resignation as Tiger manager, effective at the end of the season. Detroit finished with a 75–79 record, good for fifth place, 25 games behind the Senators.

Another event in August that didn't seem significant at the time was the major league debut of a side-arming right-hander named Elden Auker. Still regarded as one of the greatest athletes to come out of Kansas State University, Auker starred in football, basketball, and baseball in college but hurt his shoulder playing football. From that point on, he was unable to throw a ball overhand with any kind of control or velocity. Pitching caused him pain, so he learned to throw submarine style, which is almost underhand like a softball pitcher, and he learned how to change speeds and throw curves and change-ups. He was 3–3 for the Tigers in 1933, but, like Bridges and Rowe, was on the verge of becoming one of the American League's best pitchers. He would also become a lifelong friend of Charlie Gehringer.

Charlie had another great year. He hit .325, drove in 105 runs, scored 103, and had 204 hits (second highest in the league), including 42 doubles, 6 triples, and 12 home runs. In the field, he had 900 putouts and assists and made only 17 errors.

Despite their losing record, the Tigers seemed poised to finally make their move, to be a contender in 1934. Gehringer had spent nearly a decade steadily improving to the point where he was regarded as a great player on a bad team. But as Charlie surveyed the cast of characters developing around him, he was encouraged. He said Schoolboy Rowe threw the ball as hard as Lefty Grove — and that was saying something considering Gehringer considered Grove the toughest pitcher he ever faced and was the guy whose fastball brought Charlie to tears when he was hit in the arm. "Schoolie," as Gehringer and others called him, was also a good hitter. Charlie said he could hit a ball as far as Babe Ruth; he just couldn't do it as often.

Bridges had a sharp-breaking curve ball that was so good, said Charlie, that sometimes batters would duck out of the way of a pitch coming at their head, only to have it break over the plate for a strike.

Rogell, the shortstop, was a good ballplayer but was short-fused. Gehringer said there would be times when an official scorer would give Billy an error on a tough play and he'd fuss and fume and get distracted, sometimes missing defensive signals like who was to cover second base on steal attempts. But like Gehringer, Rogell became a mainstay in the Tiger infield for many years to come.

Greenberg was to become the premier power hitter not only on the Tigers but in the American League. Gehringer said Greenberg had extremely long arms and big arc in his swing so that even if he was fooled on a pitch, he had the quickness to recover and hit the ball a long way.

At long last, the pieces were coming together for the Tigers. Two key transactions occurred toward the end of the year. On December 3, 1933, A's owner Connie Mack sold catcher Mickey Cochrane to Detroit for $100,000 and reserve catcher Johnny Pasek. That same day, Cochrane was named player-manager of the Tigers. Eleven days later, Detroit traded veteran outfielder John Stone to Washington for Leon Allen "Goose" Goslin, a 33-year-old outfielder with a lifetime batting average over .300. Goslin was also a bit of a character. In 1928, he and Heinie Manush of the Browns were running neck-and-neck for the American League batting title. As it happened, the Senators and Browns played each other on the last day of the season. As Goslin was coming up for his last at-bat, he was leading Manush by a couple of percentage points. Goose wanted to be taken out for a pinch hitter, but his teammates encouraged him to get up and take his swings. He went to the plate and started an argument with

Hank Greenberg was an RBI machine for the Tigers and hit 58 home runs in 1938. Charlie Gehringer said Greenberg had a big arc in his swing and was quick enough to make an adjustment and hit balls he was fooled on. Greenberg is shown in a 1935 plate appearance (photograph courtesy of the National Baseball Hall of Fame).

the home plate umpire, hoping to get tossed out of the game. That didn't work, so he was forced to get into the batter's box. He hit a dribbler and beat it out for a base hit, giving him a .379 batting average and edging out Manush, who hit .378.

The addition of Cochrane and Goslin gave the Tigers something they hadn't had since the days of Ty Cobb — players with winning experience who had been through the pressure of pennant races. Goslin played on the only Washington Senator teams to ever appear in a World Series — in 1924, 1925, and 1933. Cochrane was part of the backbone of the Connie Mack A's juggernaut that won American League championships in 1929, 1930, and 1931.

Most everyone who followed baseball in Detroit — writers, fans, players, the management — went into 1934 hoping that better days were ahead for the Tigers — finally.

CHAPTER 6

"What in the hell is he talking about?"

Detroit was a blue collar city that enjoyed the "Roaring '20s" when the auto industry, which made up much of its workforce, was thriving. Men who toiled during day at one of the city's many assembly plants came home at night, cleaned the grease from their elbows and under their fingernails, scrubbed their faces and hands, ate supper, and looked for ways of enjoying the good life. They might stroll down to the local speakeasy to tip a few, or they might take their spouses out for a night of dancing or take in the latest motion picture show. On weekends or when they could get an afternoon off, many took the trolley or got in their automobiles and made their way to the corner of Michigan and Trumbull, where the Tigers played ball at Navin Field.

In October 1929, the stock market crashed, and few cities were harder hit than Detroit. In the next few years, as one auto plant after another was forced to cut back, there was a spiraling impact on the city's overall economy. The mom-and-pop grocery stores, clothing stores, cleaners, drug stores, barber shops, and beauty salons — places that often offered credit to patrons from the neighborhood who fell on hard times — were now struggling to survive. In the past, they had thrived because of business from customers who worked at plants that were now closing down. By early 1932, more than 220,000 men and women found themselves without a job and without much hope of finding one. Sometimes, the hopelessness turned violent.

Henry Ford, the millionaire who amassed his fortune selling automobiles made by loyal employees, fired 67,000 workers in a span of about

6. "What in the hell is he talking about?"

three years. Unemployed auto workers' disenchantment with Ford management turned brutal on March 7, 1932, when 3,000 protesters marched on Ford's River Rouge plant in Dearborn, Michigan. When they refused to disperse, police used fire hoses and tear gas on them. But instead of leaving, many of the protesters tried to fight back. A melee ensued that caused police officers to draw their guns and open fire. Five protesters were killed; 60 were wounded.[1]

Baseball, like other recreation industries, experienced the economic sting because thousands of Americans were in soup lines, not lines to get into the ball game. In 1930, before the full force of the Depression had settled in, attendance at major league ballparks was just over 10.1 million, the highest it had been in the 20th century. By 1932, it was down to about 8.1 million, and it would bottom out at 6 million before it began to turn around. Nationally, average attendance at major league games was about 5,000, but it was only about 4,100 in Detroit, where a little over 300,000 people attended Tiger games in 1933.

Navin lost a small fortune in the stock market crash but not everything and was willing to spend some of what remained to improve his ballclub. He wanted a manager who knew baseball and who would be a big draw. His first choice was Babe Ruth, whose career was on the downside with the Yankees and who had expressed his desire to manage someday. Navin contacted Ruth and wanted the Bambino to come to Detroit to talk terms. Ruth said he'd like to, but he had a commitment in Hawaii that would take a couple of weeks. The Babe said he would call Navin when he got back, but the Hawaiian trip probably cost him the chance to manage a major league team. Right about that time, Connie Mack was having one of his "fire sales," dumping experienced, expensive ballplayers in return for cash to help keep his business (the ballclub) afloat. Mickey Cochrane was available, and Navin jumped at the chance to get him. In one transaction, the Tigers had bagged a manager, a catcher, and a competitor. Cochrane emphasized the kind of spirit he had, and that he expected from his team, when he spoke to the ballclub early in spring training in 1934. He told them simply, "We've gotta ballclub here that can win a pennant."

Tiger players must have looked at each other in disbelief as they listened to their new manager. This was a team that hadn't been in a World Series since 1909, had been over .500 only twice in the last eight years, and had finished in the second division in each of the past six years. Their three top pitchers were Bridges, who was 27 with two years experience, Rowe who was 24 with one year of experience, and Auker who was 23 with about a month's experience in the big leagues. Auker said the players' first reaction was to think to themselves, "What in the hell is he talking about?"

Gordon Stanley "Mickey" Cochrane was born April 6, 1903 — about a month before Charlie Gehringer — in Bridgewater, Massachusetts. He was not used to losing and didn't tolerate it very well. At Boston University, he played baseball and was also the quarterback, running back, and punter on the football team. The quarterback position suited him well. As a catcher in baseball, Cochrane was the signal caller, just as he had been in football. He didn't know any other way but to exert control and great influence over the athletes who became part of his life. He was almost destined to be a big league manager.

Cochrane signed with the Philadelphia A's in 1925 and hit .330 his rookie year, the first of nine seasons in which he hit over .300. He was behind the plate for the A's in 1929, 1930, and 1931 when they made it to the World Series, and he retired with a lifetime batting average of .320, the highest for any catcher in baseball history.[2]

When Ty Cobb had stepped down as manager in 1926, he was succeeded by George Moriarty, who took a temporary exodus from his umpiring career to take the wheel of the Tiger ship for a couple of years. When Detroit management was ready to make a change, Moriarty quickly resumed his old job as umpire. His days as the Tiger manager do not make a headline but rather a footnote in the ballclub's history. He was followed by easy-going Bucky Harris, who avoided confrontation and seemed content to be everyone's friend. Cochrane came in like a 3 A.M. fire alarm.

He told the ballclub they had the best first baseman in baseball in Greenberg, the best second baseman in Gehringer, and the best double play combination in Rogell, Gehringer, and Greenberg. He told his young pitching staff that they were as good as any staff that he had caught in Philadelphia. He told them he would be catching them much of the time, but he wanted them to be confident on the mound, so they were to shake him off any time he was signaling for a pitch they didn't want to throw. From day one of spring training, Cochrane worked to instill a winning

6. "What in the hell is he talking about?"

Mickey Cochrane brought an aggressive, fighting spirit to the Tigers and led them to two American League championships and one World Series championship. He is shown here in typical form in the early 1930s (photograph courtesy of the National Baseball Hall of Fame).

attitude in his ballclub, teaching them to fear no one. He understood that his first job was to get the players to believe in themselves.[3]

Gehringer said Cochrane was the right man at the right time. "Mickey was a super guy and we needed him so badly, what with all of these young pitchers we had coming along, like Schoolboy Rowe and Tommy Bridges," he said. "It was like getting a good quarterback in football. You're dead without one and it's the same way with a catcher."

Third baseman Marv Owen said he was impressed with how the new manager changed the attitude of the ballclub. He remembered Cochrane telling the team, "You guys are accustomed to losing. There's not much difference between winning and losing. I don't want you fellas to talk about losing."

Cochrane gained the respect of the players almost immediately, and that made it a lot more palatable when he got tough with them. Herman "Flea" Clifton, a reserve infielder who only played four years in the major leagues, was a fast runner and tried to be another Ty Cobb on the base paths. In one game, he scampered all the way home from second on a sacrifice bunt. Cochrane approached him in the dugout and said, "You know, son, if you wouldn't have scored, I would have shipped your ass so far away it'd cost you $75 to mail a postcard from there."[4]

Cochrane's arrival in Detroit, later heralded in the *Detroit Free Press* as pulling the city out of the Depression, could have plunged the Tigers' veteran catcher, Ray Hayworth, into a depression of his own — but Hayworth was upbeat about it. He said he knew Cochrane was the best catcher in baseball, and even though Hayworth had been around for years, he learned a lot from Mickey, like the art of pulling high pitches down and low pitches up to try to "steal" a strike on balls out of the strike zone. Hayworth summed up his feelings by saying he would rather be a backup catcher on a championship team than a starting catcher on a mediocre team.

Hayworth was a bit of a character in his own right and found himself on the receiving end of one of Charlie Gehringer's classic, if infrequent, quips. Hayworth was a better-than-average hitter, but one pitcher who always seemed to get him out easily was Herb Pennock of the Yankees. Hayworth fretted about Pennock. He stewed. He cussed. He swung hard. He let up on his swing. But nothing seemed to work. In a game against the Yankees in 1933, Hayworth faced Pennock and grounded out his first time up and then hit a weak fly ball his next time up. In his third at-bat, Pennock jammed him, and Hayworth hit a harmless little pop-up that didn't get more than 10 feet off the ground and traveled about 60 feet. Pennock caught it on the mound without having to move. He could have caught it bare-handed. Hayworth returned to the dugout fuming, and his teammates kept their distance. As he was putting on his shin guards, stomping his feet and cursing, Gehringer, sitting next to him, leaned over and said, "I know how you feel, Ray. When they rob you of a hit with a great catch like that, it's really tough." There was silence for a moment, and then everyone, including Hayworth, exploded in laughter.[5]

Cochrane made a decision prior to opening day that changed the dynamic of the ballclub. He wanted to find more playing time for Joyner

6. "What in the hell is he talking about?"

Clifford "Jo-Jo" White, who got his nickname because of the way he seemed to pronounce his home state of Georgia. White was a light-hitting outfielder but a fleet-footed base runner who set records in the minor leagues for stealing bases. White had played sparingly for the Tigers in his first two years, but Cochrane wanted to give him more playing time and decided to try him as a lead-off hitter, someone who could set the table for Gehringer, Goslin and Greenberg.

The Tigers got off to a decent start in 1934, winning their first two games, and were 6–4 at the end of April. Marberry had two of the wins. Rowe pitched twice without picking up a decision. But the ballclub seemed to have new life as Cochrane demanded hustle and led by example. And already, the season showed the promise of exciting baseball, even if the breaks didn't always go the Tigers' way. For instance, on April 28, Goose Goslin had the dubious distinction of hitting into four consecutive double plays — but the Tigers still managed to beat Cleveland, 4–1. Marv Owen had an unassisted double play at third base, and the next day he executed another unassisted double play, the second time in baseball history that a third baseman turned that trick two games in a row.

Gehringer, batting third in the lineup behind White and Cochrane, was doing what he did consistently — waiting for his pitch and getting on base any way he could ahead of the big bat of Hank Greenberg. By mid–May, Gehringer was once again on pace to bat over .300, drive in more than 100 runs, and hit 50 doubles. Because he reached base so often and was hitting ahead of Greenberg, he seemed assured of scoring more than 100 runs as well. Writers began referring to Gehringer, Greenberg, and Goslin as the "G-men" in the Detroit lineup, a term fans quickly picked up.[6]

On May 5, Goslin started a month-long hitting streak in which he hit safely in 30 consecutive games. During that span, he hit .381 with 11 doubles, 2 triples, 5 home runs, and 24 runs batted in.

The Tigers, like any team, had their bad days as well. On May 6, the Red Sox beat Detroit 14–4, scoring 12 runs in the fourth inning, including four consecutive triples with Carl Reynolds, Moose Solters, Rick Ferrell, and Bucky Walters doing the damage. Marberry was the loser. The next day, the Tigers bounced back with an 8–6 win with Schoolboy Rowe pitching and also belting a home run.

On June 6, Bob Weiland of Cleveland threw a one-hitter against the

The heart of the Detroit lineup during their championship years included (from left) manager/catcher Mickey Cochrane, second baseman Charlie Gehringer, shortstop Goose Goslin, first baseman/outfielder Hank Greenberg, and third baseman Marv Owen, shown in 1935, when they led the Tigers to a World Series Championship (photograph courtesy of the National Baseball Hall of Fame).

Tigers but lost the game 2–1. The only hit for Detroit was Gehringer's RBI single that proved to be the game-winner. Goslin went hitless for the first time in 31 days, ending his hitting streak at 30. But the game had much more significance than individual achievement. The Tigers had inched their way into first place — the latest in a season they had held the top spot in 10 years, since August 24, 1924, when Ty Cobb's ballclub snuck into first place for one day and then relinquished it to the Yankees. In five of those 10 years, the Tigers were never in first place at any point in the season, not even after opening day. It had truly been a long, dry spell.

6. "What in the hell is he talking about?"

Under managers Cobb, Moriarty, and Harris, the latest date the Tigers had been on top is as follows:

1933 — Never
1932 — April 24
1931 — Never
1930 — April 17
1929 — Never
1928 — Never
1927 — Never
1926 — April 20
1925 — April 14 (after a win on opening day)
1924 — Aug. 24

Baseball in Detroit had become fun again. The *Detroit Free Press* heralded the Tigers' ascension with a three-word headline on June 7: "This Is Exciting." Schoolboy, Mickey, and, of course, the "G-Men" became part of the everyday vocabulary in the Motor City.

On June 20, Gehringer, Owen, Cochrane, and Greenberg each banged out three hits as the Tigers beat Washington 13–10. Heinie Manush of the Senators, the ex-Tiger, had four hits in the game, giving him 102 for the year, the quickest to this day that anyone has accumulated 100 hits in a season.

On July 10, the second annual major league All-Star Game was played at the Polo Grounds in New York. Once again, Charlie Gehringer was the starting second baseman for the American League, and once again he played every inning. The American League broke open the game with a six-run fifth inning and then held on to win, 9–7. Frankie Frisch became the first man to homer in two consecutive All-Star Games, but the contest has long been remembered for the performance of the Giants' great screwball pitcher, Carl Hubbell. In the first two innings, he struck out 5 future Hall of Famers in a row — Babe Ruth, Lou Gehrig, Jimmy Foxx, Al Simmons, and Joe Cronin. One detail that has become lost in telling and retelling of the story is that Gehringer got a hit off of Hubbell before the strikeout onslaught began. Charlie opened the game with a single and went to second on an outfield error. Heinie Manush followed with a walk. Then the two of them pulled off a double steal. Hubbell then struck out Ruth, Gehrig, and Foxx to end the inning. He opened the second inning by fanning Simmons and Cronin. Bill Dickey, the Yankee catcher, then

Batter, catcher, and umpire are all pictures of concentration as Charlie takes a rip at a pitch in 1937. He probably had two strikes on him (photograph courtesy of the National Baseball Hall of Fame).

singled, but Hubbell struck out Lefty Gomez to end the inning. Hubbell's six strikeouts in two innings remains an All-Star record that may be tied but will probably never be broken.[7]

Charlie had two hits in three at-bats. The double-steal in the first inning was the first in the All-Star Game's brief history, and Gehringer was the first to have a stolen base in consecutive All-Star Games.

In the second half of the season, Detroit was in a fight with the Yankees for the American League championship. On July 29–30, the Tigers played back-to-back doubleheaders in two cities. They beat the hapless White Sox 16–15 and 6–4, then boarded a train for Cleveland, arriving early in the morning and then splitting with the Indians that afternoon, losing the opener 9–7 and coming back to win the second game 4–2. At the end of the day, the Yankees held first place by the narrowest of margins. The standings were:

6. "What in the hell is he talking about?"

New York	59–36	.621	—
Detroit	60–37	.619	—
Cleveland	54–42	.563	5.5
Boston	52–47	.525	9.5
St. Louis	42–49	.462	15.5
Washington	44–53	.454	16.5
Philadelphia	38–55	.409	20.5
Chicago	34–64	.347	26.5

The win against Cleveland in the second game was the start of something big, but no one realized it at the time. The Tigers were fatigued with a grueling schedule and the dog days of August ahead of them. But Gehringer said they had something that had been lacking for many years — confidence — the Cochrane-inspired belief that they could win every day. After all, this was the man who told them in spring training that they could win the pennant.

Detroit didn't lose a game for the first two weeks of August. Including their July 31 win in the second game against the Indians, the Tigers reeled off 14 straight wins. Rowe, Bridges, and Auker all contributed shutouts, and the trio went 4–0, 3–0, and 2–0 respectively during the streak. On August 14, a crowd of 77,000, the largest weekday crowd in baseball history, jammed Yankee Stadium to watch the Tigers and the Bronx Bombers in a doubleheader. The Tigers had moved into sole possession of first place during their streak. If the Yankees could sweep the twin bill, they could move to within 2½ of Detroit. But with quiet Charlie Gehringer leading the way, the Tigers prevailed in both games, winning 9–5 and 7–3. Gehringer homered in each game to provide the offensive thrust for Detroit.

The next day, the Yankees won, and Detroit's winning streak was snapped at 14. But during that time period, August 1–14, the Yankees went 7–7, so they trailed Detroit by 6½ games on August 15. They never caught up, and Detroit never looked back.

The Tigers had picked up some pitching insurance on August 4 when they acquired Alvin "General" Crowder on waivers from the Senators. Crowder had been the top pitcher in the American League with records of 26–13 and 24–15 in 1932 and 1933 but was struggling in 1934, having won only 4 games and losing 10. The Senators may have thought Crowder's best days were behind him, but Cochrane thought the 35-year-old still had some life in him. With Mickey behind the plate, the "General" won five of six decisions down the stretch for the Tigers — and won 16 games for Cochrane the following year.

Crowder got his nickname because his last name was the same as Gen. Enoch Crowder, who was best known as the man who originated the military draft during World War I. Crowder, the ballplayer, was no relation. He had some great years in the majors and was 21–5 for the St. Louis Browns in 1928 and led the American League in winning percentage with .808. He also has the distinction of being traded for two Hall of Famers in 1930 when St. Louis traded him to Washington for Heinie Manush and Goose Goslin. While Crowder didn't make it to the Hall of Fame, he finished his career with 167 wins and only 115 losses. In 1934, he gave the young Tiger pitching staff something it didn't have, a wily veteran who knew how to win and who had experienced the pressure of pennant races.[8]

The Tigers traveled from city to city on a private train Navin arranged for them called "The Tiger Special." It had relatively comfortable seating, sleeper cars, and a dining car. Gehringer was sociable with teammates but was mostly a spectator in the high jinx that often occurred on long road trips. Rowe, Auker, Rogell, Owen, Gee Walker, and Jo-Jo White often passed the time playing card games such as hearts, bridge, and poker. Crowder's arrival livened up the games because he was a master at card tricks and had a "gambling" background from the days of his youth in North Carolina, where he worked as a "runner" in a house of prostitution and gambling, serving drinks and running errands for the proprietors and their patrons. He probably could have squeezed a lot of money from his teammates, but from all accounts, he just added some fun and some good stories to long road trips.

Meanwhile, as the Tigers were devouring their opposition in early August, another remarkable streak was in progress. Schoolboy Rowe was unbeatable. On June 16, he was the winning pitcher as Detroit beat Boston 11–4. That was the start of a 16-game winning streak that didn't end until August 29. During that time he had 13 starts and won them all, plus three games in relief. The 16 wins in a row tied the major league record set by Lefty Grove of the A's, and the streak ended with a 13–5 loss to the A's.

Gehringer said the pressure on Schoolboy was immense: "The newspapers were driving him crazy. He wasn't getting any sleep. They were in his room and calling him at all hours of the day and night." Charlie was

6. "What in the hell is he talking about?"

having the best year of his career but was overshadowed by his more colorful teammates. Charlie didn't mind; in fact, he preferred it that way.

Schoolboy became kind of a folk hero in Detroit, a different sort of adoration than fans gave to Gehringer, the quiet, dependable "Mechanical Man" who had earned their love and respect through years of quality play. Schoolboy, the big, lumbering right-hander, had achieved something more like instant success, like a singer who comes out of nowhere to have a number-one hit.[9]

About the time Schoolboy came along, Detroit fans were enjoying a relatively new way of following their team — on the radio. And Rowe provided a memorable moment when he participated in his first live radio interview. At one point during the interview, thinking the microphone was not on, he looked over at his girlfriend standing nearby and said, "How am I doin,' Edna?" It wasn't long before bench jockeys on teams throughout the league needled him with shouts of, "How's he doin,' Edna?"

Another player who contributed mightily to the Tigers' success was Elon Chester "Chief" Hogsett, whom fans cheered on with war hoops whenever he appeared even though, as Tiger historian Richard Bak put it, he had just a little more Indian blood in him than a Cleveland Indian. Hogsett was the left-handed version of Elden Auker in that he too threw side-armed and was a relief specialist, much like Marberry had been with the Senators.

Hogsett roomed with Gehringer for five years, and they became close friends. They shared a common trait in that neither one of them was talkative — and that trait produced one of the classic anecdotes about Charlie. As the story goes, he and the Chief were eating breakfast one day in a hotel restaurant, and Hogsett said, "Pass the salt, please." Charlie handed him the salt shaker and said, "You could have pointed." The story sounds far-fetched, like it came out of the imagination of an overzealous publicity agent. In an interview years later, Hogsett said he had heard the story a thousand times — but he did not deny that it happened.

H.G. Salinger, a longtime Detroit sportswriter, once wrote a column that was a spoof depicting a typical conversation between Charlie and the Chief. They had finished dinner and were discussing plans for the evening. According to Salinger, at 7:30, Charlie asked Hogsett if they should go see a movie. At 8:00, Hogsett replied that might be a good idea. At 8:30 Charlie asked him what he'd like to see. At 9:00, Hogsett responded that it didn't matter to him. At 9:30, Gehringer looked at his watch and said, "It's getting kind of late." At 10:00, Hogsett agreed. So they decided to stay in for the night.[10]

Charlie and the Chief often enjoyed having a few beers together, one of the few "vices" ever associated with Gehringer. One time in Boston, the two met a priest who was a friend of Charlie's, and the three of them enjoyed an evening of drinking together that lasted into the wee hours of the morning. The Tigers played the Red Sox that afternoon and, uncharacteristically, Charlie showed up late at the ballpark, plagued with a headache and a queasy stomach. The game that day was rained out, a circumstance the Chief attributed to "divine intervention."[11]

The Tigers kept their momentum going in September and quietly clinched their first American League championship on September 24. It was an off-day for Detroit, but Boston beat the Yankees, clinching the pennant for the Tigers, their first championship since 1909, the days of Ty Cobb, Sam Crawford, and Hughie Jennings.

Cochrane had accomplished in one year what some managers never achieve in a lifetime. The Tigers roared with their bats, on the mound, and in the field. Gehringer played every game for the third straight year and, for the second time in his career, had a string of more than 500 consecutive games. Obviously, he led the league in games played. He also led the league in hits with 214, and in runs scored with 134. He hit 50 doubles, second only to Greenberg's 63. Charlie was also second in the league in batting with a .356 average and second in on-base percentage, .450, and finished second to his teammate and manager Cochrane in the Most Valuable Player balloting, even though Lou Gehrig won the Triple Crown for the Yankees with a .363 average, 49 home runs, and 165 runs batted in.

The Tigers hit .300 as a team and had five starters who hit over .300—six if Rowe is included. The pitcher hit .303 with two homers and 22 runs batted in. The "G-men"—Greenberg, Gehringer, and Goslin—combined for 366 runs batted in, an average of 122 each. The infield of Greenberg, Gehringer, Rogell, and Owen combined for 462 runs batted in, an all-time high for an infield. Their RBI totals averaged out to 115 each. Yet another amazing statistic from the Tiger infield is that combined, they played all but one game in 1934—and that was because Greenberg had an excused absence to observe a Jewish holiday. Detroit was first in the league in hitting with its .300 average, first in the league in stolen bases with 125, committed the fewest errors with 156, and the pitching staff tied with the Yankees for most shutouts, 13. Schoolboy Rowe was 24–8, Tommy Bridges was 22–11, Firpo Marberry was 15–5, and Elden Auker was 15–7.

Dan Daniel, the often caustic New York sportswriter, said one of the biggest differences between the 1933 and 1934 Tigers was the development of the infielders, particularly Rogell, for which Daniel said Gehringer deserved much of the credit. Daniel, who over the years had trouble giving Charlie a straight compliment, wrote that Gehringer is "the best second baseman in the major leagues. Until this year, Charlie was just a colorless, if great, ballplayer. He has all mechanical skill but no fire nor the ability to inspire teammates." Cochrane tried to change this, according to Daniel, by making Charlie the "captain" of the infield. He consulted with him on infield strategy and assigned him to work with Rogell as his personal project. The result was that Rogell turned into "an infield dandy."[12]

Daniel's colleague at the *World-Telegram*, Joe Williams, also criticized Charlie's personality, echoing that he was a player "without color." Williams wrote, "Considering his class, he is the least interviewed player in the major leagues." Bad reviews didn't bother Charlie. As he had said many times, "you don't hit with your mouth."

One of the most impressive statistics of the year came not from the players or management but from the fans. Attendance at Navin Field was 919,000, highest in the league and highest in team history. Detroit was in love with its Tigers. As they prepared to play the St. Louis Cardinals in the World Series, a seven-story banner was hung from the upper floors of the J.L. Hudson building downtown. The huge smiling Tiger on it captured the mood of the city, still reeling in the throws of the Depression but in some ways seeing their beloved ballclub as a symbol of how desire, spirit, commitment, and fortitude can prevail in the most dire of circumstances.

CHAPTER 7

"Every time I turn around, the guy's on second base."

The 1934 St. Louis Cardinals are one of baseball's legendary teams. Their pitching staff was led by the Dean brothers — Jay Hannah "Dizzy" Dean and his brother Paul. Dizzy won 30 games — the last National League pitcher to accomplish that feat — and Paul won 19. In a doubleheader against Brooklyn on September 21, Dizzy threw a one-hitter in the opener, and Paul tossed a no-hitter in the nightcap. Dizzy said afterward, "If I'd a known Paul was going to throw a no-hitter, I'd a throwed one, too." Though overshadowed by the flamboyant Dean brothers, the rest of the pitching staff were no slouches. Tex Carlton won 16, and Bill Walker won 12. Dazzy Vance joined the staff late in the season and, after many great years with mediocre Brooklyn teams, played a fill-in role for the Cardinals and was rewarded with his first World Series appearance.

Rip Collins, the Cardinal first baseman, put up big numbers. He hit .300 with a league-leading 35 home runs and 128 runs batted in. Frankie Frisch was considered the best second baseman in the National League. Like Cochrane of the Tigers, Frisch was a player-manager and a firebrand who demanded hustle and embodied the winning spirit. Another big offensive weapon for the Cardinals was outfielder Joe "Ducky" Medwick, a great clutch hitter who batted .319 with 18 home runs and 106 runs batted in. Along with third baseman Johnny Leonard Roosevelt "Pepper" Martin and shortstop Leo Durocher, this band of players became known in baseball lore as "The Gas House Gang." Martin got his nickname in the minor leagues because of his fiery play and hustle, but preferred to be called Johnny or Leonard. When he came up with the Cardinals, general manager Branch Rickey told the press to call him "Pepper" because Rickey felt it fit the image that he wanted for the Cardinals. Rickey was the boss, so "Pepper" it was.

As for the "Gas House Gang," Durocher is believed to have coined the phrase because of how other teams regarded the rough-and-tumble Cardinals. The St. Louis players seemed to enjoy their reputation of being tough, rowdy individuals from the wrong side of the tracks who were not intimidated by anybody or anything. "Gas house" was a familiar term of the era, referring to manufacturing plants that made gas for lighting and cooking from coal. The gas houses usually had a foul smell, and their workers emerged from their jobs every day sweaty and grimy.

Unlike the Tigers, the Cardinals and their fans were accustomed to winning. The 1934 pennant followed National League championships for St. Louis in 1926, 1928, 1930, and 1931. But they had to scrap for this year's pennant. The New York Giants held first place for most of the second half of the season but went into a tailspin in September. They still had a chance to win on the last weekend of the year but a loss to the Dodgers while Dean was winning his 30th game for St. Louis clinched it for the Cardinals. Losing to the Dodgers with a pennant on the line was a particularly bitter defeat for Giant manager Bill Terry who, before the season started, had said to a sportswriter, "Brooklyn? Are they still in the league?"

The World Series opened in Detroit. Despite all the hype and hoopla the Cardinals brought with them, the Tigers were slight favorites to win the series. They had won 101 games during the regular season, had pitching that could match the Cardinals, and up and down the lineup had a better-hitting ballclub. They also had the advantage of playing four home games if the series stretched to seven games. Even Henry Ford, the auto tycoon, got caught up in the excitement. Although his business had plummeted to such as extent that he had laid off thousands of workers in the past few years, Ford found enough cash to spend $100,000 to sponsor radio broadcasts of the Series.

Cochrane decided to save Rowe, his ace, for the second game and started General Crowder, a veteran of two previous World Series events, in the opener. The strategy might have worked if Detroit's defense hadn't fallen apart. The Tigers, who committed fewer errors that season than any team in the American League, made five in game one of the World

Series — all by infielders. Gehringer, Greenberg, and Rogell each had one, and Owen had two. The Cardinals coasted to an 8–3 victory. Greenberg and Medwick each had home runs. Gehringer had two singles and an RBI.

In game two, Schoolboy went the distance in a 12-inning thriller which the Tigers won 3–2. At one point, Rowe retired 22 batters in a row to set a World Series record, broken 22 years later when Don Larsen threw a perfect game for the Yankees. The Cardinals scored runs in each of the first two innings. Detroit scored one in the fourth and was on the verge of losing again when Gee Walker, pinch-hitting for Jo-Jo White, singled home the tying run in the bottom of the ninth. In what had become an all-too-familiar scene, Walker, representing the winning run, got picked off first. The Tigers evened the series in the bottom of the 12th when Goslin singled to score the game-winning run. Bill Walker took the loss, pitching his fourth inning in relief of Wild Bill Hallahan. Gehringer was 1-for-4 and had a stolen base.

The series shifted to Sportsman's Park in St. Louis, where Paul Dean locked horns with Tommy Bridges. For the third straight game, the Cardinals scored early, with runs in the first and second innings. This time they held up as St. Louis won 4–1. Greenberg tripled home the Tigers' only run in the ninth inning. Gehringer had two hits in five at-bats, including a double.

Elden Auker, the side-arming right-hander, got the call to start game four for the Tigers with a mission of trying to prevent the Cardinals from going up three games to one. His mound opponent was 16-game winner Tex Carlton. St. Louis jumped into an early lead for the fourth straight game with a run in the second inning. But the Tiger bats finally came alive as they scored three in the third, one in the fourth, one in the seventh, and five in the eighth to win easily, 10–4 and even the series at two games apiece. Gehringer had two singles in four at-bats and, except for his fielding error in game one, was putting together a pretty good series. He had at least one hit in each of the first four games and seven hits in 17 at-bats.

A bit of drama occurred in the fourth inning when Dizzy Dean, in the game as a pinch runner, was struck in the forehead by a throw from Rogell, who was trying to throw to first as Dean was sliding into second. The ball bounded into centerfield, but Dean wasn't going anywhere. He

7. "Every time I turn around, the guy's on second base."

was transported off the field on a stretcher and taken to a hospital for X-rays of his head, prompting a hospital report that has lived in baseball history: "The X-Rays showed nothing."

The fifth game, to determine who would have the series lead going back to Detroit, featured mound opponents Bridges and Dizzy Dean, fresh out of the hospital. Diz wasn't as sharp as he was in his first start, and Bridges was better than he had been a few days earlier, so Detroit prevailed 3–1 with Gehringer contributing his first World Series home run, a booming drive that one newspaper called "Ruthian" and another said was hit so far it "demoralized" Dean. Frisch was criticized by some in the press for allowing Dean to pinch run the day before — and then to start him the day after he was leveled by Rogell's throw.

The teams returned to Navin Field in Detroit for game six. Cochrane and the Tigers were in exactly the position they hoped to be in on their return to their home field. They were up three games to two and had Rowe going in game six and Auker in game seven — if it was necessary. Rowe's mound opponent was Paul Dean, and both starting pitchers went all the way with neither team using a pinch hitter or pinch runner. St. Louis once again got the early jump, scoring a run in the first inning. The Tigers countered with a run in the third to tie it. The Cardinals tacked on two more in the sixth, but Detroit rallied with two in the sixth to tie it again. St. Louis pushed across its fourth run in the seventh inning, and the Tigers could not come up with another run off of Dean as St. Louis won 4–3, forcing a seventh game. Rowe pitched well but had trouble with the bottom of the Cardinal batting order. Light-hitting Durocher, eighth in the lineup, had three hits, and Paul Dean helped his own cause by singling home Durocher in the seventh. Rowe, a .303 hitter during the regular season, batted for himself with two out in the ninth inning and brought the crowd to its feet when he launched a Paul Dean fastball deep into centerfield, only to be caught at the wall for the final out. Had he pulled it or sliced it, he would have had a game-tying home run.

The Tigers thought they were robbed on a bad call by umpire Brick Owens in the sixth inning. Gehringer said it turned out to be the turning point in the series. Rogell said afterwards that pictures of the play showed that Owens blew the call. With the Tigers down 3–2, they had Cochrane on second and Gehringer on first with nobody out. Goslin laid down a bunt in front of the plate. Delancey, the Cardinal catcher, scooped it up and fired to third. Gehringer, who had advanced to second, and Rogell, watching from the on-deck circle, both said afterwards, no doubt about it, Cochrane beat the throw to third. But Owens didn't see it that way and called Mickey out. So instead of having the bases loaded and nobody out, Detroit had runners on first and second and one out. Rogell then hit a long fly to right centerfield. Gehringer advanced to third, and Greenberg singled him home. Owen then flied out to end the inning. Had Cochrane been called safe at third, the two subsequent fly balls could have been sacrifice flies, scoring runs to give the Tigers the lead. As it was, the Cardinals won, and now to win the World Series, the Tigers would have to beat Dizzy Dean in the seventh game.

Auker took the mound for the Tigers against Ole Diz, who was appearing in his fourth World Series game, counting the one in which he appeared briefly — and painfully — as a pinch runner. The game was scoreless for two innings, but in the third, Detroit's stellar defense stood still on a couple of plays. Dean hit a pop fly that dropped between Goslin, Rogell, and Owen in short leftfield as each thought the other would make a stab at it. Dean wound up on second when Gehringer was slow getting over to the bag to cover. Then Pepper Martin hit a ground ball to Greenberg and was safe when Auker didn't get over in time to cover first. Rothrock, the right fielder, then walked to load the bases. Auker made a good pitch on Frisch, jamming him, but Frankie flailed at the ball and blooped it weakly over Greenberg's head. Before the inning was over, the Cardinals had seven runs and Auker was in the showers, having given up a walk, what should have been a routine ground out, and two bloop hits. He only got one out and was charged with giving up six runs on six hits in his 2⅓ innings. The Cardinals scored another one in that inning and added four more against a parade of Tiger pitchers — Rowe, Hogsett, Bridges, Marberry, and Crowder — before it was all over. The Cardinals won 11–0.

The most memorable play of the game was an unfortunate one involving Medwick and Marv Owen. In the sixth inning, with the Cardinals well on their way to the championship, Joe Medwick slid into third base hard and collided with Owen, the Tiger third baseman. The fans, already out of sorts because of the lopsided score of the game, let Medwick have it when he took his position in left field in the bottom of the sixth, pelting him with fruit, vegetables, newspapers — just about anything they could

7. "Every time I turn around, the guy's on second base."

find. The game had to be halted three times because of all the garbage being tossed on the field. Medwick and the rest of the Cardinals scampered to the safety of the dugout. Managers Cochrane and Frisch as well as Medwick and Owen were summoned to confer with Commissioner Kenesaw Mountain Landis, who was in attendance in the box seats just beyond the Tiger dugout. Landis ordered Medwick removed from the game for his own protection and to thwart the possibility of a riot. Chick Fullis replaced him — and got a base hit in his only time at bat in place of Medwick.

In recounting the episode, Owen said the score was 8–0 when Medwick hit what looked to be an easy double off the right field wall but instead of stopping, he rounded second and came barreling into third. As Owen reached to catch the throw coming into third, his spike landed on Medwick's right foot. As soon as he realized it, he instinctively withdrew his foot and got on his haunches, said Owen. Medwick then kicked him three times. "That made me mad. When a guy slides hard but clean, that's okay. You don't give a damn, but when he gives you a few extra digs, well, you get a little mad," said Owen, who admitted he was frustrated with the way the whole game was going. As Medwick got up and brushed himself off, he offered to shake hands with Owen, but Owen ignored him. That too set off the fans who were waiting for Medwick to take the field.

Owen said the meeting with Landis was quick. He asked the third baseman what happened, and Owen replied, "You saw what happened." Landis asked Medwick what happened, and Medwick replied, "I slid into third base." The judge asked what else happened, and Medwick said "Nothing." To which Landis replied, "You're out of the game."

Rogell had his own take on what happened. He made the relay throw to third that started the action. Rogell thought Medwick was showboating with an 8–0 lead. "Medwick was fancy-danning it. When you're out in front like that, I guess your hat gets that big," he said. From Rogell's vantage point, Medwick hit Owen with his spikes when he slid into third. In trying not to fall, Owen wanted to step around Medwick but stepped on him instead. Rogell said the fans in left field threw everything they could find at Medwick. If there had been an old Ford parked in the stands, they would have thrown that, too, he said.[1]

Auker's version of the incident had Medwick sliding into third, spik-

Joe Medwick was a scrappy outfielder for the St. Louis Cardinals. His hard slide into third base in the 1934 World Series led to his removal from the game by order of Commissioner Kenesaw Mountain Landis after fans pelted him with fruit in the outfield (photograph courtesy of the National Baseball Hall of Fame).

ing Owen, and Owen returning the favor by tagging Medwick with the ball on his face. Auker, exhausted and dejected, left the clubhouse before the game was over and listened to the last two innings on his car radio.

Medwick said as he was heading for third base, he got the stand-up signal from the third base coach. But as he neared the bag, Owen made a motion like he was about to tag him, so he slid at the last minute and apparently spiked him. "I stuck up my hand to show that I hadn't meant to hurt him and he said something and I said, 'Well ____ you, too.'"[2]

Gehringer said he watched what was happening and, in his typical wry, brief way, stated that there must have been a fruit truck making deliveries in left field, based on all the stuff that was thrown at Medwick.

Landis also had his say on the matter after the game. "I saw as well as anyone what Medwick did. When Umpire Klem took no action and the players quieted down, I hoped the matter was ended. But when it became apparent that the demonstration of the crowd would never terminate, I decided to take action."[3] Paul Gallico, writing in the *New York Daily News*, wrote, "Landis did the sane and reasonable thing. Flames were creeping toward a powder mine. He extinguished the flame."

Medwick said friction between the two teams had been brewing from the time they arrived at the ballpark for the first game. He said when the Tigers were taking batting practice, Dizzy Dean walked by Hank Greenberg in the batter's box and began taunting him. A fight almost broke out then, before the first pitch was even thrown in the series, said Medwick.[4]

Fulfilling Dizzy's boast, the Dean brothers won every Cardinal victory in the Series. Gehringer was the leading Tiger hitter and tied for leading hitter in the series, getting 11 hits in 29 at-bats for a .379 average with one home run. Medwick of the Cardinals had identical stats, but when Landis removed him in the sixth inning of game seven, it prevented him from an attempt to tie the all-time series record of 12 hits. Greenberg had the only other Tiger homer and hit .321 for the series. Gee Walker hit .333.

When the World Series ended, Dan Daniel, the New York sportswriter who had trouble saying anything nice about Gehringer without throwing in a barb, acknowledged Charlie's stellar play in the Series. He wrote, "As had been expected, Charlie Gehringer proved a great ballplayer and a fine hitter.... As a matter of fact, Gehringer was something of a disappointment in spite of his hitting. He was flat and colorless as compared to the Gas House gang."⁵

Charlie didn't need Dan Daniel's endorsement, nor did he care. His work ethic and his life ethic hadn't changed. He went to mass every morning, went to work every afternoon, and was home or in his hotel room at decent time every night. He was still Detroit's most eligible bachelor primarily because of his devotion to his mother, who had been a widow for 10 years. Charlie had become successful enough that he bought her a home and looked after her constantly. For her part, Theresa Gehringer had long ago accepted the fact that her son was a ballplayer and understood the game enough that now, when he came over after going 0-for-4 against Herb Pennock or Lefty Grove, she no longer asked, "What's the matter? Aren't you trying?" like she did when he first broke in.

Charlie had a lifetime batting average of over .300, had played every inning of the first two All-Star Games, had the first steal and participated in the first double steal in All-Star history, and hit .379 in his only World Series appearance. His peers were noticing. Greenberg called him "the greatest second baseman who ever lived." Lefty Gomez took note of Charlie's penchant for hitting doubles — 44, 42, and 50 in the past three years. "Every time I turn around, the guy's on second base," said Gomez. Lefty said Charlie's only problem was that he was in a rut. "He goes 2-for-5 on opening day and stays that way all year."⁶

Bill Werber, a third baseman who played against Gehringer for nine years on the Yankees, Red Sox, and A's, called Charlie "a marvelous ballplayer." He pointed out how seldom Gehringer struck out even though he often took pitches until he had two strikes on him. "He was only going to swing once, and when he did, he usually hit the ball with authority," he said. Werber also praised Gehringer's fielding ability and said Charlie was "mechanical" in that he made plays look easy only because he positioned himself so well for every batter. Werber, who was a good base stealer, said he noticed only one weakness in Charlie's defense: he would get in front of second base to take throws on steal attempts. Werber used to slide to the back of the bag on Charlie to avoid the tag.⁷

Doc Cramer, an outfielder and teammate, marveled at Gehringer's consistency. "All you have to do is wind him up on opening day and he runs on and on, doing everything right," said Cramer.

The Tigers went into the off-season tired and disappointed but

7. "Every time I turn around, the guy's on second base."

confident they would return next year and win the World Series. Time heals all wounds, as was demonstrated in something Cochrane wrote seven years later in his 1939 book, *Baseball: The Fan's Game*. But apparently Mickey overlooked the 11–0 drubbing in the seventh game when he told fans "we lost out to the Cardinals in a heartbreaker."[8]

CHAPTER 8

"May you live ten thousand years."

Less than a month after the World Series ended, Charlie Gehringer went on a baseball goodwill mission to Japan with several other American ballplayers. They played ballgames and held clinics with Japanese youngsters to show them the finer points of the game. The ballplayers, in effect, were not only ambassadors of their sport but also of their country.

World politics were volatile. Many disturbing elements were at work in 1934 that would not fully play out until a few years later. In Germany, the powers that be combined the positions of chancellor and president, and thus, Adolph Hitler became the Fuhrer. In Austria, Chancellor Engelbert Dollfuss, trapped in an ideological tug-of-war between Fascist and Nazi extremists, was assassinated by Austrian Nazis. In America, President Franklin Delano Roosevelt was offering domestic programs to stifle the Great Depression while keeping a wary eye overseas where, among other things, the empire of Japan had an expansionist government committed to regional domination.

The American ballplayers on board the Empress of Japan weren't talking world affairs as they left British Vancouver on October 20, crossed the Pacific Ocean, and arrived 12 days later at Yokohama on November 2. Those greeted with a hero's welcome were Gehringer of the Tigers; Babe Ruth, Lefty Gomez, Lou Gehrig, all of the New York Yankees; Earl Averill, Clint Brown, and Morris "Moe" Berg of the Cleveland Indians; Jimmy Foxx, Eric McNair, Frank "Gabby" Hayes, Hal Warstler, Joe Cascarella, and Ed Miller of the Philadelphia A's; and Earl Whitehill, the old Tiger pitcher, now with the Washington Senators. Also on the trip was Connie Mack, who would manage the team during the games it played.

Flash bulbs popped as the players emerged. Ruth was the center of

8. "May you live ten thousand years."

attention and greeted the crowd warmly. The players and their wives then took the train to Tokyo, where a huge crowd awaited their arrival. Somewhere in the sea of voices of the thousands who had gathered, there came the cry of "Banzai, Gehringer of Detroit." Other players received similar greetings, enough so that they wanted to know what *banzai* meant. "May you live ten thousand years," they were told.[1]

Not all the players who made the trip were big names, but perhaps the most obscure player, from an achievement standpoint, was Morris Berg, who had never been anything more than a second-string catcher with Brooklyn, the Chicago White Sox, Cleveland, Boston, and Washington. Only once in his 16-year major league career had he appeared in more than 100 games in a season, and only three times had he appeared in more than 60 in one year.

But Berg was the only one of the ballplayers who knew what *banzai* meant. He had graduated with high honors from Princeton University in 1923 with a major in Romance languages and was also a graduate of the Columbia University Law School. But he decided to pursue a career in baseball, an odd occupation for someone with his education and ethnic background. Berg was Jewish and could speak several languages fluently, including Japanese. In the U.S., sportswriters had fun with him, saying "he can speak 10 languages but can't hit in any of them."[2]

The players were wined and dined and had audiences with the hierarchy of the Japanese government. They also played ball and worked with the kids. Charlie showed the youngsters how to position themselves in the infield and how and where to move every time a ball was hit. Gomez and Whitehill taught the youths some of the finer points of pitching. Ruth and Gehrig were popular figures in the batter's box. Moe Berg showed young catchers how to block the plate and how to "frame" pitches to get the best possible calls from umpires.

One of Charlie Gehringer's lasting memories of the trip had nothing to do with the doubles he sprayed to all fields and the home runs that he hit. Charlie said he'd never forget how sometimes, Moe Berg, the linguist, would correct the Japanese children if they used improper grammar.

Berg missed many of the social functions set up for the ballplayers, always begging off for one reason or another or just not showing up. But he was there for every game until Friday, November 29. On that day, the Americans played against a team of Japanese all-stars at the Omiya

Grounds, 17 miles north of Tokyo. Charlie and the Babe each hit long home runs that thrilled the crowd and gave the Americans the lead in the ballgame.

Meanwhile, Moe Berg, dressed in a black kimono and carrying a bouquet of flowers, entered St. Luke's International Hospital in the heart of Tokyo. He had read in the newspaper a couple of days earlier that Mrs. Cecil Burton Lyon, daughter of American ambassador to Japan Joseph Clark Grew, had given birth to a baby. He spoke in Japanese when he told a receptionist he was a friend of the ambassador's and wanted to pay his respects to the new mother. He showed her the bouquet of flowers. The receptionist told him to go to the seventh floor. Berg took the elevator, got off on the seventh floor, walked unassumingly down the hall, and opened an exit door leading to a stairwell. Closing the door behind him, he then bolted up steps that led to the rooftop. Once on the roof, he put the flowers down, reached in his kimono, and pulled out a motion picture camera. From atop the hospital roof, Moe took pictures of everything of interest below him — manufacturing facilities, military bases, industries, roads, bridges, railroads, and, as best he could, the landscape of the outlying areas. He then put the camera back inside the kimono, retrieved the flowers, went

Moe Berg was a catcher who did some espionage work for the United States government when a group of ballplayers went to Japan on a goodwill tour in 1934. Berg, a scholar, was said to be able to speak ten languages — but couldn't hit in any of them (photograph courtesy of the National Baseball Hall of Fame).

8. "May you live ten thousand years."

back inside and down the steps to the seventh floor, where he walked unassumingly to the elevator, descended to the ground floor, and left the hospital.

Or at least, that's the best account that historians have been able to discern. Nobody on the Americans' trip, certainly not the ballplayers, knew that Moe Berg had with him a letter from U.S. Secretary of State Cordell Hull, dated October 20, 1934, which read:

> To the American Diplomatic and Consular Officers:
> At the insistence of the Honorable Chester C. Bolton, representing the Congress of the United States from the state of Ohio, I take pleasure in introducing to you Mr. Morris Berg of Newark, N.J., who is about to proceed abroad.
> I cordially bespeak for Mr. Berg such courtesies and assistance consistent with your official duties.

Why would the secretary of state write a letter like that? None of the other ballplayers had a letter. What courtesies and assistance would Moe Berg need from American diplomats while he was playing baseball in Japan? The answer, history has revealed, is that they were to look the other way when Berg wasn't playing baseball in Japan, for he was an American spy. The motion pictures he took from the roof of St. Luke's International Hospital were used several years later by American military officials planning Gen. Jimmy Dolittle's attack on the Japanese mainland in April 1942, the first American direct attack on Japan in the five months after the Japanese bombed Pearl Harbor.[3]

Meanwhile, back at the ballpark, Gehringer hit a second home run as the Americans won 25–3. Gehringer said later he hadn't realized that Berg wasn't at the ballpark because Frank Hayes had been doing most of the catching in recent games. But Charlie had no idea that his teammate was a spy. "He certainly didn't let on to anything," said Gehringer, the hitting star for the Americans. "I know I didn't have any State Department letter and I know of no other ballplayers who had one."[4]

Back in the states, the Tigers had become the darlings of baseball. In somewhat of a surprise, Cochrane and Gehringer finished one-two in the balloting for Most Valuable Player, both finishing ahead of Gehrig of the Yankees, who had won the Triple Crown.

There were rumors, fueled by columnist Bob Ray in the *Los Angeles Times*, that Charlie would be offered the job of managing the Cleveland Indians in 1935. Ray said it was "common knowledge" that Frank Navin had offered the Detroit managerial job to Charlie after Bucky Harris exited in 1933 and that Charlie had turned it down. Why would he now be interested in the Cleveland job if he wasn't interested in managing the Tigers, asked Ray. Charlie was content to stay with the Tigers with the responsibility of playing second base. Detroit made few changes in the off-season, content to go into 1935 with the nucleus that had brought home the American League championship — "to dance with who brung ya" as Dizzy Dean once explained why teams shouldn't tamper with success.[5]

Pete Fox, Goose Goslin, and Jo-Jo White would be the starting outfielders, with Gee Walker seeing plenty of playing time, but his recklessness on the base paths was still a sore spot with Cochrane and many of the players. The infield of Owen, Rogell, Gehringer, and Greenberg was the best in baseball. Cochrane remained behind the plate, ably and willingly backed up by Hayworth. Schoolboy Rowe, Tommy Bridges, Elden Auker, and General Crowder formed the best corps of starting pitchers in the American League, and Chief Hogsett and Firpo Marberry were available for spot starts and relief appearances. The Tigers, not that long ago annual dwellers of the second division, were now loaded with talent. And they had something to prove. They wanted to return to the World Series and win it.

Greenberg had something to prove. Though he hit .321 in the Series and drove in seven runs, the most of any player on either team, he also struck out nine times and drew some criticism for not coming through in the clutch. In the seventh game, with the Cardinals winning 11–0, Hank showed his frustration by striking out swinging on a Dizzy Dean pitch that was head high. Auker and Rowe felt like they had something to prove, too. Schoolboy lost a game that would have been tied if his ninth-inning drive had gone three feet further. Auker was the losing pitcher in the 11–0 shellacking even though he was victimized by a couple of bloop hits and a defense that fell asleep.

Charlie made some adjustments in his personal life in 1934, though having a steady girlfriend wasn't one of them. His mother had been a widow for 10 years now, and Charlie still felt an obligation to look after her. He was making pretty good money in baseball and didn't have many obligations, so he convinced his mother to leave the farm, the family homestead on the outskirts of Fowlerville. Charlie bought a house on Grand River in the Rosedale section of Detroit for $10,500 and moved his mother

8. "May you live ten thousand years."

in with him. Many years later he said he might have married sooner, but he just felt obligated to take care of his mother, who was a diabetic, and didn't think that was a good situation to bring anyone else into.

The Tigers began the 1935 season as the favorites to repeat. But baseball has a way of laughing in the face of the obvious, and it happened again in April and May. The Tigers got off to their slowest start in more than a decade, and the Chicago White Sox, doormat of the league a year ago, got off to their fastest start since the Black Sox expulsions had reduced the team to mediocrity. Detroit lost nine of its first 11, with Bridges and Carl Fischer getting the only wins. Rowe won a game in relief on April 21 as the Tigers beat Cleveland 3–2 in 13 innings but didn't win as a starter until May 13, a month into the season. Auker had to wait until May 22 for his first win when the Tigers beat Philadelphia 4–1. The previous day, they made one of only two player moves they transacted during the entire season, selling Fischer to the White Sox.

On May 17, when the Tigers and Rowe lost to the Senators 10–8, Detroit found itself again in sixth place. The American League standings were the surprise of the baseball world:

Chicago	15–7	.682	—
Cleveland	13–8	.619	1.5
Boston	13–9	.591	2
New York	14–10	.583	2
Washington	12–12	.500	4
Detroit	11–13	.458	5
Philadelphia	6–15	.286	8.5
St. Louis	5–15	.250	9

When Joe Sullivan, a rookie spot starter and reliever for the Tigers, won one of six games he would win all year on Sunday, May 19, the Bengals reached the .500 mark, 13–13, for the first time all season. The season had not been without at least some highlights for the Tigers. On April 20–21, they played consecutive marathon games against the Cleveland Indians, losing 2–1 in 24 innings, then coming back and winning 3–2, behind Schoolboy Rowe, in 13 innings. On April 29, they drubbed the Browns, as they would all year, 18–0 with Tommy Bridges picking up the shutout win. Charlie Gehringer was on his way to his third straight 200-hit season, but it was Greenberg, hitting behind him, who would have the monster year. He'd tell Charlie, "Just get on base. I'll knock you in." Charlie told Greenberg, "I'll bet if someone was rounding third with you coming to bat next, you'd hope they'd trip so they'd have to stay at third and you could drive him in."

On May 20, Connie Mack ordered Charlie to be intentionally walked in the 11th inning to set up a double play situation for Greenberg. Hank singled, driving in two runs in a game the Tigers won 8–6. Earlier in the month, the Tigers released Firpo Marberry, who had come over in the Goslin deal two years earlier and had been 15–5 in 1934. This year, he had trouble getting the ball over the plate, and when he did, someone usually hit it hard. He was 0–1 and had given up 22 hits and 9 walks in just 19 innings.

On May 25, in the National League, Babe Ruth hit three home runs for the Boston Braves, who had acquired him from the Yankees earlier in the year. They were the last three homers of the Babe's career, and the final one cleared the right field roof at Forbes Field. In the American League, Greenberg continued to hit the ball hard. At Boston, he hit a game-winning homer as Detroit beat the Red Sox 3–2. In his previous at-bat, Greenberg lined a pitch off the jaw of Boston pitcher Fritz Ostermueller, who left the game with a broken cheekbone and a few less teeth.

By June 1, the Tigers had righted their ship. They were over .500 at 20–18 and in fourth place but just 3½ games behind the front-running Yankees and were starting to put it all together, just as they had in the previous year.

On July 8, the third annual All Star Game was played before a record crowd of 69,000 at Municipal Stadium in Cleveland. The game lacked the drama of the first two in which Ruth hit the first All-Star home run at Comiskey Park and Hubbell struck out five future Hall of Famers in a row at the Polo Grounds. In Cleveland, Jimmy Foxx hit a two-run homer off Bill Walker in the first inning, and the American League never trailed as they won for the third straight time, 4–1. Gehringer, starting again at second base, had two hits in three at-bats, including a double. In his three All-Star appearances, Charlie had four hits in nine at-bats.

Prior to the All-Star Game, the Tigers had started a hot streak which continued after the break. Between June 30 and July 7, they won 10 in a row. Between July 31 and August 11, they won another nine in a row. In that span between June 30 and August 11, Detroit had a record of 30–8 and took control of first place that they never relinquished. By Septem-

8. "May you live ten thousand years."

ber 8, when they beat the A's in a doubleheader, they owned a 10-game lead. They clinched their second straight American League championship on September 21.

Greenberg, the darling of the Jewish community throughout the nation, found himself in a bit of a personal dilemma in the heat of the pennant race. Rosh Hashanah, a Jewish holy day, was on September 10. Rabbis and other Jewish leaders questioned whether the ballplayer should play that day. The Tigers were scheduled to play the Boston Red Sox. Greenberg was not a particularly religious man, but he did not want to offend anyone. At the same time, he had a job to do and didn't want to hurt the ballclub.

He made a decision that seemed to be a reasonable compromise. He announced that he would play on Rosh Hashanah but would not play on Yom Kippur, ten days later. As it turned out, the Tigers won on Rosh Hashanah and lost on Yom Kippur.

Greenberg returned to the lineup on September 21, and the Tigers clinched the pennant that day.

Gehringer had another good year although some of his numbers were down from the previous season. He hit .330 with 201 hits, including 32 doubles, 8 triples, 19 home runs, and 108 runs batted in. The second 500-consecutive-game string of his career ended in mid-season, but he did play in 150 games, the seventh time in eight years he played in at least that many. But Gehringer's chief role in the batter's box was to be a set-up man for Hank Greenberg, and his success at doing that allowed him to score 123 runs.

The year belonged to Greenberg. He hit .328 with 36 home runs and 170 runs batted in — 103 of them before the All-Star break. He came within two of having 100 extra base hits — 46 doubles, 16 triples, and 36 home runs. He also scored 121 runs. He was the American League's Most Valuable Player. However, Greenberg and Gehringer had some help. Cochrane hit .319, White .321, Goslin .292, and reserves Hayworth and Walker hit .309 and .301 respectively.

The Tiger pitching corps did not disappoint. Bridges won 21, giving him 43 wins in the past two years. Rowe won 19 while losing 13, also giving him 43 wins in the past two years. Adding to Rowe's value was the fact that he hit .312 with three home runs and 28 runs batted in. Auker was 18–8, and General Crowder, having his last good year in the majors, won 16 while losing 10. Chief Hogsett made 40 appearances, mostly out of the bullpen, and won six games.

Gehringer, Greenberg, Goslin, and Cochrane shared a unique experience that year while the ballclub was in Washington. They were invited to the FBI headquarters to meet the agency's gung-ho director, J. Edgar Hoover, who at that time was becoming an American folk hero because of the FBI's war on organized crime. While they were there, Hoover gave the ballplayers a tour of the place and took them down to the shooting range, where they got the opportunity to shoot at some targets.[6] For a man with a reputation of not getting around much, Charlie was doing all right. Within a span of two years, he had met both Al Capone and J. Edgar Hoover.

Charlie Gehringer ran into all sorts of interesting people in his travels, among them the gangster Al Capone and J. Edgar Hoover (above), director of the FBI, who allowed Charlie and some teammates the opportunity to shoot in the FBI firing range (author's personal collection).

The next task for the Tigers was to take on Charlie Grimm's Chicago Cubs in the World Series. At least, said Auker, the Cubs were a gentlemanly group, compared to the cocky, raucous Gas House gang of the Cardinals. Maybe so, but the Cubs were the hottest team in baseball, winning a record 21 in a row in September.

CHAPTER 9

"The entire town was ga-ga."

Elden Auker guessed wrong about the Cubs. They were not the choir boys he thought they were. They began taunting Greenberg almost from the moment they saw him on the field, often calling the Jewish man a "kike." When manager Grimm was asked why the Cubs got on Greenberg so much, he said, "You always needle the star. What's the point of riding substitutes?"

Navin Field was filled to overflowing on Wednesday, October 2, when more than 47,000 came to see Schoolboy Rowe and Lon Warneke match up in the first game of the World Series. Warneke was 20–13 for the Cubs during the regular season, the second straight year he had 20 or more wins for Chicago. "The Arkansas Hummingbird," as he was called in recognition of his home state, won 192 games in his major league career and had the distinction of throwing two consecutive one-hitters. Against the Tigers, he gave up four meaningless hits — doubles by Fox and Rowe and singles by White and Fox — as the Cubs won 3–0. Frank Demaree, an outfielder who had hit two home runs all year for the Cubs, hit the first home run of the World Series off of Rowe. Reminiscent of the first game of the 1934 series, Detroit made three errors, one by Rowe in the first inning. Only two of the runs off Schoolboy were earned. Nonetheless, the win was an important road victory to start the Series for the Cubs, a game in which neither team made any substitutions.

In game two, Tommy Bridges and Charlie Root were the mound opponents. Bridges was coming off his second straight 20-plus win season for Detroit. Root was 15–8 for the Cubs and a tough competitor. He had once won 26 games for Chicago and had won 15 in three out of the last four years. He is forever remembered in baseball lore as the man who served up the pitch to Babe Ruth in the 1932 World Series when legend has it that the Babe called his shot, pointing and then homering into the centerfield stands. Root went to his deathbed saying it never happened, but the truth or fable, whichever it was, remained permanently attached to accounts of his career, in which he won 201 games.

On this day, however, Root was no match for the Tigers. White, Cochrane, and Gehringer opened the game with singles, and Greenberg followed with a home run. Bridges went all the way in the 8–3 Detroit victory. Charlie went 2-for-3 but said his best hit of the game didn't count for any-

Chicago Cubs manager Charlie Grimm was known as "Jolly Cholly," but he led the needling of Tiger players during the 1935 World Series, especially Hank Greenberg (photograph courtesy of the National Baseball Hall of Fame).

thing. "I hit the hardest ball I ever hit in baseball in the second game off Charlie Root," he said. "It went over the temporary scoreboard in right field. I usually didn't hit for very good distance but this one went out. The only trouble was, it was foul." Gehringer then walked and came home when Greenberg, continually mocked by the Cub bench, hit a home run.[1]

The Tigers won the game but suffered a terrific blow when Greenberg broke his wrist in the seventh inning as he tried to score all the way from first on a single. He collided with Cub catcher Gabby Hartnett, who fell on Hank's left wrist. Greenberg finished the game, but afterwards doctors determined the wrist was broken. Detroit would have to play the rest of the Series with their 170-RBI man out of the lineup.

Cochrane had to scramble to find a suitable replacement for Greenberg. He decided to move Owen from third to first and inserted Flea Clifton at third for the remainder of the series. Owen resisted when Cochrane first approached him but accepted the change when Mickey told him the decision was final. But Owen refused to wear a first baseman's glove, preferring instead to use his regular mitt, which was smaller and had no big webbing to scoop up throws but was nonetheless more comfortable for him. The next day, he had 11 assists at first base without an error.

Auker, who by now realized the Cubs were no more gentlemanly than the Cardinals had been the year before, started game three but did not finish. It was a see-saw battle at Wrigley Field. The Cubs mounted a 3–0 lead at the end of five innings. The Tigers clawed back with one in the sixth and four in the eighth to take a 5–3 lead. But Chicago scored two in the bottom of the ninth to tie. The Tigers pushed across a run in the 11th inning when Jo-Jo White singled, driving in Marv Owen for the 6–5 victory. Rowe got the win in relief of Hogsett, who had relieved Auker. Gehringer went 2-for-5, including a double. Demaree hit his second homer of the Series for the Cubs, matching his season total.

In game four, the Tigers prevailed 2–1, with General Crowder out-dueling Root, who pitched better this time around but received no offensive support. The Tigers took a 3–1 lead in the series. But once again, just as in the 1934 Series, a controversial call at third base had players, fans, writers, and even an umpire buzzing. And Charlie Gehringer was right in the middle of it. Gehringer, who was 2-for-4 including a double, an RBI, and a stolen base, said, "I slid into third base and the Cubs thought I was out. The Cub infielders — Hack, Jurges, Woody English — they told umpire George Moriarty what they thought of his vision. If it hadn't been a World Series, he would have thrown them out." This was one of many skirmishes between Moriarty, the former Tiger manager, and the Cubs.

The trouble between the Cubs and the umpire actually started in the third game when "big, beefy, loud-voiced George Moriarty," as *Time* magazine described him, called Cub captain Cavaretta out on a close play at second base. Grimm and other Cubs argued with Moriarty, and he shouted at them, ordering Grimm back to the dugout. "I didn't swear at him but he swore at us," Grimm said afterwards. Coach John Corriden said, "He (Moriarty) was guilty of antagonizing and demoralizing our ballclub." Coach Ray Johnson said subtly that Moriarty made reflections on the Cubs'

Phil Cavaretta, Cubs' first baseman, made a spectacular catch of a ball hit by Charlie Gehringer in the 1935 World Series that Charlie said one of the hardest he ever hit (photograph courtesy of the National Baseball Hall of Fame).

9. "The entire town was ga-ga."

ancestry. Even National League President Ford Frick offered an opinion. "Moriarty used blasphemous language," he said.

Clearly, Judge Landis, for the second consecutive World Series, had to get involved. He told Moriarty and several Cubs he wanted to see them in his office when the Series was over. He wound up fining Grimm, several players, and Moriarty. At their hearing, Landis asked each man individually what he had said to the others. Landis later wrote, "In my time in this world, I have always prided myself on a command of lurid expressions. I must confess that I learned from these young men some variations of the language even I didn't know existed."[2]

The Tigers had a chance to win their first World Series championship since 1909 in game five, matching Rowe against Warneke for the second time. The Cubs scored twice in the third inning on a Billy Herman triple followed by a Chuck Klein home run. As it turned out, that's all they needed because Detroit could only push across one run against Warneke, and Bill Lee, who pitched the last three innings when Warneke developed a sore shoulder. The final was Chicago 3, Detroit 1. Gehringer went 1-for-4.

In the sixth game, Tommy Bridges tried to close it out for Detroit. Larry French took the mound for the Cubs. Going into the ninth inning, the score was tied 3–3, and both starting pitchers were still in there. Stan Hack, the Cubs' affable third baseman, led off the ninth with a triple, Chicago's 12th hit off of Bridges. Though he was obviously tired, Cochrane decided to stay with him. The next batter was shortstop Billy Jurges. A hit, a long fly ball, or possibly even a ground ball hit in the right spot would deliver the go-ahead run for the Cubs. Jurges struck out. Then, in a move second-guessed by Cub fans for years, Grimm had the pitcher, French, bat for himself. He had gotten a hit earlier in the game off Bridges. This time, however, French tapped weakly to the mound, and Bridges threw him out easily for the second out. Augie Galan then flied out to end the inning.[3]

In the bottom of the ninth, Mickey Cochrane singled, bringing Gehringer to the plate. Already with two hits in three at-bats, Charlie hit a scorching line drive toward the right field line that he thought would win the game and the series. Somehow, Phil Cavaretta, the Cub first baseman, was able to knock it down with his glove, retrieve it in the coach's box, and step on first for the out. "Nine times out of 10, that's a double," said Charlie, who knew a little something about hitting doubles. Although Gehringer was out, he had done his job, advancing the winning run into scoring position. Goslin, who hadn't had a hit all day, then singled to right, and Cochrane scampered home with the winning run. Detroit had won its first World Series in 26 years.

Auker was sitting in the dugout next to Goslin when the Tigers came to bat in the bottom of the ninth. The Goose, who knew he was to be the fourth man up, leaned over to Auker and said, "I've got a hunch. I'm gonna be up there with the winning run on base and we're gonna win this game." A few minutes later, when Goslin lined the ball over Billy Herman's head to score Cochrane, Goose ran through the throng of joyous players until he found Auker. He shouted "What did I tell ya, what did I tell ya?"[4]

The Tigers had won despite losing Greenberg, the RBI machine, midway through the Series. Clifton, who was inserted at third base when Owen moved over to play first in place of Greenberg, went 0-for-16. Owen was 1-for-20. The hitting stars for the Tigers were Pete Fox, who had 10 hits including three doubles and a triple for a .385 average, and Gehringer, who had nine hits including three doubles. Charlie also drove in four runs.

Just as he had been in All-Star Games, Charlie was the model of consistency in two World Series appearances in which he played every inning of every game. His two-year World Series totals were:

Year	G	AB	R	H	D	T	HR	RBI	AVE.
1934	7	29	5	11	1	0	1	2	.379
1935	6	24	4	9	3	0	0	4	.375
Totals	**13**	**53**	**9**	**20**	**4**	**0**	**1**	**6**	**.377**

The Tigers had waited a long time to win a World Series and felt they had been robbed the year before. They celebrated wildly as they hit the clubhouse after the game. "With blood-curdling yells that rocked the rafters, the victorious Tigers charged into their dressing room ... to cut loose in a wild, hilarious celebration ... all yelling, swearing and sweating," the *Chicago Tribune* reported.

A jubilant Mickey Cochrane hugged Goslin but singled out Tommy Bridges for retiring three Cubs in the ninth inning after Hack got the leadoff triple. "A hundred and fifty pounds of courage," said Cochrane. "It was the finest exhibition of pitching I ever saw in a World Series game."

9. "The entire town was ga-ga."

Judge Landis came in to congratulate Cochrane, Goslin, Gehringer, and the rest of the Tigers. "I never saw a greater World Series game," said Landis.[5]

The citizens of Detroit poured into the streets to celebrate their Tigers' championship. For many, it was the first Tiger title in their lifetime. Detroit police estimated 500,000 in the streets, an impromptu parade that started in the ballpark where fans had streamed on to the field, and outside, at Michigan and Trumbull near the main entrance to the ballpark, and then stretching for as far as the eye could see in all directions. There were no reports of willful vandalism or looting, but the sheer force of numbers led to overturning street cars.

After the clubhouse celebration died down, Gehringer and his teammates showered, dressed, slapped each other on the back, and tried to figure out a way of leaving the ballpark unnoticed so they could go celebrate in their own way. Auker and his wife Mildred went to the Detroit Athletic Club for dinner with Harvey Frauhoff and his wife, two close friends. Chefs at the club had made a huge Detroit Tiger insignia out of ice and wheeled it in front of the Auker table while the band played "Hold That Tiger." A young singer from the South was accompanying the band that night. Not yet established, she was working her way up by appearing in places like the Detroit Athletic Club. Her name was Dinah Shore.[6]

Gehringer, who had his own way of describing things, said "the entire town was ga-ga." He left the ballpark and wanted to go downtown with a friend, but going anywhere was next to impossible because of the pedestrian traffic jams. "You couldn't cross the streets. The city was such a mess. First championship for Detroit. Seemed like everyone was downtown whoopin' and hollerin,'" he said. While reminiscing about it years later, he punctuated his remarks in typical Gehringer enthusiasm. "Golly," he said.[7]

"Good, clean fun," said Rogell. "Everybody was going crazy, but nothing vicious." Rogell might have had an eye for proper citizenship. When his playing career was over, he was elected to the Detroit City Council and was re-elected so often that he served for nearly 30 years.

The Cubs, meanwhile, seethed over the umpiring of Moriarty, but, under orders of Landis, had to do it silently. That's because, according to Edward Burns of the *Chicago Tribune*, Judge Landis told Grimm if he or any player or coach swore again at Moriarty, they would forfeit their World Series paycheck.

Burns told his readers, "Thus, a good ripe oath, or even a little bitsy one, would have cost the emitter thereof $4,554. On the basis of standard Cub tribute to Moriarty, this would run $569 a syllable or $759 a word — pretty high-priced cussing, as enjoyable as cussing may be."[8]

Burns said it was fortunate that Landis did not fine the Cubs for what they said under their breaths. He pointed out that while the Tigers blamed umpire Brick Owens for missing a call and possibly costing them the 1934 World Series, the Cubs did not put that allegation against Moriarty. They dared not. But Burns reminded his readers that Moriarty was a former Tiger player and manager.

Burns also pointed out that Charlie Gehringer had been in the middle of yet another controversy involving Moriarty. In the sixth game, which the Cubs had to win to keep the series alive, they took a 3–0 lead into the ninth inning. Bill Lee faced Gehringer and got two strikes on him — not unusual considering Charlie's habit of waiting for his pitch. Lee's next offering was strike three in the minds of the Cubs but not according to home plate umpire Moriarty. Charlie then singled and later scored Detroit's only run.

The Tigers were the toast of the town, but a little more than a month after the season ended, tragedy struck the baseball family. On November 13, 1935, Frank Navin, who was president of the Tigers for 32 years, a span that stretched from Cobb to Cochrane, was riding one of his horses at the Detroit Riding and Hunt Club when he suffered a fatal heart attack. He was 64. William O. Briggs, one of the majority stock holders, took over as president of the team. It was not long before his imprint replaced Navin's in every aspect of Tiger baseball, including the name of the ballpark, which was changed from Navin Field to Briggs Stadium in 1937.

Charlie had his ups and downs with Navin. He had signed Charlie to his first contract in 1923 but okayed the docking of his meager minor league pay when Charlie took three days off to attend his father's funeral the next year. But Charlie understood that baseball was a business, and year after year he signed his contracts in the off season without ever giving serious thought to holding out, even though he had become one of the best all-around players in baseball. In contrast to the Dean brothers in St. Louis, Dazzy Vance in Brooklyn, and Babe Ruth in his productive years with the Yankees, any negotiations between Gehringer and Navin were private and apparently fruitful.

Gehringer was quiet and efficient on and off the field, content to take care of his business without flair or fanfare. It didn't make for gaudy headlines, but it made good sense to Charlie who steadfastly stuck to the philosophy that he made a living with his bat and glove and not with his mouth. All the while, he was developing a keen sense of how businesses operated that would serve him well long after his baseball career was over. Auker, whose friendship with Charlie lasted 70 years, said, "Charlie wasn't one to go around talking about how great he was. He didn't have to promote himself. He was so damn good, only a fool wouldn't notice he was among the very best in the game."

Lyn Lary, the Yankee shortstop, would get particularly frustrated when Charlie robbed him of hits in the field. One day at Yankee Stadium, Gehringer raced to his left, snared a Lary ground ball hit up the middle, and threw him out at first base. His next time up, Lary zinged a ground ball past Greenberg headed for right field when Charlie glided over to his right, gloved it, and fired to first to get him out. Lary looked at Gehringer, threw up his hands and said, "Gehringer, you're just like horseshit. You're all over the place."[9]

During the World Series, Chicago writers got an insight into Charlie's personality. One of them wrote, "Although having a year of university life at Ann Arbor, and having worked as assistant librarian at the Fowlerville library, he talks in monosyllables, especially when being interviewed about his own career. And he has never smoked, chewed or drank." Rather than criticizing him for his shyness, the reporter simply concluded that Gehringer might be the most modest player in all of baseball.

The Tigers, fighting for respectability just a few years earlier, entered the 1936 season with a swagger. They were now king of the hill in the American League in an era when it seemed that certain teams took turns dethroning the Yankees from that position. For a couple of years in the 1920s, the Washington Senators did it. Then the Philadelphia A's dominated for a few years. And now the Tigers were on top.

Detroit had made good use of some personnel from those Washington and Philadelphia teams. As good as Gehringer was at bat and in the field, and as solid as the pitching staff was with Rowe, Bridges, Auker, Crowder, and Hogseth, it was the addition of Goslin from the Senators and Cochrane from the A's that seemed to make the team complete. Goslin now had the distinction of playing on the only two Washington teams ever to be in a World Series and on the first Tiger team to win one since 1909.

On December 10, 1935, Detroit purchased outfielder Al Simmons from the Chicago White Sox for $75,000. Aloysius Harry Simmons was often referred to as a right-handed Charlie Gehringer because of his ability to make contact and to spray the ball all over the field. Like Gehringer, he was not a home run hitter but was always among the league leaders in doubles. He too had been part of the Philadelphia A's juggernaut but had been the victim of one of Connie Mack's "fire sales" and was sent to Chicago in 1933. He hit .344 for the White Sox in 1934 but had the worst year of his career in 1935 as his batting average plummeted 77 points to .267. The Tigers picked him up to add some experience and some extra punch in their lineup.

Charlie was glad to have Simmons as a teammate for another reason. He said Simmons always hit the ball hard and in a way that was difficult to field at second base. Simmons, batting from the right side, was notorious for stepping "in the bucket." He would turn his left foot toward the third base dugout as he swung so that the front of his body was practically facing the pitcher. From this seemingly awkward position, he would smoke the ball to all fields. But when he hit the ball on the right side of the diamond, it would slice like a golf shot. Charlie called it a "fade ball," hit hard enough to get out of the infield fast and fading away from the fielder trying to catch up with it.

Another baseball note of interest occurred on December 14 when Firpo Marberry signed with the New York Giants. Marberry, who had some good years pitching for the Tigers, had retired as a player and had become an American League umpire in 1935. He returned to pitching with the Giants in 1936 before returning to the Washington Senators, with whom he had his greatest years.[10]

The Tigers were a confident bunch as they headed into the 1936 season. The team that had won two American League championships and one World Series championship was essentially intact, and now Al Simmons had been added. Few teams in baseball history could boast of a lineup with five future Hall of Famers, but the Tigers had one with Goslin and Simmons in the outfield, Cochrane behind the plate, Greenberg at first and, of course, the "Mechanical Man," reliable Charlie Gehringer at second.

9. "The entire town was ga-ga."

Most observers thought that Schoolboy Rowe was also well on his way to Hall of Fame stardom and Tommy Bridges was building a pretty good resume, although both pitchers needed a few more good years under their belts to warrant the same accolades as the others.

In the eyes and minds and hearts of most baseball followers in Detroit and elsewhere, a third pennant seemed almost certain.

CHAPTER 10

"Too much time to think."

If there's anything certain about baseball, it's the uncertainties, as the Detroit Tigers found out in 1936. They lost four out of their first six games to start the season, the only wins coming from two shutouts by Schoolboy Rowe, 3–0 against Cleveland on opening day and 5–0 against Chicago five days later. Then they reeled off five straight wins. On April 29, the Senators snapped the Tiger win streak with a 7–3 victory, but the defeat was minor compared to another loss. Senator base runner Jake Powell plowed into Greenberg at first base. The force of the collision snapped Hank's wrist back, the same wrist he injured in the World Series the previous fall. The wrist was broken again — and Greenberg was out for the rest of the season.

Cochrane, who was now the general manager in addition to being field manager and catcher, had to do something to fill the gap at first base. On April 30, he acquired first baseman Jack Burns from the St. Louis Browns. But in order to get Burns, he had to give up Chief Hogsett, Charlie Gehringer's roommate and a veteran of the Tiger mound staff. Burns hit .283 and played first base adequately, but his 63 runs batted in were 107 short of what Greenberg had driven in the year before.

In trading away Hogsett, Cochrane was relinquishing a man who had made 109 relief appearances for the Tigers in the past three years. In the space of 24 hours, Detroit was without the services of its number-one hitter and its number-one relief pitcher, who were crucial elements in the championship years.

Things would get worse. The day after Greenberg got hurt, Cochrane got hit with a foul ball on his instep and had to leave the game. The ball was hit off the bat of Powell, the man who collided with Greenberg the

10. "Too much time to think."

day before. The Tigers weren't dead yet, but they were limping. The only thing that kept them afloat was a starting pitching staff of Rowe, Bridges, Auker, and Crowder that was as good a foursome as any in the league — and the hitting of Charlie Gehringer who was hitting over .350 and on a pace to break Earl Webb's mark of 67 doubles in one season. Gee Walker was also having the best year of his career.

On June 4, Cochrane, back in the lineup and seemingly healthy, hit an inside-the-park grand slam home run against the A's but collapsed after crossing home plate. The cause appeared to be exhaustion, and Mickey sat out a couple of games. Then in Boston, a week later, Cochrane suffered a nervous breakdown. He was sent home and was admitted to Henry Ford Hospital in Detroit to rest and recuperate. Not long after that, he and his family flew to a friend's ranch in Wyoming, where he continued his recovery period. While he was gone, third base coach Del Baker served as acting manager.

More trouble occurred when Alvin "General" Crowder, the man who had come over from Washington with Goose Goslin and added some much-needed experience to a young pitching staff, developed chronic stomach problems. He came on in relief in a game against Boston on June 22 and picked up the victory as Detroit won 8–7. But it was his last appearance in the big leagues. In early July, Crowder announced his retirement and went home to try to get healthy again.

Rookie lefthander Jake Wade was pressed into service. Wade made 13 starts and had a 4–5 record, which wasn't bad for a rookie but was far from what the Tigers had expected when they started the season with Crowder as the fourth starter.

To make matters worse, while Detroit was trying to fill the voids left by the injury to Greenberg, the trade of Hogsett, the retirement of Crowder, and the illness of Cochrane, the New York Yankees were showing signs they were ready to once again take over as leaders of the American League.

Babe Ruth was gone, but Lou Gehrig was still there, and so were Tony Lazzeri, Bill Dickey, Lefty Gomez and the two "Reds" — Red Rolfe at third base and Red Ruffing on the mound. But the talk of the American League was a young rookie named Joe DiMaggio, who was like Charlie Gehringer in many ways — he could hit, field, throw, was fast on the base paths, and was quiet and unassuming. DiMaggio did not seek all the publicity he was getting, he just wanted to show up every day and play ball.

On July 7, the fourth All-Star Game was played at Braves Field in Boston. Charlie Gehringer was once again at second base for the American League. He went 2-for-3 against Dizzy Dean and Carl Hubbell, including a double, but the National League prevailed, 4–3, before about 26,000 fans, which remains the smallest crowd in All-Star Game history. It was the National League's first win in All-Star competition.

When regular season play resumed, the Tigers weren't able to generate any momentum. They simply could not overcome the loss of Greenberg, Hogsett, Crowder, and Cochrane. Detroit managed to win 83 games, 10 less than their total in 1935, and they finished in second place — something they would have reveled in five years ago — but they finished 19 games behind the champion Yankees. In years when they finished lower in the standings, they had been fewer games out of first place than they were in 1936.

Several players had decent years. Bridges won 23, lost 11, and logged 297⅔ innings. The curve-balling right-hander had won 20 or more three years in a row and had 66 wins in the past three years. Rowe won 19 and lost 10, his second straight year of falling one short of a 20-win season. He had 62 wins in his first three seasons in the big leagues. Auker was 13–16, an off year for him, but he was still an important part of what was now the Big Three and had 56 wins in the past three years. Among hitters, Gee Walker had his best year in the majors, smacking 55 doubles on his way to a .353 batting average.

But once again, the hitting star for the Tigers was Charlie Gehringer. His .356 average was fourth in the American League. He was third in the league in runs scored with 144 and second in hits with 227. He had reached base 314 times via hit, walk, or being hit by a pitch, and that was second highest in the American League. Despite his penchant for taking pitches, often drawing two called strikes before he took a swing, he struck out only once every 49 at-bats. Only Joe Sewell had a lower strikeout percentage. Where Charlie had no equal in 1936 was in his ability to hit the ball in the gaps and down the lines. He hit 60 doubles, seven short of the all-time record set by Earl Webb. Through 2007, no one else in baseball history has hit 60 doubles since Charlie did it in 1936.

Charlie had a big following not only in Detroit but throughout the state. While he avoided events in which he would be required to speak, he accepted the duty of public appearances as part of his job. Charlie liked

10. "Too much time to think."

to play badminton in the winter as a way of keeping in shape. Because he had the same dexterity and fluid movement that he had on the baseball field, he was an excellent badminton player. He discovered that if he could show up at charity events and play badminton without having to make a speech, that was a pretty good trade-off.

One night, he went to Port Huron, a town of about 40,000 not far from Detroit, to play in a badminton exhibition at the local Elks Lodge. Ten-year-old Jim Fitzgerald was there. His father, an Elks member, had brought his son so that the boy could meet his hero, Charlie Gehringer. Charlie shook the youngster's hand and gave him his autograph — Chas. Gehringer — and the boy went away ready to tell all of his friends that he and Charlie were buddies. Scenes like that were recreated often, a responsibility of popularity — but never for publicity as far as Charlie was concerned.[1]

The Tigers didn't make any major moves in the off-season. When everyone was healthy, they still had the best infield in baseball with Greenberg, Gehringer, Rogell, and Owen, and the outfield was set with White, Goslin, and Walker. Cochrane had no peer behind the plate, with the possible exception of Bill Dickey with the Yankees. Rowe, Bridges, and Auker remained a mighty threesome on the mound, although Cochrane was becoming increasingly concerned about what he considered Rowe's attitude, particularly toward keeping in condition.

The winter passed with no major deals being made. On April 1, 1937, the Tigers acquired Floyd "Babe" Herman, most recently of the Reds but who had been a terrific hitter a few years back with the Brooklyn Dodgers. Babe was a character who could hit a ball a country mile but had trouble catching even routine fly balls. He once drove to spring training in Florida from his home in California and pulled into training camp with an automobile full of dents, loose fenders, and nicks. His teammates razzed him that his car caught more than he did. He once did an interview with a newspaper reporter and, when the interview was done, reached in his pocket, pulled out a lit cigar, and resumed smoking it. It was treated as pure coincidence that Babe was acquired on April Fool's Day.

With Herman signed, Cochrane felt he could do without the services of Al Simmons, the future Hall of Famer, who had a good year with the Tigers but had trouble dealing with the sometimes dictatorial style of his manager. Neither of them was disappointed when Simmons was shipped off to Washington for $15,000, a very low price tag for a player of that caliber.

Detroit went into the 1937 season with its typical potent offense, but the Tigers hadn't acquired a suitable replacement for Crowder in the starting pitching rotation. That role would be shared by rookie George Gill and Roxie Lawson, who had spent much of his five-year career as a relief pitcher. In fact, in 1936, of Lawson's 41 appearances with the Tigers, 33 had been in relief. He was 8–6 on the season. The year before, he was 3–1 for the pennant-winning Tigers but did not appear in the World Series against the Cubs.

Baseball's knack for supplying the unexpected emerged once again for the Tigers in 1937, which would turn out to be Charlie Gehringer's best year in terms of statistics. But the team was falling apart around him. Schoolboy Rowe, winner of 24, 19 and 19, games in his first three big league seasons, showed up for spring training out of shape. Cochrane fumed. He was not one to coddle his ballplayers and had no use for athletes who let the team down by not holding to high personal standards both on and off the field.

In a move reminiscent of Joe McCarthy dealing with Grover Cleveland Alexander 11 years earlier, Cochrane suspended Rowe for the first month of the season and told him to go home and shape up. The message Cochrane delivered was clear: "I don't care who you are; you play by my rules or you don't play."[2]

So the Tigers opened the season with a pitching rotation of Tommy Bridges, Elden Auker, George Gill, and Roxie Lawson, obviously lacking the depth and experience of the past few years. But Detroit's offense was once again a run-producing machine with a healthy Greenberg, Gehringer, Goslin, Cochrane, Owen, Rogell, Walker, Fox, and White.

On April 20, Walker became the only player in baseball history to hit for the cycle on opening day, and he did it in reverse order — homer, triple, double, and single — as Detroit edged Cleveland 4–3. On May 13, Gill made his first major league start and shut out the Browns, 4–0. Auker, coming off his worst season, was on his way to his best season. On June 8, his sidearm deliveries handcuffed the Browns as he gave up only one hit, a fourth-inning double by Bob Johnson in a 6–4 Detroit victory.

But by that time, near tragedy had struck the Tigers, and they never

10. "Too much time to think."

fully recovered. On May 25, in a game against the Yankees, Cochrane homered off Bump Hadley in the third inning. In the fifth inning, Mickey leaned into a pitch that he said later he didn't really see. The fastball hit him squarely in the temple, and he went to the ground as if he had been shot. Witnesses heard the thud of the ball hitting his head and saw him lying on the ground unconscious, saying it was the most sickening sight they had ever come across on a ball field.

Gehringer, in the on-deck circle, was stunned. "My goodness, he went down like someone had hit him with an ax," he said. "He got hit right above the ear. The ball bounced right back to the pitcher."[3]

Cochrane was carried off the field unconscious and taken to St. Elizabeth's Hospital, where he regained consciousness. It was determined he had a fractured skull, a cracked sinus, and a concussion. Cochrane remained there for two weeks and then was transferred to Henry Ford Hospital in Detroit, where he could continue his recuperation closer to home.

An irony of the Cochrane beaning was that on the same day Mickey went out, Schoolboy Rowe, the man he had suspended, made his first start of the year and was the losing pitcher as the Yankees won 4–3. On June 8, Cochrane's name was removed from the active player list. On that same day, third baseman Owen broke his wrist. The Tigers were truly a broken ballclub.

The 1937 All-Star Game was played in Washington. President Frank D. Roosevelt threw out the ceremonial first pitch and stayed and watched part of the game. He saw the American League win once again, this time by a score of 8–3 with Charlie Gehringer getting three hits in five at-bats while playing every inning at second base. The game is remembered in baseball lore as the one in which Dizzy Dean, pitching for the National League, was struck in the foot by a line drive off the bat of Earl Averill. Dean was sidelined for several weeks with the broken foot, and while he returned to the mound and pitched several more years, he was never as effective as he had been before the injury.

In late July, Cochrane rejoined the ballclub, but his playing days were over. From now on, he would manage from the dugout. Charlie said he was never the same manager again. "He had too much time to think," said Gehringer. When he was behind the plate, he didn't have time to think, so he couldn't outguess himself. He managed almost by instinct — but not when he watched the game from the sidelines. He simply had too much time on his hands, and it hurt his managing abilities, at least according to Charlie.

Through it all, the Tigers stayed in the pennant race. On the day that Owen went down and Cochrane was officially through as a player, the Tigers found themselves at 45–25 in fourth place, but just a 1½ games behind the White Sox and Yankees, who were in a virtual tie for first place. Part of the reason for Detroit's success was that Auker and Roxie Lawson were having stellar years on the mound, and Gehringer and Greenberg were having their best years at the plate.

And then there was the emergence of big Rudy York, who had been called up from Toledo to catch in place of Cochrane, play some third base in place of Owen, and occasionally spell Greenberg at first base. York was a poor, uneducated fun-loving boy who quit school in the third grade to work in the mills in Georgia. When finally in a position to earn some big league money, he spent it as fast as he could — by his own admission, on booze, women, and cars. He and Charlie Gehringer couldn't have been any further apart in temperament and lifestyle, so they made an interesting combination when they roomed together on the road.

Charlie said one of York's really bad habits — a step below his usual bad habits which were just raucous — was that he smoked in bed and would fall asleep with a lit cigarette between his fingers then wake up when the cigarette burned his finger. York admitted sheepishly that he led the American League in burned mattresses. After a year, Charlie got a new roommate, saying he didn't want to be in the same room on the day Rudy burned a hotel down.

But York could hit. In August, he set a major league record (since broken) when he clobbered 18 home runs, helping the Tigers to a 19–12 record for the month. But the Yankees went 21–8 during the same time period, and by the end of the season, New York was the champion for the second straight year. Detroit finished second — incredible considering the injuries and other setbacks they incurred — but they were a distant second, finishing 13½ games behind the Yankees.

The Tigers overcame their many obstacles because of a league-leading team batting average of .292, including four players with 200 hits or more — Gehringer, Greenberg, Fox, and Walker. Greenberg hit 40 home runs and drove in 183, one short of Lou Gehrig's American League record.

10. "Too much time to think."

And Charlie Gehringer, at age 34, became the oldest player in baseball history to win his first batting title with an average of .371.

Roxie Lawson, who was to average about five wins a year in a nine-year career, was the chief beneficiary of the Detroit explosive offense. Roxie won 18 and lost only 7 despite having an earned run average of 5.26. He led the Tigers in wins. But the comeback pitcher on the staff was Auker, who returned to form with a 17–9 record after his sub-par season in 1936.

No single circumstance can ever be the cause of a team's rise or fall, and the Tigers could point to many unexpected developments in 1937 — the injuries to Cochrane and Owen, too much dependence on young players like Gill, Lawson, and York, the absence of Al Simmons, and the lack of punch from Babe Herman (no homers, three RBIs, and appearing in only 20 games.)

But one statistic that jumps out is the record of Schoolboy Rowe. Averaging almost 21 wins a year in his first three seasons, Rowe won only one game for the 1937 Tigers, 18 less than his total for 1936. The Tigers, even with their potent offense, simply had no way of overcoming that big of a decline from their number-one pitcher.

CHAPTER 11

"The Michigan Mummy."

Charlie Gehringer not only won the batting title but was voted the American League's most valuable player in 1937. Though Charlie had a great year, many argued that DiMaggio had a better one, and they might have had a point. Gehringer's numbers were lower than the Yankee Clipper's in just about every offensive category except doubles and batting average:

	G	AB	R	H	D	T	HR	RBI	AVE.
Gehringer	144	564	133	209	40	1	14	96	.371
DiMaggio	151	621	151	215	35	15	46	167	.346

Moreover, the Yankees won their second consecutive American League championship while the Tigers finished a distant second. Gehringer backers claimed the Yankees could have won the pennant without DiMaggio but the Tigers would have never finished second without Charlie. In fact, they said, DiMaggio might not have even been the most valuable player on his team, let alone in the league.

Dan Daniel, writer and columnist for the *New York World Telegram*, informed his readers that Gehringer's longevity and sterling character had a lot to do with his winning the award. "The selection of Gehringer, who has been the second baseman of the Tigers for a dozen years, and is one of the best-liked players in the game was rather expected," wrote Daniel, who was not a part of the selection committee. "It was believed that with Charley nearing his 35th birthday and perhaps not again likely be a contender for the award, sentiment would stuff the ballot box."[1] Daniel acknowledged that "qualified experts" believed Gehringer was the best sec-

11. "The Michigan Mummy."

ond baseman in the history of baseball and there was no deep resentment over him winning the award because he is "quiet, well-mannered and a credit to himself and the game." In this case, the qualified experts were eight sports writers — one from each city in the American League.[2]

Daniel's tone changed considerably as he pondered the process of picking a most valuable player. On November 13, 11 days after the MVP announcement, Daniel told his readers that the selection of Gehringer "presents a powerful argument for the abandonment of the present system and a substitution of a general poll of the experts." He continued, "It is quite obvious that the current scheme of placing the selection in the hands of only eight writers is far from a satisfactory one."[3]

Joe Williams, another New York columnist, also questioned the selection. Like Daniel, Williams considered Gehringer dull, not someone who made a good interview, but could not deny his ability as a ballplayer. Calling Charlie "the Michigan Mummy," Williams wrote, "Gehringer will probably receive the news with mixed feelings of fear and misery" because it might mean he would have to give a speech. "Any time the gentleman says more than 'good morning' or 'nice day' he becomes what practically amounts to a chatter box."[4]

Williams also claimed that Cochrane lobbied on behalf of Charlie when he attended the World Series. Cochrane told writers that DiMaggio, who had just completed his second season with the Yankees, had many more years to excel whereas this might by Charlie's last chance to win the award. Williams also observed that had Gehringer played for the Yankees instead of the Tigers, or if the Tigers had won the championship, his selection might have been unanimous.

The hometown newspaper was kinder. "It's about time the Baseball Writers Association got around to naming Gehringer the league's best ballplayer. He's been that for years," proclaimed the *Detroit News*.

Charlie had been in a tight race for the batting title with Gehrig and DiMaggio most of the second half of the season. A writer asked Gehringer in September what he thought about it. He said he didn't know what he was hitting, that he never paid any attention to batting averages. In September, his teammate Gee Walker said to him, "You were hitting .368, the last time I looked." Charlie replied, "Well, I'll be down where I belong pretty soon." By season's end, he had gone up three points, finishing with a .371 average.[5]

Even late in his career, Charlie continued to wait for his pitch and then drive it with a level swing. In 1937, he won the batting title with a .371 average and was the American League's Most Valuable Player (photograph courtesy of the National Baseball Hall of Fame).

11. "The Michigan Mummy."

Gehringer won the batting title — and probably the Most Valuable Player award — because of a torrid August. A look at his month-by-month statistics in 1937:

Month	G	AB	R	H	AVE.
April	6	22	5	6	.273
May	21	80	22	29	.360
June	24	93	17	34	.387
July	26	105	28	36	.342
August	32	122	38	59	.483
September	32	129	21	42	.308
October	3	5	2	3	.600
Totals	**144**	**564**	**133**	**209**	**.371**

Gehringer was first in the league in hitting, second in on-base percentage, second in number of singles, fifth in runs scored, fifth in hits, and sixth in number of walks. Charlie hadn't changed much over the years — and winning the American League's top honor wasn't likely to change that. He still looked after his mother, went to mass every morning, and worked at low-profile jobs in the off-season. He stopped working at the Hudson department store and sold coal wholesale one winter. He also leased two gasoline stations in the Detroit area and hired people to run them. Charlie believed an athlete's name had good marketing value for a while, but eventually, the product and service were what had lasting value — the same philosophy that had served him so well on the ball field.

Gehringer had developed an interest in automobiles almost from the time he was able to afford a car and had purchased a Hupmobile in the early 1930s from a Detroit-area salesman named Ray Forsyth, a sports fan who provided good service on Charlie's vehicles. Over the years, Gehringer bought two more Hupmobiles from Forsyth, and later, when Forsyth began operating a Buick dealership, Charlie started buying Buicks. The two men developed a personal and professional friendship that lasted 50 years.

The city of Detroit was going through tough times again as the Great Depression wore on. As one might expect, as the auto industry went, so went Detroit. And the auto industry was struggling. By the spring of 1938, about 40 percent of Detroit's 700,000 auto workers were jobless. Workers tried desperately to organize to have some way of protecting themselves from ruthless, insensitive bosses. Walter Reuther, who would rise to be a powerful union boss, was beaten to near death as he passed out leaflets promoting the fledgling United Auto Workers union outside the Ford Motor Company's Rouge plant in Dearborn, the site of the violence five years earlier.[6]

Charlie had been scouting around looking for a stable job in the off season, something that could sustain him when the day arrived that he would have to retire from baseball. In 1938, he formed a partnership with Forsyth that would be a new venture for both of them — automobile accessories. A friend of both men, J.M. Kisselle, was a patent attorney and had worked with Ann Friedolph, a New York businesswoman, on a patent for a button that would go on automobile upholstery. She needed someone to market the buttons to automakers. Neither Gehringer nor Forsyth were given to jumping blindly into business deals, but they thought this one had promise, and with very little investment on their part.

In the 1930s, any buttons on automobile upholstery had metal stays. With usual wear and tear, the buttons came loose or the metal clips would poke through and scratch the motorists or, worse, tear their clothes. In short, they were a nuisance. Mrs. Friedolph's invention solved all of that. Gehringer and Forsyth decided to give it a try.

The automakers were aware of the upholstery problems. Always the first to hear the complaints, they were interested in the solution. Chrysler Corporation and the Ford Motor Company were the first customers. General Motors was next. "We sold them by the jillion," said Charlie.[7] The Gehringer and Forsyth firm was born, and in the next 30 years, they would add heating alloys, leather and vinyl upholstery, carpeting, and various gadgets to their product line. Charlie and Ray were the executives, but they considered themselves sales representatives, and each made the rounds of their built-in market — Detroit's auto industry.

Meanwhile, in the front offices of the Detroit Tigers, Walter Briggs and general manager/manager Cochrane, neither of them known for their patience, wanted to find a way of returning the Tigers to championship level. Briggs had spent millions renovating the ballpark, putting in an upper deck and providing comfort for fans. He renamed the ballpark Briggs Stadium to remind everyone who was now running the show, and he wanted a "show" that would be second to none in the American League. It was Cochrane's job to deliver, not only as manager but as general manager. And Cochrane believed, as every general manager of every team believes, that the ballclub needed more pitching.

11. "The Michigan Mummy."

So Cochrane acquired pitcher Vern Kennedy from the Chicago White Sox. Kennedy, a right-hander who had thrown a no-hitter against the Cleveland Indians in 1935, was 11–11 in his first full season and won 21 games in 1936. Kennedy was named to the American League All-Star team in 1937 and won 14 games for the White Sox that year. He looked to be a good acquisition for the Tigers, but to get him, Cochrane had to give up a lot, starting to break up the team that had won the previous championships. Kennedy came to Detroit along with infielder Tony Piet and outfielder Fred "Dixie" Walker. But the Tigers gave up veteran third baseman Marv Owen and possibly the most popular Bengal with the fans, Gee Walker. Mike Tresh, an up-and-coming catcher, also went to the White Sox as part of the deal.

Cochrane figured that on balance, the Tigers came out alright. They gave up an infielder, Owen, and got one in return, Piet. They gave up an outfielder, Gee Walker, and got one in return, Dixie Walker. And they got a pitcher, Kennedy, without having to give up anyone from their mound staff.

Owen had a feeling he would be traded but thought he was going to Cleveland. But Walker was surprised by the trade, and so were Tiger fans. They mounted a petition drive to have the trade rescinded, which of course did not work. Cochrane said publicly that if the trade turned out to be a dud, he would take the blame.

On October 3, 1937, Detroit released 37-year-old Goose Goslin, who had slowed considerably and whose best days were clearly behind him. Goose hooked on with his former team, the Washington Senators, for one final season in the majors. But the departure of Goslin and Walker within the space of a couple of months, and the retirement of Cochrane after his near-fatal injury the previous summer, meant that the 1938 Tigers would have a new look. Gone was two-thirds of an outfield that had brought glory to the Motor City, and without Owen, one-fourth of what most people considered the best infield in baseball was gone as well.

The Tigers would be depending on the slugger Greenberg and the reliable Gehringer, a man approaching the status of old-timer, to carry the offensive load. Concerned about filling all those seats he had added to his stadium, Briggs issued a statement from his winter home in Florida that he had approved the Gee Walker deal. Briggs hoped to appease disgruntled fans and take some of the heat off Cochrane.

Detroit's opening day lineup featured several new names. Kennedy was the starting pitcher, Rookie Don Ross was at third base, Dixie Walker and rookie Chet Morgan were in the outfield, and Rudy York was behind the plate. The Tigers lost five out of their first six games and spent most of the first half of the season fighting to get back to .500. However, there were a few bright spots. Kennedy made Cochrane and Briggs look like geniuses when he won his first nine decisions. Greenberg, playing without injuries that had plagued him the past few years, was hitting home runs in bunches and was on a pace to challenge Babe Ruth's 1927 record of 60. York was avoiding the "sophomore jinx" and was on a pace to once again hit 30 home runs or more. The surprise of the early season was Charlie Gehringer, who was also experiencing a power surge and was among the league leaders in home runs in April.

But Schoolboy Rowe continued to struggle. His relationship with Cochrane had soured in 1937 when Mickey suspended him for not being in condition, and now he had a sore pitching arm. The result was that Rowe, a 62-game winner in his first three seasons, was sent down to the minors to work out the kinks. This left Bridges and Auker to anchor a starting rotation that also including Roxie Lawson and George Gill.

The Tigers didn't climb over .500 until May 30, when they were 18–17. They showed signs of life in June when a four-game winning streak pushed them up to 32–29 on June 24. But they lost seven in a row in July. Then they put together an eight-game winning streak to once again put them at .500 with a 46–46 record on July 30. They continued to win about as many as they lost in August but put together two six-game winning streaks in September. By season's end, they had snuck into the first division, finishing in fourth place with an 84–70 record, 16 games behind the front-running Yankees.

Kennedy, after winning his first nine decisions, won only three of his next 12 and finished with a 12–9 record. Bridges' numbers were down partly because he didn't have the run support he had enjoyed in previous years. He was 13–9 and led the ballclub but was well off his pace of the previous few years. Auker was 11–10, and Rowe, who spent most of the year in the minors, was 0–2.

The big-hitting star for the Tigers was Greenberg, who chased Babe Ruth's home run record all year but finished with 58. On the last day of the season, Detroit played a doubleheader with the Indians at Municipal

11. "The Michigan Mummy."

Stadium in Cleveland. Most of the attention was on Hank, but a young Cleveland pitcher stole the show. Bob Feller set a major league strikeout record by fanning 18 Tigers in the first game, including Greenberg twice. In the second game, Hank got three singles and a walk off of the Indians' Johnny Humphries in a meaningless contest in the standings. As darkness set in, home plate umpire George Moriarty, the old Tiger, tried to keep the game going as long as he could. Finally, when he had to call it on account of darkness, he apologized to Greenberg but said he had no choice. Greenberg told him there was no need to apologize, that he had gone as far as he could.

Charlie Gehringer hit over .300 again, but not by much. His batting average was .310, 61 points below what he had hit in 1937, when he won the batting championship and the Most Valuable Player award. He attributed the drop to two things. When he began the season hitting for power, he started swinging for the fences more than he had in the past — which was really out of character for him. "I thought I was Babe Ruth," he said with a laugh years later. But also, he explained, "I was a year older."[8] His attention on power hitting showed up in other ways. For the first time since his injury-plagued year of 1931, he failed to get 200 hits, finishing well below that mark with 174. He hit 32 doubles, a credible number for most players but only about half of what he had hit just two years earlier.

In July, Charlie appeared in his sixth consecutive All-Star Game and, once again, played every inning. He had a single in three-at bats and played flawlessly in the field, but the National League won the game, 4–1. The game was played in Cincinnati, and fittingly, the starting pitcher for the National League was the Reds' Johnny Vander Meer, who that season became the only pitcher in baseball history to pitch two consecutive no-hitters.

Charlie never played in another All-Star Game, but his statistics for six games include 20 at-bats with 10 hits, including 2 doubles, for a .500 average. He scored twice, batted in one run, and stole 2 bases.

The Tigers' woes in 1938 were best personified by the fate of their feisty manager, Cochrane, who was never the same after his beaning the year before. Mickey was a guy who always had to be in the middle of everything, but now on the sidelines he could not fight and lead like he could when he was part of the action. When his playing career came to an abrupt end and he was relegated to the dugout, he became, in effect, a caged Tiger. He had the falling out with Rowe and had trouble getting along with another Tiger pitcher, Cletus "Boots" Poffenberger, a free spirit whom the Tigers had acquired in 1937 and who liked to do things his own way — totally in contrast to Mickey's style of control. Owen once described Boots as being "a little rocko."[9]

But Mickey's biggest problems were with Tiger management — in particular Walter "Spike" Briggs Jr., the ballclub's secretary. After a loss to the Boston Red Sox on August 6, Detroit fell three games below .500. Cochrane and Briggs exchanged heated words with Mickey telling "Spike" he didn't have the players he needed to win. Briggs suggested that maybe the manager was the problem. In typical fashion, Cochrane reacted immediately and quit.

Gehringer, like fans, writers, and other players, couldn't believe it. Cochrane was the heart and soul of a ballclub that floundered for years and then won two American League championships and a World Series in his first two years at the helm. But Charlie could see how it happened. "Mickey was pretty quick on the draw with his temper, as was Briggs," said Gehringer. Charlie thought for sure Cochrane would land a position in the Detroit organization, but it did not happen. Mickey was through.

Briggs named coach Del Baker as the new manager. After a slow start under the new man, the Tigers seemed to jell. They put together three six-game winning streaks in the last six weeks of the season and finished at 84–70, another fourth-place finish. But they were 37–19 after Baker took over, giving some hope, at least for the future. The Tigers not only rode the crest of the Greenberg home run barrage, but also the slugging of York, who hit 33 homers, including four grand slams, and drove in 127 runs.

Charlie said he and the other players enjoyed playing for Baker. He was totally different in personality than Cochrane — more low-key, not given to temper tantrums, not overbearing, and yet extremely knowledgeable. "I liked to play for him," said Gehringer. "He was all baseball, morning, noon and night."

Meanwhile, Jack Zeller, the Tiger farm system director, was promoted to general manager to replace Cochrane, and became busy morning, noon and night himself, revamping what he considered a once-great ballclub that was getting old and could not compete for a championship

11. "The Michigan Mummy."

with the likes of young Joe DiMaggio and the New York Yankees, winners of three straight World Series championships.

Because of his experience in the farm system, Zeller had a good feel for the up-and-coming ballplayers and wanted to mesh them with some veterans to rebuild the franchise. It was clear from the beginning that there were only two "untouchables" on the Tiger roster — Hank Greenberg and Charlie Gehringer.

The revamping began on December 12, when Zeller purchased the contract of Fred Hutchinson, a tall, skinny, right-handed pitcher from Seattle who had been pitching for his hometown minor league team. Hutchinson was considered good enough to enter the Tiger starting rotation right away. Two other minor league pitchers Zeller had his eye on were Paul "Dizzy" Trout, a big, bespectacled, hard-throwing right-hander, and Hal Newhouser, a moody southpaw with great stuff who had trouble controlling both his pitches and his temper. Detroit also expected big things from speedy rookie outfielder Barney McCosky. The Tigers had the same hope for young catcher George "Birdie" Tebbetts, the heir apparent to the throne behind the plate that Hayworth and Cochrane had occupied for a decade.

Three days after the Hutchinson deal, Zeller tried to fill the void left by the previous season's departure of third baseman Owen to the White Sox. But to get what he wanted, Zeller had to give up something in return, which is the way of the world in the business of baseball. He wanted Mike "Pinky" Higgins, the Red Sox third baseman. To get him, he traded one of the mainstays of the old pitching staff, Elden Auker, along with pitcher Jake Wade and infielder Ed Morgan. The Tigers picked up pitcher Archie McKain as part of the deal.

As the 1939 season started, Schoolboy Rowe was back with the ballclub, promising both his arm and his attitude had new life under Del Baker, the new manager. But it was evident early on that Auker was sorely missed in the starting rotation. Bridges was sharp as ever, but Rowe was still trying to get back in his old groove, and Hutchinson was finding that life in the big leagues was a little different than in the balmy Pacific Northwest.

In his major league debut, May 2, 1939, Hutchinson lasted less than an inning and gave up eight runs on four hits and five walks as the Yankees clobbered the Tigers 20–2. Hutchinson's debut is an obscure footnote on the game that day. Far more significant in baseball history is the story of someone who did not play. Lou Gehrig, hitting under .200 with only one RBI for the season and experiencing weakness in his bones, took himself out of the Yankee lineup, ending a streak of 2,130 consecutive games played. He would be dead within two years of amyotrophic lateral sclerosis, a degenerative bone disease which came to be known as "Lou Gehrig's Disease."

Searching for a dependable big gun to thrust into the starting rotation, on May 13, Zeller pulled off one of the biggest trades of the 20th century in terms of movement of players. The Tigers traded three of their pitchers — Vern Kennedy, George Gill, and Roxie Lawson — along with three other players — pitcher Bob Harris, outfielder Chet Laabs, and infielder Mark Christman — to the St. Louis Browns for three fringe players — outfielder Roy Chester "Beau" Bell, veteran infielder Ralph "Red" Kress, and pitcher Jim Walkup — and the key player in the deal, Louis "Bobo" Newsom.

Newsom was a 20-game winner with the Browns in 1938 and had won 16 in 1937. He was big, brash, and oozed self-confidence — some called it bragging — an American League counterpart to what Dizzy Dean had been to the St. Louis Cardinals. Newsom was quite the opposite in personality to Gehringer, but Charlie laughed at some of Bobo's antics. He recalled a time when Newsom was pitching against the Tigers and had two strikes on Hank Greenberg. Suddenly, Bobo trotted off the mound and into the dugout. He stuck his hands in a pail of water, rinsed off his face, and toweled himself off. It was as if he had mistakenly thought the inning was over. Meanwhile, Greenberg bided his time at the plate, wondering what was going on. Then Newsom bolted back out to the mound, got his signal from his catcher, and threw strike three past Greenberg.

Charlie said as a member of the Tigers, Bobo had trouble saying no when someone offered him a beer. And he liked to play practical jokes. Schoolboy Rowe was often one of his victims because Schoolboy was a little slow on the uptake, according to Gehringer. Newsom once nailed Rowe's spikes to the floor. But on the field, said Charlie, Bobo knew what he was doing. Zeller hoped Newsom would light a fire under the Tigers, but equally important, he needed to eat up some innings and at least come close to his 20-win performance of 1938 to make up for the departures of Kennedy, Gill, and Lawson from the pitching staff.

11. *"The Michigan Mummy."*

Bobo Newsom was the pitching ace of the 1940 pennant-winning Tigers. His father died after watching him win the World Series opener (photograph courtesy of the National Baseball Hall of Fame).

On May 20, Detroit picked up another pitcher, Bud Thomas, on waivers from the Washington Senators. He had pitched for Connie Mack's A's until early in 1939. On April 23, he gave up Ted Williams' first major league homer. Not long after that, Mack shipped him to Washington, where Thomas barely had time to unpack before the Senators sent him to the Tigers.

While all the wheeling and dealing was going on, Detroit was playing baseball. For Charlie Gehringer, it was a far different clubhouse than it had been in years past. He had been there in the days of Ty Cobb and Harry Heilmann (who was now a Tiger radio broadcaster) and Earl Whitehill and Bob Fothergill, and the championship years with Mickey Cochrane. Now, less than four years after they won the World Series, only six players remained from that team—Gehringer, Greenberg, Bridges, Rowe, Rogell, and Fox. By the end of the year, Rogell would also be gone.

On May 27, Charlie added to his long list of accomplishments by hitting for the cycle in a 12–5 win over the Browns. He singled, then doubled, then tripled, then homered, becoming the first player in baseball history to hit for the cycle in that sequence. He had another good year, hitting .325, the seventh consecutive year he was above .300, but age was starting to catch up with him. He was 36 and appeared in only 118 games, his fewest since 1931 when he was out with injuries. His 86 runs scored—a good amount for most players—was his lowest since 1926, his first full season. His 132 hits were his fewest since 1931, and his total of 29 doubles and 86 runs batted in were also his lowest in the past eight years.

Greenberg also had an "off year" of sorts, hitting "only" 33 home runs. That was just five shy of home run champion Jimmy Foxx but 25 fewer than Hank hit in 1938 when he challenged Babe Ruth's single-season record. York hit 20 home runs, down from 35 and 33 his two previous years. Rudy was now catching and playing some innings at first base. The Tigers wanted Greenberg to move to the outfield, a shift he eventually gratefully accepted—for a cash bonus of $10,000.

There were some bright spots. Newsom won 17 for Detroit and, coupled with the three wins he had for the Browns, turned in his second straight 20-win season. Rowe won 10 games, a far cry from his glory days but better than his last two seasons when he won only one game altogether. Tommy Bridges had another great year with a 17–7 record. Bud Thomas did not disappoint. He was 7–0 in mostly a relief role. Barney

11. *"The Michigan Mummy."*

Hal Newhouser was a youngster on the 1940 championship team but was already developing into a Hall of Fame hurler for the Tigers (photograph courtesy of the National Baseball Hall of Fame).

McCosky hit .311 and became a fan favorite with his timely hitting, daring base running, and flashy play in the outfield, much like Gee Walker had been for so many years. Hutchinson struggled the entire season and finished with a 3–6 record.

Despite all the changes and high hopes, the Tigers finished fifth in the American League with a record of 81–73. The Yankees won their fourth consecutive World Series championship, something that the Bronx Bombers of the Ruth-Gehrig era had never achieved.

But more distressing to Briggs, Zeller, Baker, and the Tiger fandom was not just the Yankees, but three other teams — Boston, Cleveland and Chicago in that order — had finished higher in the standings than Detroit, which ended up 26½ games out of first place. For all their effort on an off the field, the Tigers were a second-division ballclub.

A clear sign that the Tigers were beginning to age — or at least one them — was in July when Charlie, elected to the American League All-Star team for the seventh consecutive year, asked to be replaced. He was nursing a pulled muscle in his leg. He would never appear in another All-Star Game. The American League beat the National League 3–1 in the mid-season classic at Yankee Stadium. Joe Gordon started at second base for the American League.

Dizzy Trout wasn't much of a factor when Detroit won the pennant in 1940, but five years later he was a mainstay on the World Series champion Tigers (photograph courtesy of the National Baseball Hall of Fame).

CHAPTER 12

"The cry babies."

Quiet, unassuming Charlie Gehringer had his share of encounters with colorful characters over the years, on and off the field. He won the respect of his nasty manager Ty Cobb, got a hit and stole a base in the 1934 All-Star Game before Carl Hubbell struck out five future Hall of Famers, was on deck when Mickey Cochrane endured the near-fatal beaning in 1937, was barnstorming in Japan when Moe Berg was doing espionage work for the U.S. government, and shared a few moments with Al Capone in the gangster's Chicago hotel room. Yet by many writers' estimation, Charlie was one of the dullest people to write about. However, in the spring of 1939, Gehringer found himself in unfamiliar territory — the subject of gossip in newspaper columns. Lorraine MacDonald Dodge, a wealthy Detroit socialite, threw a party for him on his 36th birthday, and Hy Goldberg in the *Detroit News* said the two were "romantically linked."[1]

What made the report sensational is that Lorraine MacDonald Dodge came upon her wealth the year before as the result of the strange, untimely death of her husband, Daniel Dodge, one of the heirs to his family's automobile fortune. Danny Dodge and Lorraine MacDonald had married in 1938 and honeymooned at an exclusive lodge her family had recently built on Manitoulin Island on Lake Huron in Canada. One day, Danny came across some dynamite in an old carriage house, lit a stick, and threw it out into some open land. The resulting explosion drew the attention of his new wife and others who were nearby. He lit another stick, but as he started to toss it in the same direction as the first, he hesitated because onlookers were now in the path. So he turned to throw it out a window on the opposite side of the carriage house. The dynamite hit the window ledge, bounced back toward Dodge, and blew up. He was severely injured as were several others just outside the carriage house.

Lorraine and some caretakers believed the nearest medical help was across the bay. They loaded Danny and the other injured people on the family's boat and tried to get them to a hospital. At one point in the trip, Danny reportedly stood up just as a huge wave rocked the boat. He fell overboard and went under. Others in the boat tried to find him but couldn't. Tragically, Danny Dodge, 21, drowned. The police and the Dodge family were not convinced that Lorraine Dodge's account of how her husband died was on the level. But after a thorough investigation, she was cleared of any wrongdoing and the death was ruled accidental due to drowning.

A year later, Lorraine hosted the birthday party for Charlie. Calling it a "romantic link" might have been an exaggeration by the columnist or wishful thinking on the part of the young widow. Charlie could have had many steady girlfriends over the past 15 years but passed up every chance because he never wavered in his commitment to take care of his mother. Even Hy Goldberg alluded to it in the same column in which he reported on the party. "That trite old line about being good to your mother is no gag as far as Charlie is concerned," he wrote. Johnny Neun, who roomed with Gehringer when he first came up, heard about the party and said, "When I knew him, you couldn't get him to look at a girl but I guess he's old enough now. He deserves a party. He's a good guy."[2]

Characteristically, Charlie didn't comment about the party or the alleged "romance" between him and Lorraine Dodge. If there was one, it was short-lived. Lorraine Dodge got married again (to someone else), and Charlie went about his business of playing baseball six months a year, selling auto accessories most of the rest of the year, and being the guardian of Theresa Gehringer.

Charlie's mother, once the biggest skeptic of her son's chances for success in making a living by playing a game, was now a big fan. Occasionally, she came to Briggs Stadium to see Charlie play, but most of the time, she listened to games on the radio. The broadcaster was Gehringer's old teammate Harry Heilmann, whose voice was as familiar to one generation of baseball fans as Ernie Harwell's would be to a future generation. Heilmann mixed anecdotes about Tigers past and present with his play-by-play and developed catch phrases that endeared him to his listeners. If an opposing batter hit a long fly ball, Theresa Gehringer and other

12. "The cry babies."

listeners could rest a little easier when they heard Heilmann exclaim, "Bugaboo — another fly is caught." Bugaboo was an insect repellant that was a commercial sponsor of Tiger broadcasts. If a long fly ball appeared to be going out of the park, Heilmann alerted fans by shouting, "Trouble, trouble." Sometimes during exciting games, he would point his microphone in the direction of the noisy crowd and say, "Listen to the voice of baseball."[3]

No one expected too much from the Tigers in 1940. The Yankees seemed to have a stranglehold on first place, and Cleveland was an up-and-coming contender with its young fireballer, Bob Feller. Boston also had a superstar in the making in outfielder Ted Williams. The Tigers still had Greenberg and Gehringer, but Charlie would be 37 on his next birthday, and there was some question as to whether Greenberg would return to his 1938 form. As usual, Schoolboy Rowe was a question mark. Bridges was dependable and consistent, but he needed help. It was clear that any chance Detroit had in overtaking the Yankees rested on the arm of Bobo Newsom.

Zeller and Baker continued to try to put the pieces together. In the off season, Billy Rogell, Charlie Gehringer's longtime double-play partner in the middle of the infield, was traded to the Chicago Cubs for Dick Bartell. Many in the press considered it swapping two over-the-hill shortstops.

During the winter, Charlie made some guest appearances here and there, tended to his auto accessory business, and continued to look after his aging mother at home. One day, while shoveling snow in front of their house, maneuvering the shovel with the same quickness and grace he used picking up ground balls in the summer, he felt a twinge in his back, a sharp pain that made him wince. He finished his shoveling with a minimum of bending and went inside to rest. As the winter wore on, every now and then he would feel the back pain again.

On March 5, 1940, at spring training in Lakeland, Florida, the pain became so great that Charlie left the practice field. He had been taking infield practice when he hurt himself again. "I came in for a slow grounder, scooped up the ball, started to throw to first when a kid ran into my line of fire," said Charlie. "I was off balance and in motion, but I held up my throw with a lurch. Then my back miseries began." Quiet Charlie also said the words that Detroit fans did not want to hear: "If this continues, I'll go home." He meant he would go home permanently. It was the first time Charlie had ever talked publicly about retiring.

For most of the rest of spring training, Gehringer played sparingly and received daily treatments to relieve the back pain. When the Tigers headed north for some exhibition games prior to the start of the season, Gehringer stayed behind. Doctors thought the Florida sun would be better for him than the climate changes he (and his back) would experience on the way to Detroit.

In early April, there was still a question whether Charlie would be able to answer the call on opening day, April 16. When the Tigers arrived in Knoxville, Tennessee, manager Baker received some encouraging news from Florida. Gehringer had been working out with the Buffalo Bisons and on April 11 had actually played in a game for a few innings. He was planning to rejoin the team in Cincinnati, where Detroit was to play a four-game series with the Reds to conclude the exhibition season. If all went well, he would be ready to take his usual place on the field and in the starting lineup.

Zeller and Baker's revamped Tigers opened the season with Tebbetts behind the plate, an infield of York, Gehringer, Bartell, and Higgins, and Greenberg, McCosky, and Fox in the outfield. The strength of the pitching staff was clearly the one-two punch of Newsom and Bridges, but there was also some depth with Rowe, Newhouser, Hutchinson, and Trout. The Tigers also had spot starters in veteran Al Benton and rookie Johnny Gorsica. Benton had started his major league career with the Philadelphia A's in 1934 and pitched for them for two years. He then spent two years in the minors before being sold to the Tigers prior to the 1938 season. He was 5–3 in 1938 and 6–8 in 1939. Gorsica was another in the string of pitchers the Tigers had developed over the years who came to the big leagues showing a lot of promise.[4]

Nearly 50,000 people showed up on opening day at Briggs Stadium, the largest opening day crowd in the major leagues, to watch Bobo Newsom take on the St. Louis Browns. Nearly all of them went home disappointed as the Browns whipped the Tigers, 5–1. The contest was a landmark game for two reasons. It was the only game all year that the Browns won in Briggs Stadium — and Bobo didn't lose another game until July 17. Living up to what Zeller and Baker had hoped for, Newsom reeled off 13 consecutive victories and was the dominant pitcher in the American League.

During that span, Bobo was 3–0 against St. Louis, 3–0 against Wash-

12. "The cry babies."

ington, 2–0 against Chicago, 2–0 against Philadelphia, 2–0 against the Yankees, and 1–0 against Cleveland. More importantly, he put the Tigers on his back and carried them in the midst of a torrid pennant race. At the end of play on July 17, the standings looked like this:

Cleveland	48–33	.593	—
Detroit	47–33	.587	.5
Boston	47–33	.587	.5
New York	42–36	.538	4.5
Chicago	36–40	.474	9.5
Washington	35–48	.422	14
Philadelphia	32–47	.405	15
St. Louis	33–50	.398	16

A flashpoint in the season occurred in June and had nothing to do with the Tigers but affected the American League pennant race as a whole. Though the Indians were winning consistently, their players were becoming upset with manager Oscar Vitt because of his constant criticism and derogatory comments. On June 11, Boston clobbered Bob Feller and beat the Indians 9–2. Vitt was overheard in the dugout saying, "Look at him. He's supposed to be my ace out there. How am I supposed to win a pennant with that kind of pitching?"[5]

Vitt had been a below average major league player. His 10-year career included seven with the Tigers when he was Ty Cobb's teammate. He didn't hit like Cobb. His lifetime batting average was .238. But he had a reputation of being a student of the game and found his niche as a minor league manager. In 1937, his Newark Bears won 109 games in capturing the International League championship. Newark's nearest foe finished 25 games out of first place. Cleveland Indians owner Alva Bradley snared Vitt to manage his ballclub, hoping Vitt would have the same success in the major leagues as Joe McCarthy, who moved up to the majors after a successful year in Louisville 12 years earlier.

The day after Vitt blasted Feller, Cleveland lost again at Boston, 9–5, with the Indians' other ace, Mel Harder, taking the loss. During the long train ride home to Cleveland, several players, including Feller, Harder, first baseman Hal Trosky, third baseman Ken Keltner, and catcher Rollie Hemsley, decided they had to talk with Bradley about their manager. The next morning, a dozen players went to his office and demanded that Vitt be fired. That afternoon, the Indians came out of their slump with a 3–2 win over the Tigers. The game was decided in a most unusual way. Charlie

Gehringer, the most sure-handed second baseman in all of baseball, made two errors on one play to cost the Tigers a run.

The Gehringer double-error played second fiddle to a bigger story in the morning newspapers. First reported by Gordon Cobbledick in the *Cleveland Plain Dealer*, the word quickly spread: Mutiny among the Cleveland Indians. It was the talk of baseball and obviously a major distraction to the Indians. After several days, the same players who organized the meeting with Bradley decided they had to put their discontent behind them for the sake of the team — or at least give the impression they had. So they signed a letter of apology and presented it to Vitt. But in terms of team morale and loyalty, the damage had been done. The Indians vowed to play hard, but many of them ignored Vitt's signals as he coached at third base and paid little attention when he talked to them.

Tiger fans feasted on the Indians' problems. The next time Cleveland came to Detroit, many fans yelled "Cry Babies" when the Indians took the field and someone put a baby bottle on top of the Cleveland dugout. Later in the season, when the Indians made another trip to the Motor City, a fan dropped a baby stroller onto the field.

Charlie's back problems plagued him off and on all season. He continued to play, but the press speculated that this would be his last year. On August 21, after watching the Tigers and Yankees in a doubleheader at Yankee Stadium, New York sportswriter Dan Daniel told his readers this would be Charlie's last year as the Tigers regular second baseman. Gehringer made no public mention of retirement. He preferred to focus on the pennant race, which had become one of the most exciting in American League history.

In early September, four teams had a shot at winning it all — Cleveland, Detroit, Boston, and New York. On Sunday, September 8, the Tigers beat St. Louis 5–4, Cleveland beat the White Sox 5–4, and the Yankees clipped Boston 9–4. The Indians and Tigers were tied for first place, and the Yankees were just one game out. The Red Sox loss dropped them five games out of the lead, so their chances were fading. Still only .31 percentage points separated the top four teams:

Cleveland	76–56	.576	—
Detroit	77–57	.575	—
New York	75–57	.568	1
Boston	72–62	.537	5

12. "The cry babies."

On September 9, the Tigers had an off day, and Thornton Lee of the White Sox handcuffed the Indians, 2–1, pushing Detroit into first place by mere percentage points. On Tuesday, the Cleveland–New York game was rained out, and the Red Sox, behind Lefty Grove, beat the Tigers 6–5, moving the Indians back into first place.

Wednesday, September 11, was a rare day in baseball history. Depending on what time of the day it was, three different teams occupied first place in the crazy American League pennant race. The Indians started the day in first place. When they lost the first game of a doubleheader to the Yankees, New York was on top, but only for a couple of hours. Cleveland won the second game of the twin bill, but when Detroit beat Boston later in the day, the Tigers took over first place.

The Tigers then took two out of three from the Yankees, with Schoolboy Rowe, having a terrific comeback season, winning the opener 6–3 and Tommy Bridges tossing an 8–0 shutout the next day. New York salvaged one game, handing Bobo Newsom a 16–7 pasting. But a Cleveland loss kept the Tigers a half-game ahead — only until the next day because Washington beat Detroit behind Dutch Leonard 6–1 while the Indians were winning a double header from the A's, putting them back in first place.

Detroit and Cleveland continued to both win and lose at about the same pace, so with ten days left in the season, each had a record of 85–61. They had eight games left — six against each other.

The first set of crucial games was at Briggs Stadium in Detroit. The pitching match-ups were sensational: Bobo Newsom and Mel Harder on Friday night, Schoolboy Rowe versus Al Milnar on Saturday, and Tommy Bridges facing Bob Feller on Sunday.

In the opener, Newsom was good, but Harder was better. Cleveland had a 4–1 lead going into the bottom of the eighth. McCosky led off with a walk. Then Charlie Gehringer characteristically took one pitch after another until he got one he liked and rapped a base hit. That was enough to convince Vitt that Harder had lost his stuff. He summoned Bob Feller, Sunday's scheduled starter, in from the bullpen. Feller gave up singles to Greenberg, York, and Higgins. Suddenly, the score was 4–3 with the tying and winning runs on base. Feller was removed without retiring a batter, and Joe Dobson came in. By the time the inning was over, the Tigers had a 6–5 lead. Detroit reliever Al Benton took care of business in the ninth to preserve the victory, giving the Tigers a one-game lead in the standings.

Players and writers said after the game Charlie's single was the key hit to ignite the rally. Harder had been tough for seven innings. After McCosky walked, if Charlie had made a quick out or failed to advance the runner, Harder might have gotten a second wind. But Charlie made a tired pitcher throw more pitches and then stung him for a hit that launched the big inning.

On Saturday, the Tigers jumped on Milnar early and often, and Schoolboy Rowe showed the form he had when he dominated opposing batters in the 1934–1935 pennant years. Detroit won 5–0 to take a two-game lead over the Indians and put some pressure on Vitt, who questioned whether to start Feller on Sunday. The young fireballer had won his 26th game of the year on Wednesday and then made the brief but faulty relief appearance on Friday night. Vitt rolled the dice and went with Feller against Bridges in the series finale. This time it was the Indians' turn to put on an offensive display. Feller didn't pitch well, but well enough as Cleveland won the ballgame 10–5, moving back within a game of the Tigers. Both teams were idle on Monday.

On Tuesday, the Indians opened a two-game series with the sixth-place St. Louis Browns and would have to face two former Tigers, Elden Auker and Vern Kennedy. Meanwhile, the Tigers had a two-game series with Chicago. Auker handcuffed the Indians, beating them 7–2 while Detroit was rained out at Chicago but still picked up a half-game and now led by 1½ games with four to play. That was the good news. The bad news was that because of the rainout, the Tigers had to play a doubleheader with the White Sox on Wednesday. If Chicago swept and Cleveland won, the two teams would be tied going into their three-game series to end the season.

The Indians beat the Browns 4–2. The Tigers battled the White Sox and won 10–9 in ten innings in the first game of their twin bill. Manager Baker used Newsom for two innings in relief, and Bobo picked up his 20th win. It was Baker's turn to roll the dice. Newsom had been scheduled to start the second game, and Baker decided to give him the ball despite his two innings of work in game one. Bobo and Johnny Rigney faced off in a dandy with Chicago winning 2–1 after six innings. In the seventh, Greenberg unloaded his 41st home run of the season to tie the game. In the eighth inning, after McCosky singled, Charlie Gehringer once again delivered in the clutch, singling to push the tying run into

12. "The cry babies."

scoring position with Charlie becoming the potential lead run. Rigney wanted no part of Greenberg and pitched especially carefully, walking him to bring up York. Rudy hit a sacrifice fly to score what turned out to be the winning run. The Tigers now had a two-game lead over Cleveland with three to play, all against the Indians. One more victory would clinch the American League championship.

As the Tigers took the train for the relatively short trip to Cleveland, Baker met with Gehringer and the other starters. He had a decision to make on his pitching rotation. Baker knew that Vitt would have to start Feller in the opening game. Even though the star pitcher had worked twice in the past week, it was do-or-die time for the Indians, and when a whole season's work is at stake, you go with your ace. Cleveland had to sweep the series, but the Tigers only had to win one to clinch the pennant. So Baker had decided to start one of his second-tier pitchers in the opener against Feller. That would give his front-line starters an extra day's rest. Schoolboy, Bridges, and Newsom would all be available for the final two games.

Baker presented his plan to the players. The question was: who should start the Friday night game — Hutchinson, Newhouser, Trout, or Floyd Giebell, a youngster who had been in the minor leagues until two weeks ago when he became one of the Tigers' September call-ups. Giebell had only one major league win, but Gehringer thought it should be him since he was the hurler most likely to be a mystery to Indian hitters. Most everyone else agreed except Greenberg, who questioned whether it was wise to put Giebell in that tight a spot. Hutchinson and Newhouser had more experience, but the consensus was for Giebell. Baker, of course, had the final say, but he too thought Giebell was the best choice.

As Charlie and the other players got off the train at Union Station in Cleveland, they were met by a band of unruly Indian fans who wanted to get even for the Tiger fans in Detroit who had taunted the Cleveland players with shouts of "cry baby" and for the incidents with the baby bottle and the stroller. The Indian fans began throwing fruit and tomatoes at the Detroit players.

Fortunately, the hotel was directly above the train station. As 25 Cleveland policemen tried to control the situation, Gehringer, in his typical quiet way, looked around in search of a quick, reasonable solution. He spotted the freight elevator not too far from where they were standing. "Follow me," he said. Following Charlie's lead, the players scurried to the safety of the elevator.[6]

The crowd at the game was just as feisty. Greenberg was pelted with fruit as he took his position in left field. Home plate umpire Bill Summers had the public address announcer plead with the fans to stop. Someone threw a bucket of objects into the Tiger bullpen, striking catcher Birdie Tebbetts and knocking him unconscious for a moment. When he came to, he noticed the police ushering the assailant out. Tebbetts ran up in the stands and punched the man.

The game was a dandy. Feller was sharp, but young Giebell was able to hang in there. Neither team had scored as the fourth inning began. Charlie, waiting as he always did for the pitch he liked, didn't get one. He walked. York got hold of a Feller fastball and hit a towering fly ball that headed foul down the leftfield line. But a wind current, blowing from leftfield to right, took the ball and pushed it fair — and into the leftfield stands for a two-run homer. Witnesses said the ball landed a foot fair and a foot past the leftfield wall. It was one of three hits the Tigers got off Feller all day. Giebell scattered six hits, but no Indians crossed the plate. Detroit won the American League championship with a 2–0 victory behind the gutsy performance of a pitcher nobody had ever heard of — until this day.

Giebell was a West Virginia farmer who had a college degree in accounting. The Tigers had signed him in 1937 after scouts saw him pitch in a semi-pro tournament in Dayton, Ohio. Despite winning the game that clinched the pennant, he was not eligible to participate in the World Series because he wasn't part of the Detroit roster until after September 1. Giebell would not win another game in the major leagues.[7] Baker said after the game, "Even if I make 100 bad guesses before I retire, they can't take this one away from me. I had a hunch the kid would deliver."[8]

Feller, who started the 1940 season by throwing a no-hitter against the Chicago White Sox on opening day, would go on to win 266 games in his career, but he also suffered some tough losses along the way. Eight years after Giebell beat him in the 1940 pennant clincher, Feller lost a 1–0 decision in his first World Series appearance against the Boston Braves. He had enormous respect for Charlie Gehringer. Years after both of their careers were over, Feller described Charlie: "He never said much and was always in the right place at the right time. He was what we call a 'guess hitter' and he guessed right a lot."[9]

12. "The cry babies."

With all the drama of the Detroit-Cleveland series to end the season, there wasn't much attention paid to the fact that the Yankees came within two games of winning their fifth consecutive championship. New York columnist Joe Williams speculated on what made the difference this year. Was it Bobo Newsom? Schoolboy Rowe? Hank Greenberg? Charlie Gehringer struggling along? No, said Williams, Denny Carroll was the Tigers' unsung hero. Carroll was the team's trainer, but he was more than that, said Williams. He was a muscle massager, and he, more than anyone else, was responsible for taking care of the aging bodies of Dick Bartell and Charlie Gehringer and putting new life into the arm of Schoolboy Rowe. Williams wrote, "He's just a rubber. His secret is that he knows how to rub and where to rub. Actually, he's what the therapeutic profession would call a muscle manipulator. He knows all about the human anatomy and he has extraordinarily sensitive fingers." The Tigers won the pennant, and "everyone out here (in Detroit) says Mr. Carroll deserves all the credit."[10]

In Cleveland, the Indians fell one game short of their goal on the field. Off the field, not long after the season was over, they got what they wanted: Alva Bradley fired Oscar Vitt.

CHAPTER 13

"I kept yelling 'home, home, home.'"

In 1940, Charlie hit over .300 for the last time in his career, finishing with a .313 average and appearing in 139 games, thanks to the magic fingers of Denny Carroll. Newsom was fabulous, winning 21 and losing only 5. Schoolboy Rowe was the biggest surprise in the American League with his 16–3 record. Tommy Bridges, Detroit's most consistent pitcher for almost a decade, was 12–9. Gorsica and Newhouser, whose roles were mainly as spot starters and to eat some innings to give others a rest, were 7–7 and 9–9 respectively. McCosky, the lead-off hitter, hit .340 and set the table for the big bangers, Greenberg, who also hit .340 with 41 homers and 150 runs batted in, and York, who hit .316 with 33 home runs and 134 runs batted in.

Detroit's World Series opponent was the Cincinnati Reds, who had a much easier time, statistically, winning the National League championship with a record of 100–53. Brooklyn was a distant second, 12 games behind the Reds. Cincinnati's offense was led by slugging first baseman Frank McCormick, who hit .309 with 19 home runs and 127 runs batted in. The only other .300 hitter was catcher Ernie Lombardi, who hit .314, and his 74 RBIs, though 53 fewer than McCormick's were nonetheless second best on the team. Cincinnati's strength was in its pitching staff. The Reds had a starting four of Paul Derringer, 20–12, Bucky Walters, 22–10, Junior Thompson, 16–9, and Jim Turner, 14–7.

The Reds were able to win the pennant despite an enormous tragedy that occurred in August. Willard Hershberger, a backup catcher, was pressed into service in late July when Lombardi went out with an injury to his finger. Hershberger had been with the ballclub since 1938 and had accepted his role well as a backup. And he was having a good year in 1940, hitting .309. But after Lombardi got hurt, the Reds went into a bit of a slump. When the Reds lost a tough game to the Giants at the Polo Grounds on July 31, Hershberger seemed to take it personally, thinking his calling for wrong pitches had cost them the ballgame. Teammates tried to console him. Then, on August 3, when Cincinnati lost the second game of a doubleheader to the lowly Boston Braves, Hershberger again acted overly depressed. Manager Bill McKechnie noticed that he seemed distracted on the field. McKechnie took him out to dinner after the game and assured him he was doing his part for the team. By the end of the dinner, they were talking about other things, and both agreed it was time to call it a night. When they parted and each went to his respective hotel room, McKechnie thought Hershberger was back in good spirits.

The Reds and Braves had another doubleheader the next day. Hershberger did not show up for practice and was not there by game time. McKechnie sent one of the club's traveling assistants to go back to the hotel to check on him. When the aide checked Hershberger's room, he found him dead in the bathroom, where he had slit his throat with a razor blade. He was 31 years old.

Team members, of course, were devastated and dedicated the rest of the season to Hershberger's memory. They even retired his uniform number, No. 5. The Reds scrapped to find another catcher and on August 12 signed one of their coaches, Jimmie Wilson, as a free agent, bringing him out of retirement. At the age of 40, Wilson caught 16 games and then played in the World Series. The Reds were sailing along with a 62–32 record at the time of Hershberger's death. They continued their winning ways, going 38–21 the rest of the season.[1]

The World Series turned out to be a classic, going the full seven games. Neither team led the other by more than one game as day after day, they traded wins and losses. Charlie Gehringer played every game, much of the time with gritted teeth because his backaches had become chronic.

The Reds felt they had something to prove. In 1939, they were swept by the Yankees in the World Series. They were an experienced bunch and not prone to the bench-jockeying antics of the Gas House Gang and Charlie Grimm's Cubs, the Tigers' last two World Series opponents in 1934 and 1935.

In the opener, Bobo Newsom faced Paul Derringer. The Tigers broke it open early by scoring five runs in the second inning, aided by five hits, two errors, and a walk. The final was 7–2. Newsom got the win. Then, tragedy struck the Tigers. Newsom's father, who was at the game and watched his son notch a World Series victory, died of a heart attack the next morning in his room at the Netherland Plaza Hotel, where the Tiger players and families were staying. Detroit would now have to regroup much as the Reds had done during the regular season when they had to deal with an untimely death.

In the second game, the pitching match-up was Schoolboy Roe for the Tigers and Bucky Walters for the Reds. "I guess I was nervous," said Walters. "I walked the first two men and Charlie Gehringer came up. Jimmie Wilson, our sub catcher came out to talk to me. He told me to be myself out there. I guess he thought I was nervous. Gehringer hit a single to score one run."

The next batter was Greenberg with a chance to break the game open. "Hank sure gave me a big break," said Walters. "He hit into a double play. If Hank had hit one out, that could have been the end of it for us." A run scored on the double play to give Detroit a 2–0 lead before the Reds ever came to bat. But Cincinnati hit Schoolboy early and often. He was in the showers before the third inning was over, and the Reds had a 5–2 lead. They held on to win 5–3 to even the series at one game apiece. Detroit managed only two hits besides Gehringer's RBI single in the first inning.[2]

Game three moved the series to Detroit, where the veteran Tommy Bridges, like Rowe appearing in his third World Series, faced Jim Turner, a 14-game winner in the regular season. They both pitched brilliantly and were locked in a 1–1 tie until the seventh inning, when Rudy York and Pinky Higgins homered, and the Tigers scored four times. They went on to win 7–4 and once again took a one-game lead in the series.

In the fourth game, Derringer went up against the youngster Dizzy Trout, a surprise starter for the Tigers. Newsom had insisted on staying with the team, despite his father's death, but was given an extra day off. Gorsica, a spot starter during the regular season, had worked six innings in relief of Rowe in game two. So Baker handed the ball to Trout, who had started 10 games in the regular season with a 3–7 record. If Floyd Giebell had been eligible, Baker might have turned to him one more time. But Baker rolled the dice in choosing Trout, and this time they came up snake eyes. Trout gave up three runs on six hits before being relieved with

13. "I kept yelling 'home, home, home.'"

nobody out in the third inning. Cincinnati went on to win 5–2, evening the series at two games each. For Derringer, it broke an 0–4 spell in World Series play, including two losses as member of the Cardinals in 1933, a loss to the Yankees in 1939, and the second loss in this Series.

Newsom, still grieving his father's death, took the mound in game five and tossed a three-hit shutout. Hank Greenberg led the Tiger attack with a three-run homer and two singles as Detroit won 8–0. Gehringer, playing in pain, had his best game of the Series, getting two hits in four at-bats and scoring two runs. The Series moved back to Cincinnati in game six with the Reds staying in the same hotel where Newsom's father had died less than a week earlier. This time it was Bucky Walters throwing a gem as he shut out the Tigers 4–0. Once again, Rowe got shelled, giving up two runs on four hits and leaving the game without getting out of the first inning. Once again, Gorsica pitched six innings in relief, trying to keep Detroit in the game. Bartell and York each had two hits, and Higgins had one, but the rest of the Tigers, including Charlie, went hitless.

For game seven, neither manager rolled any dice. Baker went with Newsom, pitching on one day's rest but with an abundance of adrenalin and emotion. McKechnie picked Derringer, his 20-game winner who was coming off his best World Series performance ever. The game was a classic. The Tigers pushed home a run in the third, and Newsom made it hold up until the seventh inning when Frank McCormick hit a double. Jimmy Ripple then followed with a long fly to right field that bounded off the wall. McCormick, who was not a fast runner, held up until he realized right fielder Bruce Campbell was not going to make the catch. Campbell fielded the ball cleanly and fired a perfect relay throw to Bartell, who had his back to the infield. Gehringer, watching the base runner, saw that McCormick had gotten a late start off of second and was just lumbering around third when Bartell got the relay. Charlie yelled "Home, home, home," but apparently Bartell did not hear him over the roar of the crowd. He looked, cocked his arm, but did not throw. McCormick scored. A moment later, Ripple scored on a sacrifice fly. That was all the scoring for the entire game. Cincinnati won 2–1 and won the World Series in a thriller over the Tigers.

In 1934, Charlie thought an umpire's call might have been the one play that stopped the Tigers dead in their tracks. In this Series, it was one play again, or the lack of it, by one of his own teammates. Bartell hesitated, and the Tigers lost. "I kept yelling 'home, home, home,'" said Charlie. "Gee whiz, with Bartell's arm, he's a dead pigeon. But he never did throw the ball. Even after he looked and still had a chance, he still didn't throw ... I don't know why."[3]

McCosky watched the play from the outfield. He said Ripple's double went between him and Campbell in right-centerfield. "Campbell picked up the ball and relayed it to Bartell at short, and he hesitated. If Bartell had thrown it right when he got it, it probably would have been close. He should have thrown it. He didn't."[4]

Charlie had been living with pain for a long time. Now he was talking about it. Coming off a World Series in which he hit only .214, Gehringer vowed he would never play in such pain again. "It was sheer torture for me to play this past season," he said. "I couldn't get out of bed most days until noontime. When I bent down to field a ball, especially to my left, I felt as if my insides were being torn loose." Charlie said there were times during the season and during the World Series when he didn't think he could move a couple of steps in the field or get the bat off his shoulder when he swung. Retirement seemed to be drawing near.[5]

Dan Daniel, the *New York World Telegram* columnist who had followed Gehringer's career closely over the years, made light of his "dullness" and minimized his 1937 Most Valuable Player award as recognition of sentiment more than achievement, now wrestled with the notion that Charlie might actually retire. In a column just prior to the World Series, Daniel mentioned Charlie's back problems and that he was receiving regular injections to stop the pain. "That situation, as well as his age, combined with the fact that he has several gas stations in Detroit, is financially well fixed and may decide to get married — all enter into the possibility that Gehringer will call it quits," he wrote.

Charlie never mentioned anything about getting married. He was still caring for his mother in the home he bought for her in Detroit. But the rumors were that he was still seeing Lorraine Dodge, the wealthy widow. Daniel put it this way: "Talk around Detroit insists on calling it a romance between the Dodge widow and Charlie."

Gehringer didn't like to talk publicly about his batting average, so he certainly wasn't going to discuss his love life — if he had one. When asked

13. "I kept yelling 'home, home, home.'"

about it, Charlie deflected the question as if he was fouling off a pitch he didn't like. He said Mrs. Dodge was an excellent bridge partner.[6]

Wish Egan, the longtime Tiger scout and jack-of-all-trades for the front office, wouldn't say anything about Charlie's private life even if he knew anything juicy. But he loved to tell stories about Charlie. Gehringer was well-known in Tiger inner circles for being the first to sign his contract every year — usually before Christmas. Egan said that when Charlie first signed with the Tigers in 1924, he went to see Frank Navin, who gave him an hour-long sales pitch about the Tiger organization, its management, and how Charlie fit into the team's plans for the future. Charlie never said a word. When Navin paused to catch his breath, Charlie saw his opportunity. "Where's the contract?" he said. Navin produced it, and Gehringer signed it. He would have done it an hour earlier but was too polite to interrupt the boss.[7]

With understandable bias, Egan said he thought Gehringer was the best second baseman of all time. And Wish had seen most of them. He said Eddie Collins was a great fielder and a good hitter, but Charlie was a greater hitter and better fielder. He said Nap Lajoie was a great hitter, but Charlie, even at age 37, could outrun Lajoie in his prime. Egan said Hornsby, Evers, and Frisch were all great ballplayers, good at everything they did and excellent at some things, but Gehringer excelled in everything. Hence, Egan rated Charlie at the top. Two other things about Charlie stood out, said the old-timer: he was a good team man and, together with Mickey Cochrane, formed the best 2-and-3 hitters in a lineup in the history of baseball. As for Charlie's possible retirement, Egan said when it happened, it would be done in classic Gehringer style: brief and without fanfare. "Gehringer will walk in some day and say 'I am finished' and that will be that."[8]

In December, Gehringer was still undecided about his plans for 1941 except for one thing. He vowed he would not play with the pain he endured during the past season and in the World Series. "I'll never go through what I did last season," he said. "I'm going to go to Lakeland (Florida spring training site), try picking up a few grounders, and then, if I get that old twitch in the back, I'm packing away my glove for good."[9]

Columnist Joe Williams told his readers in March that while watching the Tigers in spring training, he heard strange noises, like animals moaning and wailing, and was trying to identify the sounds. As he pondered, he said someone hit a ground ball to Bartell at shortstop. He picked it up and tossed to Charlie at second who whirled and threw to first. Williams said he turned to an observer and told him he was shocked by the abuse he was witnessing. "We are talking about man's inhumanity to man, the brutality of the capitalistic system, the horrors of human slavery. About Bartell and Gehringer. Their legs creak and rattle every time they take a step. That's the noise we've been hearing. Their ancient dogs growling in protest."[10] Williams said he was particularly saddened to see Charlie going through the paces because it wasn't the same Charlie he had seen in the past. "It is always depressing to see an old star fade, but it's the one dead sure thing about the game; sooner or later, all the old stars fade and this may be the last year, big or otherwise, for Charles Leonard Gehringer."[11]

Charlie knew the end was near. But he could still play — and the Tigers didn't have anyone better to play second base. Even with a sore back, Gehringer still hit .313 in 1940 and could still field his position. But Father Time was bothering him more than his back these days. "You get (to be) 37 or 38, it doesn't seem to be too old, but it is in sports," he said. "I'd played 18 years and it takes a lot out of you. You lose your zip in hitting and you lose a certain amount of speed fielding." Charlie said he didn't notice much difference in his fielding other than he was a step or two slower than he had been. "I'm sure balls got through that wouldn't have 10 years earlier. I suppose the fans and the manager notice."[12]

There was no greater evidence of that than on July 4, 1941, when the Tigers played the White Sox in a doubleheader. In the ninth inning of the second game, with Detroit ahead 10–6, Del Baker made a defensive replacement that, as necessary as it seemed at the time, must have turned his stomach. He sent Boyd Terry in as a defensive replacement for Charlie at second base. Terry had only been in the big leagues for two weeks.

The Associated Press took note of Baker's move this way: "The abrupt end of the 16-year major league career of Charles Leonard Gehringer, Detroit's mechanical man second baseman, was believed to be in sight today." Gehringer was considered in the same class as Napoleon Lajoie and Eddie Collins, and while he didn't talk publicly about retirement, it was pretty well known that he wanted to go out while fans still held him in high esteem.

For the Tigers, any prospects for repeating as American League cham-

13. "I kept yelling 'home, home, home.'"

pions nose-dived on May 7 when Hank Greenberg was inducted into the U.S. Army. The Tigers simply had no way of replacing 150 runs batted in. Rip Radcliff, his replacement, only drove in 40. York hit 27 home runs, the only real power in the Detroit lineup. Newsom slumped to 12–20 and Bridges was 9–12. Most of the rest of the staff hovered around the .500 mark: Trout 9–9, Newhouser 9–11, Gorsica 9–11, and Rowe 8–6. The only bright spot on the mound was the veteran Al Benton, pitching mostly in relief, 15–6.

Charlie's troubles were not confined to the field. He hit .220, 100 points below his lifetime batting average and scored 65 runs in 127 games, fewest since 1926, his first full year in the big leagues. His total of 96 hits were especially anemic for a man who had seven seasons with more than 200 hits. His 19 doubles, four triples, and three home runs were his lowest since 1925.

For Detroit, all of this added up to a 75–79 record and a fifth-place finish for the defending American League champions. Once again, the Yankees were back on top and the Tigers had to regroup.

CHAPTER 14

"If my chatter bothers you too much..."

On November 11, 1941, thousands of Detroit residents lined the streets for the annual Armistice Day parade, complete with floats, music, politicians, pretty women, and cute kids, all in their own way commemorating the event of 23 years earlier when the armistice was signed that ended what President Woodrow Wilson called "the war to end all wars."

One of the participants in the parade who drew huge applause was Army Sgt. Hank Greenberg, riding on top of a tank and waving to spectators who cheered him as if he had just hit a game-winning homer. Greenberg was one of 16 million American men between the ages of 18 and 35 who had fulfilled their duty and registered for the military draft in the fall of 1940. Other ballplayers had also registered, of course, but Greenberg was the biggest name player to be called up for active duty. On May 6, 1941, he hit two home runs — his first two of the year — as the Tigers beat the Yankees. The next day, he headed for Camp Custer in Battle Creek.

On December 5, a little more than a month after the parade, Greenberg was discharged from the Army because of his age. He was a month shy of his 33rd birthday. Two days later, in what President Franklin D. Roosevelt would call "a day that will live in infamy," the Japanese bombed Pearl Harbor. The next day, Congress declared war on Japan. And Hank Greenberg re-enlisted.

Baseball Commissioner Kenesaw Mountain Landis, a staunch Republican but a patriot through and through, wanted to make sure Major League Baseball did its part to help in the war effort. Baseball players would serve honorably in the armed forces; there was no question about

14. "If my chatter bothers you too much..."

that. But should the 1942 season be suspended altogether? Was it proper for men at home to be playing a game when those overseas were risking their lives? Landis wrote to Roosevelt expressing his concerns and assuring the president that he would follow through on whatever executive order he received.

On Jan. 15, 1942, Landis received a reply from the president. Roosevelt wrote:

My dear Judge:

As you will of course realize, the final decision about the baseball season must rest with you and the Baseball Club owners — so what I am going to say is solely a personal and not an official point of view.

I honestly feel that it would be best for the country to keep baseball going. There will be fewer people unemployed and everybody will work longer hours and harder than ever before. And that means they ought to have a chance for recreation and for taking their minds off their work even more than before.

Baseball provides a recreation which does not last over two hours or two hours and a half and which can be got for very little cost. And, incidentally, I hope that night games can be extended because it gives an opportunity to the day shift to see a game occasionally.

As to the players themselves, I know you agree with me that individual players who are active military or naval age should go, without question, into the services. Even if the actual quality of the teams is lowered by the greater use of older players, this will not dampen the popularity of the sport. Of course, if any individual has some particular aptitude in a trade or profession, he ought to serve the government. That, however, is a matter I know you can handle with complete justice.

Here is another way of looking at it — if 300 teams use 5,000 or 6,000 players, these players are a definite recreational asset to at least 20,000,000 of their fellow citizens — and that in my judgment is thoroughly worthwhile.

The same day Roosevelt wrote what came to be known as the "green light letter" to Judge Landis, an announcement in Detroit had a jarring effect on the Tigers and their fans. Charlie Gehringer was let go.

By mutual agreement, Charlie's name was omitted from the spring training roster, but the Tigers made it clear they wanted him to stay with the organization. It was up to Charlie to decide whether he wanted to devote his energies fulltime to his auto accessories business and to take care of his growing aches and pains or to stay with the Tigers in some capacity. One thing was certain from the Tiger standpoint: they were not putting their great star out to pasture. "Charlie has the final word as to whether he wants to remain in baseball," said general manager Zeller. "And the coaching job is open for him. Naturally we want to see how well our younger players can fill the second base job without putting extreme pressure on them in competition with Charlie."[1]

Four days later, Gehringer took Zeller up on his offer and signed a one-year contract to be a coach. Rookie Jimmy Bloodworth was to get the first shot at replacing him at second base. Charlie got the first base coaching assignment, so fans would get to see him every game, as they had for the past 18 years. As the *New York Herald Tribune* told its readers, with his personality and penchant for silence, he was hardly qualified to be a train announcer. When the 1942 season started, bench jockeys had a lot of fun with him, shouting at him to "quiet down" as he manned his position in the coaching box.

In a game against Washington early in the year, Charlie got Senator first baseman Mickey Vernon laughing when he leaned over to him and said, "If my chatter bothers you too much, you can tell the umpire." His manager, Baker, said, "He may not be noisy, but he's the best-dressed coach in the league, I'll tell you that. Boy, he sure can make his clothes harmonize."[2]

Gehringer's new role became official with the league when the Tigers formally released him as a player on February 4. But on May 22, the Tigers reactivated him, making Charlie a player-coach so that he could fill in occasionally in the field and hopefully contribute a little with his bat. As it turned out, he contributed little. Gehringer appeared in 45 games and batted just 45 times. He managed to get 12 hits to give him a .267 average in his limited appearances. But the Tigers, once again missing Greenberg and, for all practical purposes missing Charlie, won only 73 games and lost 81, finishing in fifth place, 30 games behind the first-place Yankees.

Greenberg's Army stint and Gehringer's semi-retirement were not the only setbacks for the Tigers at the start of the 1942 season. Bobo Newsom, whose spectacular 21–5 record in 1940 helped the Tigers to the World Series, was unhappy with the salary cut he was asked to take after his dismal 12–20 mark in 1941. So Bobo held out. He had missed most of spring training when owner Briggs decided a 12–20 pitcher wasn't worth the trouble he was causing — so he sold him to the Washington Senators on March 31 for $40,000. Briggs also had enough of Schoolboy Rowe's inconsis-

14. "If my chatter bothers you too much..."

tency. Rowe, once depicted in a *Detroit News* cartoon as sitting on top of the world, was unceremoniously shipped to the Philadelphia Phillies.[3]

Baker had to make a lot of adjustments. He had rookie Bloodworth at second base. Bloodworth and veteran outfielder Doc Cramer had been acquired from Boston during the winter in exchange for outfielder Bruce Campbell. Rookie Ned Harris was also in the outfield along with McCosky. Baker moved Benton, the bullpen ace, into the starting rotation along with Bridges, Newhouser, Trout, and rookies Virgil Trucks and Hal White. From the outset, it didn't look like a lineup that could compete with the Yankees, and it didn't.

There wasn't a .300 hitter in the starting lineup. McCosky hit .293. Harris .271, third baseman Higgins .267, and Cramer .263. All the other regulars were below .250, including Charlie's replacement, Bloodworth, who hit .242.

Trucks might have been rookie of the year had there been such an award in those days. He won 14 games and lost only 8 despite the meager run support that he and his fellow pitchers received. White, the other rookie in the rotation, managed to break even at 12–12. Big, bespectacled Trout and the temperamental Newhouser were 12–18 and 8–14 respectively. Curve-balling Tommy Bridges, the lone remaining starter from the glory years, was 9–7.

On September 27, the last day of the season, the Tigers were shut out for the second day in a row by the Cleveland Indians. That game was Charlie's last as an active player. He finished his career with 2,839 hits, 574 doubles, 146 triples, 181 home runs, and a lifetime batting average of .320. His All-Star Game performances were superb, playing every inning of the first six games and banging 10 hits in 20 at-bats for a .500 average. He played with championship teams in 1934, 1935, and 1940 and had a World Series batting average of .321, almost identical to his lifetime batting average. The man known for his consistency also had the same lifetime fielding percentages in regular season and World Series play —.976.

Sixty-five years after he retired, Gehringer was still fourth all-time in most seasons with at least 100 runs scored (12), behind only Henry Aaron (15), Rickey Henderson (13), and Lou Gehrig (13). He was tied for fourth place in most seasons with at least 200 hits (7), fourth in most seasons with 40 or more doubles (7), and 10th all-time in career doubles with 754. His 60 doubles in 1936 are the sixth highest all-time and through 2007,

70 years after Charlie did it, no one else had reached that total in one season.

Defensively, through 2006, he was 6th in most career games at second base (2,206), second to Eddie Collins in most career assists at second base (7,068), sixth in most career putouts at second base (5,369), and seventh all-time in most career double plays by a second baseman (1,444).[4]

Gehringer was the mainstay in one of the most durable, powerful infields in baseball history with Marv Owen at third, Billy Rogell at short, Charlie at second, and Greenberg at first. Their collective feat of driving in 462 runs in 1934 is still a major league record for infield productivity in one season. That was the year that between them, they missed only one game, and that was because Greenberg stayed home to observe a Jewish religious holiday.

As the Tigers regrouped — again — for the 1943 season, they would be without yet another cog from their pennant-winning days of 1940. At the end of the season, Baker was fired and was replaced by Steve O'Neill, an old catcher who had managed the Cleveland Indians at one time but now was managing the Tigers' minor league club in Buffalo. Despite rumors to the contrary, Charlie Gehringer was never considered for the managerial job, nor did he want it or seek it. Charlie wanted to retire like he did everything else. Quietly.

CHAPTER 15

"He simplified where others dramatized."

"I won't be back," Charlie informed the Detroit ballclub in the fall of 1942 when he accepted a commission into the U.S. Navy as a lieutenant. He was destined to become a lieutenant commander in the Navy's fitness program, a job for which the 39-year-old bachelor was eminently qualified.

"A ballplayer can feel it coming," said Charlie, reflecting on retirement. "You lose that extra step in fielding a ball. I can probably run as fast in a straight line as a lot of rookies. But I've lost the jump on the ball." He said he had lost some bat speed as well. "I've lost a little snap in my wrists. Pitchers I used to own now overpower me."

As he always had, Charlie rated Lefty Grove as the toughest pitcher he ever faced. "He'd just fog it through and dare you to hit it," said Gehringer. He said Grove in his prime had a fastball better than either Walter Johnson or Bob Feller. In fact, he said, Feller wasn't overpowering. "If he didn't have the greatest curve in the game, he wouldn't get anybody out."

There wasn't much more Gehringer could have done for the Tigers. He had been a mainstay on three American League championship teams, had represented himself and his team admirably in six All-Star Games and in three World Series and had led a priestly life off the field. He was almost always the first to sign a contract for the upcoming season and reported to spring training on time and without complaint. Frank Navin once described Charlie this way: "He's everything a ballplayer should be. He has all of the virtues and none of the faults. I don't think there has ever been another player just like him, meaning a player who was Charlie's equal as a hitter and as a fielder and whose deportment on and off the field was so near perfect."[1]

One individual accolade that eluded Gehringer was inclusion among baseball greats who attained 3,000 hits. Charlie finished with 2,839. Just four more hits in each season that he played would have put him over the top. Gehringer never fussed about it. "It wasn't that big a deal back then," he said years later.

Charlie spent three years in the Navy, first assigned to St. Mary's Pre–Flight School in California. There, among other duties, he served as the school's baseball coach for two years. Then he was transferred to the naval station at Jacksonville, Florida, where he also coached the baseball team and even played some second base. His 1945 team included Billy DeMars, later an infielder for both the Philadelphia A's and St. Louis Browns, and Alf Anderson, an outfielder who played briefly with the Pittsburgh Pirates. Gehringer's Navy teams posted a record of 85–15 during his three years as coach.

Charlie's shyness followed him into the Navy, and even the military publications had a little fun with him. The *Jax Air News*, the newspaper at the Jacksonville Air Base, published an item that related a story told by J. Taylor Spink, editor of *The Sporting News*. Charlie's former manager, Mickey Cochrane, said Lt. Gehringer was so non-talkative that he once went an entire season saying only four words to his manager. He said, "Hello, Mickey" at the start of spring training and "Good-bye Mickey" at the end of the season. When Lt. Gehringer was asked by the *Jax* editor if the story was true, Gehringer shook his head in disagreement and said wryly, "He overstated it."[2]

When Charlie was discharged from the Navy in 1945, he told reporters his only baseball from then on would be at family reunions and picnics. With spring training for the 1946 season right around the corner, Watson Spoelstra of the *Detroit News* asked him if he was sure he wouldn't be going to Florida in a few weeks. "Not unless someone gives me an orange grove," said Charlie, once again displaying his quiet wit.[3]

Gehringer's 19 years in the big leagues left him one year shy of qualifying for a full pension from the players' pension fund. That was later rectified when he was given credit for the three years he would serve in the Navy. Upon his discharge from the Navy, he spent a few days in New

15. "He simplified where others dramatized."

York and ran into Hank Greenberg at Toots Shor's restaurant. Greenberg had been discharged from the Army in 1945 in time to help the Tigers win the American League pennant and then beat the Chicago Cubs in the World Series. In fact, he hit a grand slam home run in the game that clinched the league championship.

Greenberg tried to entice Charlie to go to spring training with the Tigers. "You better stay in baseball," he told him. "This American League is a hitter's paradise."[4] But Gehringer had other ideas. He figured baseball had been good to him, and he had been good to baseball. Now it was time to move on to other things. "I came out of the service in such good shape that I felt I could have played a few years," he said. "But we had a good business going by that time so I said what the heck."[5]

Gehringer had always been meticulous about taking care of personal business and planning for the future. While still looking after his elderly mother, he saved a little money each year from working at Hudson's in the early days, from the gas stations he owned but let others operate, from selling coal wholesale, and from his lucrative business relationship with Ray Forsyth.

Representing Gehringer and Forsyth, a firm specializing in selling automotive accessories, Charlie went around to various auto makers to pitch his product. In the Detroit area, the name Charlie Gehringer opened a lot of doors that might not be open to other salesman. "The name would get you in but it wouldn't get the job done," said Charlie. "I put in an eight-hour day and worked hard. Some of those prospective customers in the automobile industry were really tough. They'd say to me: What do you (a ballplayer) know about this business?" As it worked out, Gehringer said some of the toughest customers turned out to be some of the best ones, and, conversely, some of the nicest ones never bought a thing. "Look about in the car you own," Spoelstra wrote in *The Sporting News*. "Chances are that Gehringer and Forsyth sold the auto company some of the interior materials."[6]

In 1946, Charlie's life took another dramatic change. Theresa Gehringer, the mother and widow he had looked after for 22 years with Biblical dedication, died. She had been the center of his family universe, the woman he loved and trusted more than anyone else. Therese, as she was called, hadn't wanted her son to go into baseball, but in the years that followed, as Charlie's career progressed, she showed her support and devotion for what he wanted to do, as only a loving mother could. She was easy to spot at the ballpark when she came, dressed in her Sunday best, gray hair pulled back in a bun, often under a hat that covered most of her hair.

With his mother gone, Gehringer could think about marriage. One of the places Charlie made regular sales calls was the Chrysler Corporation in Detroit. He became acquainted with a secretary there, one of the people he had to see before he could gain entry to the main office. The secretary's name was Josephine Stillen, a devout Catholic about 20 years younger than Charlie who knew nothing about baseball. The name Charlie Gehringer meant nothing to her except that he was that salesman who

Charlie and Jo Gehringer share a happy moment together after their marriage in 1949. When they first met, she knew nothing about baseball. To Jo, Charlie was just a salesman who called on the office she worked in. They were married for nearly 44 years (photograph courtesy of the National Baseball Hall of Fame).

15. "He simplified where others dramatized."

always came to call. So when he took a liking to her, he was a little chagrined that she was not equally impressed.

Lifelong friend and former Tiger teammate Elden Auker said in their playing days, Gehringer was the most eligible bachelor in town. "He was a handsome guy and the most popular player on the team. Girls were falling all over each other to get at Charlie," Auker said. "But not Jo. He was just a salesman to her."[7]

So Charlie had to woo her, something totally foreign to his personality. They dated and eventually fell in love. The stories of their courtship contain some amusing moments that show how, even in romance, he never stepped too far out of character. One night, while they were driving together on a country road, Jo looked over at Charlie and said, "Charlie Gehringer, I just love you to death." Charlie didn't change expression. He drove on for several minutes and then answered her with one word: "Why?"[8]

Meanwhile, Gehringer was once again getting some attention in the baseball world. In the 1945 Hall of Fame balloting by the Baseball Writers Association of America, no player received the required 75 percent approval for induction, but Charlie, who had been out of baseball for only three years, received 10 votes. In 1946, many Hall of Fame balloting rules were changed because only one player had been inducted in the past six years. One change was that the elections would be held every year, rather than every three years as had been the case. Even with the emphasis of getting someone elected, once again no player received the required 75 percent. Charlie got 23 votes.

In 1947, four players were elected — and they all had a connection with Gehringer in one way or another. The new inductees were: Carl Hubbell, the masterful New York Giants pitcher who gave up a base hit to Charlie in the 1934 All-Star Game before striking out Babe Ruth, Lou Gehrig, Jimmy Foxx, Al Simmons, and Joe Cronin in succession; Frankie Frisch, whose Gas House Gang St. Louis Cardinals defeated Gehringer and the Tigers in the 1934 World Series; Mickey Cochrane, the great catcher for the A's and Tigers who put together two consecutive pennant-winning seasons as player-manager of the Tigers; Robert "Lefty" Grove, the fireballing pitcher for the A's and Boston Red Sox who Charlie thought was the toughest to hit and who plunked Charlie on the arm with a pitch that brought him to tears years ago.

That would have been great company for Gehringer to be in, and he came close. He received 105 votes, 16 shy of the 121 needed to represent 75 percent of the 161 total votes cast. He was 6th in the voting, behind the four inductees and Pie Traynor, the great Pittsburgh Pirate infielder, who fell just two votes shy of induction. Traynor made it in 1948 along with Yankee pitcher Herb Pennock. Al Simmons finished third in the voting and Charlie was fourth.

In 1949, nobody received 75 percent of the vote when balloting was done in February. Under yet another rules change, the writers cast a second ballot, this time selecting from the top 20 players who received votes the first time around. The second vote took place in April. The only winner was Charlie Gehringer. The top vote-getters were: Gehringer, Mel Ott, Jimmy Foxx, Dizzy Dean, Al Simmons, Paul Waner, Harry Heilmann, Bill Terry, Hank Greenberg, Bill Dickey, and Rabbit Maranville.

Announcement of Charlie's election brought accolades from baseball people all over the country. Detroit writers and fans were elated that Charlie was to be inducted just two years after Cochrane had been honored. Gehringer became the fourth Tiger in the Hall of Fame. Ty Cobb and Hughie Jennings had also both been previously elected.

J. Taylor Spink of *The Sporting News* could hardly contain his excitement. Spink, who had seen Charlie play many times, wrote, "He had ease, grace and the poetry of motion. He made all the plays look simple. Few ever matched him and none surpassed him in going back after a fly ball."[9]

H. G. Salsinger, who followed Gehringer's entire career while writing for the *Detroit News*, wrote that Gehringer was "a ballplayer's ballplayer" just like Carl Hubbell was "a pitcher's pitcher" and that only a ballplayer could fully appreciate Charlie's awesome skills in the field and at the plate. "Many players intentionally make every play look as difficult as possible; Charlie managed to make them all look easy. He played second base in the same way that Bobby Jones played golf. He simplified where others dramatized." It was because of this quality, wrote Salsinger, that the public never fully appreciated Gehringer's talent.[10]

Newspapers published a photograph of Gehringer taking the phone call in which he received the good news. Undoubtedly staged for the cameras, Charlie is pictured sitting behind his desk at Gehringer and Forsyth, wearing a suit and tie, with suitcoat buttoned and handkerchief neatly in the coat pocket. He has just a hint of a smile. The picture captures the

15. "He simplified where others dramatized."

classic Gehringer nonchalance even for such a momentous occasion in his life.

The Hall of Fame ceremonies were held June 13 in Cooperstown. Hundreds gathered to honor and cheer their baseball heroes of yesteryear — Gehringer, Kid Nichols, Pie Traynor (1948 inductee) and, posthumously, Herb Pennock and Mordecai "Three Fingers" Brown. Branch Rickey, president of the Brooklyn Dodgers, presided over the affair and spoke warmly about each of the men being inducted. He heralded Charlie as "a man of mechanical precision, obscure as far as showmanship was concerned, but a great player." In his keynote speech, Rickey said baseball can be held up to the world as the nation's national pastime. It has three great qualities, said the Dodger executive: beauty, comparative freedom from injury, and "the marvelous exactitudes and precision of measurements relating to human skills."[11]

In the annual Hall of Fame game following the ceremonies, the Washington Senators banged out 15 hits and defeated the Pittsburgh Pirates 8–7.

It was a glorious day — a fitting tribute to the game and to the men who made it a great game — or at least that's what Charlie heard about it. He wasn't there. Nobody was sure where he was. Hall of Fame officials had received word that he had another commitment. Understandably, it would have been difficult for them to imagine what could be a more important commitment than his induction into the Hall of Fame.

Within a week, the truth was known. While Charlie was being honored at Cooperstown, he and Josephine Stillen were on their way to California, where they were married on June 18. Charlie handled his marriage like he had handled everything else in his life — without fanfare. The wedding was in San Jose. Newsmen learned that the marriage would take place at St. Clare's Catholic Church and headed there to get pictures and comments from the newlyweds after the ceremony. While they were waiting at St. Clare's, Charlie and Jo exchanged their vows at St. Patrick's Catholic Church across town. Charlie wanted it to be private and made sure that it was.

When he learned the circumstances, J. Robert Quinn, director of the Hall of Fame, remarked, "He may have married the girl and although I am not acquainted with her, knowing Charlie as I do, I can't believe he ever popped the question in the first place."[12]

Dan Daniel, recounting the series of events in the *New York World-Telegram*, was not amused. He admired Gehringer's baseball ability over the years but seemed to detest what he characterized as Charlie's dullness. Writing about what he considered Gehringer's apathy towards the induction, Daniel said Mel Ott was more deserving of being in the Hall of Fame than Charlie. That notwithstanding, Daniel felt Gehringer should have been there, according to Daniel. "Any living person receiving the superlative honor which goes with induction in the Hall of Fame should regard it as a most emphatic mandate to take part in the ceremonies."[13]

Charlie and Jo did it their way, making official a love affair that was to last for almost half a century. And with both his marriage and his Hall of Fame induction, Charlie accomplished what he strived to do with everything in his life — without a lot of fuss.

Just as he had always put devotion to his mother ahead of any other thing in his personal life, he was prepared to do the same for Jo, and he started by putting her ahead of the Hall of Fame. He was prepared to return to Detroit, resume his highly successful auto accessories business, and go home every night to be a devoted, loving husband. His association with the Tigers, he had decided, would be as a fan.

CHAPTER 16

"I didn't know who was and who wasn't."

The Tigers had some good years under Steve O'Neill. In 1943, Charlie's first full year of retirement, when he joined the Navy, the club finished fifth with a 78–76 record. But there were signs of better days ahead. Trout, the stout right-hander, was getting control, and Newhouser, the lanky lefty was gaining self-control. In 1944, Newhouser won 29 and lost 9, Trout won 27 and lost 14, and the Tigers finished second to, of all teams, the St. Louis Browns, who won their only American League championship that year. Detroit had been just a couple players short of what they needed to get them over the top, and they got them in 1945 when first Hank Greenberg and then Virgil Trucks were discharged from the armed services. Once again, Newhouser and Trout had big years, going 25–9 and 18–15 respectively. Greenberg hit the game-winning homer in the pennant-winning game, and Trucks returned just in time to work in a key ballgame down the stretch. Putting it all together, the Tigers won their fourth championship in 12 years and then beat the Chicago Cubs in the World Series, just as they had in 1935. Trucks was the winning pitcher in game two.

Newhouser won 26 and lost 9 in 1946, dispelling the theory that he had been great only because the best hitters were off at war. However, the Tigers slipped to second place and finished second again in 1947. When they tumbled to fifth place in 1948, O'Neill was excused from further managerial duties.[1]

Red Rolfe, the former Yankee infielder, took the helm and guided the Tigers to a fourth place finish in 1949. In 1950, they won 95 games, finishing second to the Yankees. But the following year, they dropped to fifth place.

While all of this was happening on the baseball field, Charlie Gehringer was enjoying life as a happy husband, good golfer, successful businessman, and an occasional participant in exhibition baseball games and charity events. One of the more unusual of these took place on April 11, 1950, in Dallas, Texas, when Dick Burnett, owner of the Dallas Eagles, pulled off a remarkable stunt in a game between Dallas and Tulsa. It was opening day, and Burnett wanted to break the Texas League all-time attendance record (16,018 at Fort Worth in 1930). A millionaire oilman, he rented the Cotton Bowl football stadium for the day then set out to hire nine famous former Major League ballplayers to appear in one more game — as the starting lineup for his Dallas Eagles. Three of the players he had in mind were a trio of old Tigers: Ty Cobb, Mickey Cochrane, and Charlie Gehringer.

Cobb, considered the greatest living ballplayer since the death of Babe Ruth two years earlier, was a key to success. Burnett believed if he could sign Cobb, it would be a huge draw and other ballplayers might follow Cobb's lead and make an appearance. Cobb agreed, and one by one, other stars of the past signed on, including Charlie.

The Eagles played the Tulsa Oilers that night — and never had such a band of baseball greats graced a minor league baseball arena. Taking the field for the Eagles were Mickey Cochrane behind the plate, Charlie Grimm (the Eagles manager) at first base, Gehringer at second, Travis Jackson at short, Frank "Home Run" Baker at third, and Duffy Lewis, Ty Cobb, and Tris Speaker in left, center, and right. And to the delight of the crowd, Dizzy Dean took the mound for the Eagles.

Burnett left nothing to chance. Charlie and the others rode in a parade through downtown Dallas late in the afternoon, and the Kilgore High School Rangerette drill team performed before the game. There was hype, there was hoopla, and there were 54,151 fans in the stands. Burnett had gotten his wish. The crowd was an all-time Texas League record.

That evening, the usually routine activity of batting practice drew rapt attention from spectators. The old-timers didn't have the power or finesse they once had, but nobody seemed to care. Charlie took his swings with the others and made contact, like he always had. However, this time the pitches were lobbed in, and the hits didn't have the zing they once had.

16. "I didn't know who was and who wasn't."

There were a lot of laughs and nobody seemed to care — except Cobb, who, at age 63, hadn't lost any of his feistiness or his quest for perfection, even in batting practice for an exhibition in a minor league ballpark. Now wearing spectacles, Cobb swung wildly at two pitches, then stepped out of the box and complained that flash bulbs from cameras were bothering him. There is no documentation, of course, as to what onlookers were thinking, but it would not be surprising had Charlie looked at the antics of his first big league manager and thought, "He hasn't changed a bit." Cobb got back in the batter's box and laid down three bunts along the first base line.[2]

As Harry Donabedian, the Oilers' lead-off man, stepped into the batter's box to start the game, the crowd roared. Gehringer was in his familiar crouch at second base, knees slightly bent, eyes intently on the batter, body swaying ever so slightly, ready to move in either direction — if his body cooperated. Ol' Diz worked the count to 3–2 as Cochrane tapped his glove behind the plate, then put one finger down, and yelled encouragement. The sixth pitch of the game was ball four. As Donabedian trotted down to first base, Charlie and his eight teammates headed off the field, replaced by the Dallas regulars.

The way some of the old-timers talked about those six pitches, listeners who didn't know any better might have thought they were talking about a World Series game. "I missed that plate by about an inch," said Dean, gesturing with his thumb and finger. "But the ump was right," he said. Cochrane chimed in, telling the press, "Old Diz was sharp out there tonight. That sidearm of his was breaking nicely." Others talked about what it felt like to take the field once again. If Charlie said anything, it wasn't quoted in any newspapers. He went back home to Detroit, to his wife and to his business.[3]

Aside from occasionally attending Tiger ballgames and a few old-timer functions, Gehringer kept his distance from baseball. In early 1951, he attended the festivities commemorating the 75th anniversary of the National League, a league he never played in, at the Broadway Central Hotel in New York. Charlie was invited along with several other Hall of Fame members who were there because of their stature in the game regardless of which league they played in.

Asked a frequent question in those days — would he be getting back into baseball anytime soon? Gehringer said no, he was happy with the life he was leading. He told the press that he attended about 10 Tiger ballgames a year, when his schedule permitted it. Then, with typical wry humor, he said, "After all, I did see a lot of baseball games years ago."

The Tigers took a tumble in 1951. Winners of 95 games in 1950, they sputtered around the .500 mark for most of the next season. It was as if the players on 1950's vibrant team had suddenly gotten old all at once. On July 29, as the Tigers were splitting a doubleheader at Philadelphia to put them at 42–48 for the season, there was big news coming out of Detroit. Billy Evans, the old umpire who had been the Tiger executive vice president and general manager since 1946, resigned, effective at the end of the season.

That was a surprise — but it was only half of the announcement. The other half was a bigger surprise. Charlie Gehringer was named to replace him — the same Charlie Gehringer who had divorced himself from baseball to devote all of his attention and energies to life outside the ballpark.

Owner Walter Briggs said Gehringer, one of the most popular Tigers of all time, was the only man he considered for the position. "My job was to persuade Charlie to take the job," he said. Gehringer said the negotiations had taken place about 10 days earlier and that he was reluctant to the end. "He just didn't give me a chance to say no," said Charlie. "He held out his hand for about 10 seconds waiting for me to shake on the bargain — and finally I got embarrassed, grasped my hand and shook it."[4]

The negotiations with Charlie began mysteriously on July 7 when he received a telephone call at his new, $75,000 ranch-style home not far from the Orchard Lake Country Club in Birmingham, a well-to-do Detroit suburb. The caller, Tigers public relations man Ed Fitzgerald, had a mysterious message. He wanted to talk to Charlie but not in his office or Charlie's. He suggested they meet the next day in the parking lot of the General Motors building in Detroit.

As the two men sat in Fitzgerald's car, the PR man said he had a message from Walter Briggs. The owner wanted Gehringer to become general manager of the Tigers. Charlie told Fitzgerald he was flattered but that he had a good business going and was leading a comfortable life so he respectfully declined the offer. Fitzgerald told him to think about it, and that they would be in touch with him later.

A week later, Briggs called and asked Charlie to meet with him at his stadium office. The feisty owner, chomping on a cigar, put on a first-class

16. "I didn't know who was and who wasn't."

sales pitch, telling Charlie he was the only man being considered for the job and that he could write his own salary. Not only that, said Briggs, the Tigers would compensate him for any business losses he sustained because of his work with the ballclub.

Charlie was still hesitant. "Would you be mad if I said no?" he asked the owner. Briggs responded by continuing his sales pitch, punctuating it by extending his right hand toward Charlie. "He held out his hand — it seemed like minutes — and I shook it," said Charlie. "I knew I would hurt him if I didn't."

At first everyone agreed to delay the announcement until the end of the season, but fearing the news would leak out well before then, the Tigers held a press conference on the morning of July 28 at Briggs Stadium. Typically, Gehringer, the man of the moment, wasn't there. He was on the golf course at Orchard Lake.

When Rolfe was informed in Philadelphia, he said, "I'm amazed. I'm not surprised that Billy is leaving, but in all the talk about who might take his place, I never heard Gehringer's name mentioned. I think Charlie will do a good job as soon as he gets the hang of things."

Jo Gehringer was proud but a little uneasy about what the new job would do to the life she and Charlie had created for themselves. "I'm happy for him because it is a big honor to be offered a position of that kind. He's always liked baseball so much and I've always wanted him to do what he thinks he ought to. But I hope it doesn't keep him away from home too much," she said.[5]

Gehringer said Briggs offered him the job because he had a "player's knowledge" of ballplayers that would help in rebuilding the Tigers. Briggs saw this as a challenge, but Charlie soon found it to be a nightmare. His headaches started sooner than he originally thought they would. Briggs decided it was best for the ballclub if Evans' resignation became effective immediately so that Charlie could get a head start on evaluating the team. "We had a lousy ballclub and I had been away from baseball for about 10 years. I didn't know who was and who wasn't," he said.[6]

The 1949 Tigers, playing under Rolfe for the first time, won 87 games and finished second, 10 games behind the Yankees. Four Tigers pitchers won 15 games or more — Newhouser, Trucks, Hutchinson, and Art Houtemann. Third baseman George Kell won the batting title — just barely — hitting .3429 to Ted Williams' .3428. Kell's 2-for-3 on the last day of the season prevented Williams from winning the Triple Crown. Slugging first baseman Vic Wertz hit 20 home runs and drove in 133 runs.

This contingent came through again in 1950 and kept the Tigers in the pennant race for most of the season. As September neared, just two games separated the top four teams — New York, Detroit, Cleveland, and Boston. On September 22, the Tigers and Yankees were tied for first. But while New York won seven of their last 10, Detroit was losing six out of 10. Though they won 95 games, the Tigers finished second.

There was reason for optimism in 1951, but the zest wasn't there. Kell and Wertz had good years again, but others slumped. And when Houtemann and another promising pitcher, Ray Herbert, were drafted into the armed services, the air pretty much went out of the Tiger balloon. It was Charlie's job to pump it up again.

He tried to do it with some blockbuster trades. In November, he offered two of his stars, George Kell and Vic Wertz, along with catcher Joe Ginsberg to the Cleveland Indians. In return, Detroit would get the Indians' slugging third baseman Al Rosen, catcher Jim Hegan, and a pitcher. The hang-up was who the pitcher would be. Gehringer wanted "one of the big four" as he called them — Bob Feller, Bob Lemon, Early Wynn, or Mike Garcia. Cleveland said no, so the deal fell through. Cleveland's general manager was none other than Hank Greenberg, Charlie's old teammate.

On March 14, 1952, the Tigers traded first baseman Dick Kryhoski and pitchers Gene Bearden and Bob Cain to the St. Louis Browns for catcher Matt Batts, pitcher Dick Littlefield, and first baseman Ben Taylor. Then on June 3, Charlie traded aging pitcher Dizzy Trout, third baseman Kell, and outfielders Johnny Lipon and Walter "Hoot" Evers to the Boston Red Sox for pitcher Bill Wight, first baseman Walt Dropo, utility infielder Fred Hatfield, veteran second baseman Johnny Pesky, and first baseman Don Lenhardt.

The deck continued to be shuffled on August 14 when Littefield and Lenhardt, both acquired earlier in the year, were sent to St. Louis along with slugger Vic Wertz and Marlin Stewart in exchange for outfielder Jim Delsing and pitchers Ned Garver, Bud Black, and Dave Madison.

In all, 23 players had changed uniforms in the three trades. While all of that was going on, Trucks and Houtemann had records of 5–19 and 8–20 respectively. In one of those quirky baseball circumstances that is

16. "I didn't know who was and who wasn't."

hard to explain, though Trucks won only five games all year, two of his wins were no-hitters. The Tigers won 50, lost 104, and finished in last place in the American League for the first time in the team's history. In fact, until 1952 Detroit had been the only team in the American League never to have finished in last place.

J.G. Taylor Spink of *The Sporting News* visited Charlie in his office at Briggs Stadium in early October, just after the disastrous season had ended. Spink was not surprised to find Gehringer in coat and tie in an unlittered office. The two men spoke about the disappointing season and that remarkably, as poorly as the team played, the Tigers drew more than 1 million fans. "What hurt me most is that we could not reward our patrons with a better brand of baseball," said Gehringer.

It wasn't a good season for anybody connected with the ballclub. Charlie said he tried to shake things up, to put some new life into the team. "We traded off some good players because they did not win for us and we were getting nowhere. The players we got for them did not improve the situation. Nothing that I did and nothing that the team did seemed to help," he said. The Tigers needed more speed, they needed a "top-notch" catcher and an infielder and an outfielder who can hit, said Charlie. It was almost as if he was thinking back to the days when he patrolled around second base, with Mickey Cochrane behind the plate, Hank Greenberg at first, and Gee Walker racing around the bases. Having a Schoolboy Rowe or Tommy Bridges on the pitching staff wouldn't hurt, either.

Since trades hadn't worked, Gehringer was convinced the Tigers needed to develop players in their own farm system — and a couple of them were almost ready. An outfielder named Al Kaline was a year or two away, and Charlie thought a kid by the name of Harvey Kuenn had a great future. "I'm as sure as I can be of anything that Harvey Kuenn will become one of the great infielders of baseball," he said. "He can hit and hit with power. He has an almost flawless batting style. He is tall and rangy at shortstop." Kaline, an outfielder, had the same tools as Kuenn, plus a great throwing arm. With kids like that, Gehringer believed Detroit had a chance to move up quickly because there wasn't much difference between the last six teams in the American League. Acquisition or development of two or three key players could allow a team to move up quickly in the standings.

Spink asked Charlie which one player in the league he would pick to build his team around. "Mickey Mantle," said Charlie. "He can hit, he

16. "I didn't know who was and who wasn't."

can field, he can throw and he can run the bases. He is the first switch-hitter in history who is equally effective batting from either side of the plate." Then Gehringer paused, sighed, and said he understood the Yankees had two or three players in their farm system who were just as good as Mantle.[7]

Probably the toughest chore for Charlie during the 1952 season was firing Red Rolfe as manager on July 5. Rolfe, who had been the *Sporting News* manager of the year just two years earlier, had seen his team suffer two eight-game losing streaks and two seven-game losing streaks in the first half of the season. The Tigers were 20½ games out of first place and 7 games out of seventh place when the change occurred. On Gehringer's recommendation, Briggs named Tiger pitcher Fred Hutchinson as the new manager. But things never got better.

For the first time in his career, sportswriters questioned Charlie's ability as well as the wisdom of Tiger brass in hiring him. "What did the old Tiger second baseman know about running the front office? Nothing, as he frankly admitted," wrote Joe Williams in the *New York World-Telegram*. "Furthermore, he didn't want the job." Williams and other writers speculated that Charlie was in over his head. "How many days will there be that he'll outsmart Weiss (Yankees), Lane (Indians), Cronin (Boston) and old Griff (Washington) in the baseball market?"

The decision to fire Rolfe and hire Hutchinson came under fire. "Fred Hutchinson, as far as is known, had never even managed a Little League team. This was a chaotic situation; it cried out for an old hand with wisdom, patience, resourcefulness," wrote Williams. He said American League club owners were uneasy with the Tigers' situation because Detroit had always been a money-maker for the league and that status was clearly in jeopardy.[8]

Charlie's tenure as general manager was a disaster, and he was the first to admit it. Less than two weeks after his interview with Spink where he reflected on the future, Charlie was replaced as general manager by his good friend Herold "Muddy" Ruel, director of the farm system. Charlie

Opposite: Charlie Gehringer didn't have many bright moments as general manager of the Tigers, but one of them was signing a young outfielder named Al Kaline in 1951, who became a Hall of Fame player for Detroit (author's personal collection).

was more than glad to turn over the reins. He was eager. "I guess a lot of people like that job but I don't see how you can sleep nights. I would've had ulcers if I had stayed another year. So much going on. So much turmoil," he said.[9]

Charlie went back to a more sedate life of selling automobile accessories. He and Forsyth became wealthy and remained business partners until Forsyth's death in 1973. Gehringer then sold his interest in the business in 1974.

Charlie would never say so publicly, but one of the things that held the Tigers back during the days he was trying to build them up was Walter Briggs' refusal to sign black ballplayers. At the time, Brooklyn was winning pennants with Jackie Robinson, Roy Campanella, Don Newcombe, Joe Black, and Junior Gilliam; the Giants were winning with Hank Thompson and Willie Mays; and Cleveland won a championship with Larry Doby and Satchell Paige. Meanwhile, the Tigers had mediocre to poor ballclubs. They had a segregationist in the front office. Tiger historian Richard Bak wrote of Briggs, "His prejudices were vocal and well known. And became increasingly strident with age. Coming at such a pivotal time in baseball, Briggs' attitude was more than shameful. It was almost criminal."

The parade of great black ballplayers continued for many years, and several became major league stars. Henry Aaron helped the Milwaukee Braves win two National League championships, Ernie Banks won two Most Valuable Player awards with the Chicago Cubs, and Minnie Minoso, a black of Cuban descent, was an outstanding outfielder with the Chicago White Sox. The New York Yankees, who already had championship ballclubs, were a little late breaking their own color barrier and signed Elston Howard, who became part of the Yankee dynasty in the 1950s and '60s. Not until 1958 did the Tigers bring up their first black ballplayer, Ossie Virgil, from the Dominican Republic.[10]

CHAPTER 17

"They won't get me in that suit again."

At the end of 1952, Charlie retreated to his home in Birmingham and his business in Detroit, two places he wished he had never left. Seeking occasional interviews, old friends like Joe Falls and Watson Spoelstra of the *Detroit News* would come out to Charlie's house, find their host almost always in coat and tie or sweater and tie, and settle down for some reminiscing. One time, as Spoelstra pulled up, Charlie had a golf club in hand and was practicing his "short game" on the massive expanse of his front lawn. He was wearing dress slacks and a white shirt and tie under a buttoned cardigan sweater.

Charlie and Jo lived in a large, red brick home on a five-acre wooded lot. The property was 1,200 feet long, and the house was 500 feet from the street, providing Charlie an ample fairway to practice his chip shots. The property was also a haven for birds, and it was Charlie's responsibility to feed them. One time, he saw 15 pheasants in his backyard.

As limited as Charlie's end of the conversation might have been, these talks almost always resulted in stories or newspaper columns. In one such interview, Gehringer talked about the question he got the most — why he always took the first pitch. Actually, he didn't always take it, but he believed that if a batter was intent on swinging at the first offering, he was likely to swing at anything. Once pitchers realized that, they would take advantage of it.

Gehringer showed disdain for batters who swung for the fences all the time. "I know all about going for distance," he said. "I did it one year, 1932. I had a great start, with eight home runs, when Babe Ruth only had three or four. I believe I still had eight when Ruth had 34. I kept going for distance and had only my third year under .300 in all my years of playing."[1]

Talking to Arthur Daley of the *New York Times* about Babe Ruth, Gehringer said the Babe hit the most towering shots he had ever seen. "He hit them so high that I've often thought it would have been physically possible for a fast second baseman to have caught some of the home runs he hit — provided there were no stands and the second baseman had running room," said Charlie. He recalled a pop up Babe hit against the Tigers one day when Charlie was at second and Johnny Neun was playing first. "The Babe hit one up into the clouds over first," said Charlie. "Johnny ran back. He ran in. He raced around in circles." The ball seemed to be suspended in space — except the wind started pushing toward second with Neun in hot pursuit. Finally, the ball descended, and Neun made a desperate lunge for it about 10 feet from where Charlie was standing. "He missed it by 10 feet. I caught it myself," said Gehringer.[2]

In 1963, the Tigers summoned Charlie to join the team in spring training to help them with a project. Dick McAuliffe was a scrappy infielder who had played everywhere but first base, but his natural position was shortstop. The Tigers wanted to groom him into being their regular second baseman and wanted Charlie, just a few weeks shy of his 60th birthday, to help. Gehringer had long ago proven that he couldn't say no when the Tigers called, so he made his way to Lakeland, to see what he could do to help. He was still one of the regulars at spring training each year but usually just as a fan.

McAuliffe broke in as a shortstop and got into eight games with Detroit at the end of the 1960 season. In 1961, he appeared in 55 games at shortstop and 22 at third base. The following year, he was shifted around frequently, playing 49 games at third base, 16 at shortstop, and 70 at second base.

Given the title of "special coach," Charlie worked with McAuliffe and Jake Wood, another infielder, showing them how to properly position themselves in the field and get a jump on the ball. He also talked to them about the importance of awareness and anticipation. McAuliffe developed into a fine second baseman and was the Tigers' starter at that position for years to come. In 1968 he was one of the anchors of ballclub that won the American League pennant behind Denny McLain's 31 wins and the World Series behind Mickey Lolich's stellar pitching.[3]

17. "They won't get me in that suit again."

In February 1965, Charlie got back into the game in an even more active role, accepting an invitation to go to Japan for two weeks as a hitting instructor for the Hanshin Tigers in Osaka, Japan. It was his first trip back since he made the jaunt with Moe Berg, the ballplayer and American spy, 30 years before.

Charlie scoffed at what he taught the Hanshin players. "If I could teach people how to hit, I'd own the Detroit club," he said. But he liked the Japanese style of trying to place the ball rather than swinging for the fences. "That's down my alley," he said. "I always like the Nellie Fox type of hitter." Fox was a spray hitter — and a second baseman — for the Chicago White Sox.

On July 31, Charlie went to Yankee Stadium to take part in an Old-Timers game. In his first at-bat, facing Jim Konstanty, the old Philadelphia Phillies pitcher, he swung like the Gehringer of yesteryear and lined a base hit into the outfield. As the 62-year-old lumbered down to first base, he felt a sharp pain in his leg and crumbled to the ground. X-rays showed he had snapped his Achilles tendon and would need surgery. He flew back to Detroit, had the operation, and was laid up for two months. When he returned to his office at Gehringer & Forsyth, he walked with a noticeable limp. Vowing he had made his last appearance in a baseball uniform, Charlie said, "They won't get me in that suit again." He was most upset that he wouldn't be able to play golf for quite a while.[4]

The Tigers, meanwhile, were starting to act like contenders again. In 1967, they were one of four teams — along with the Red Sox, White Sox, and Twins — that had a chance to win it all going into the last weekend of the season. Boston finished on top, with Detroit and Minnesota tied for second, each one game out of first. Chicago ended up third just three games behind.

In 1968, the Tigers jelled, much like the teams Charlie played on under Mickey Cochrane in 1934 and 1935. Denny McLain and Mickey Lolich gave them a formidable one-two, righty-lefty combination in the starting rotation. First baseman Norm Cash, catcher Bill Freehan, and outfielder Gates Brown provided some power. But two of the leaders on the ballclub were future Hall of Famer Al Kaline, whom Gehringer had signed 17 years earlier, and Dick McAuliffe, the infielder he had worked with in 1963 spring training to turn him into Detroit's full-time second baseman.

When Kaline appeared in his 2,000th game as a Tiger in April 1968,

Gehringer, wearing his customary coat and tie, was on hand to congratulate him. Only three other Tigers had achieved that milestone — Ty Cobb, Sam Crawford, and Gehringer. Charlie finished with 2,323 and hit the 2,000 mark in 1939 when he was 36 years old. He assured Kaline that he would surpass the Gehringer figure if he stayed healthy — and as it turned out, he was right. Kaline retired in 1974 after 2,834 games with the Tigers, second only to Cobb.

On May 11, 1968, Charlie turned 65 and observed his birthday by doing what he liked to do best. He was on the golf course at the Bloomfield Hills Country Club and played 18 holes despite a steady rain. He shot an 82, not bad for most golfers, but Charlie was disappointed. "I was even par for a while, but in the rain, my game went to pot," he said. *The Sporting News*, in reporting on Charlie's 65th birthday, mentioned that he and his business partner, Ray Forsyth, were both $100,000-a-year-men in the auto accessories sales business. Some in the Detroit area thought the newspaper underestimated their incomes.[5]

One way Charlie stayed connected with baseball through the years was his work with the National Baseball Hall of Fame Veterans Committee, which he served on from 1953 to 1990, helping recognize great ballplayers of the past who had been passed over by the Baseball Writers Association of America during their years of Hall of Fame eligibility. The committee was formed in 1953 with a mix of baseball personnel and media. The first committee consisted of Gehringer, J.G. Taylor Spink of *The Sporting News*; Paul Kerr, a Hall of Fame staffer; Warren Giles and Will Harridge, presidents of the National and American Leagues respectively; Frank Shaughnessy, former president of the International League; and sportswriters Warren Brown, Frank Graham, and John Malaney.

Gehringer was one of the longest-serving members of the committee, which found itself in controversy many years, either because of its failure to elect anyone or for selecting players many people thought were either undeserving or just "hometown favorites" of some committee members. Through all of this, Charlie's longtime standing on the committee can be attributed to his reputation — the same reputation he had as a player — of doing his job quietly and efficiently and doing his best to stay out of the limelight.[6]

But Gehringer always tried to respond to fans even long after he retired. An example is a letter he wrote to someone who apparently met

17. "They won't get me in that suit again."

him or called to request some information. The letter is dated October 22, 1979, and the salutation contains only the person's first name:

Dear Jack:
 Confirming our recent conversation, I am responding to your request regarding highlights in my baseball career.
 As you know, every game has thrills contributed by a single person or team play. To give you an account of the major thrills in my life, I will give them in sequence as I remember them.
 My first big league game in the fall of 1924.
 My first home-run hit in New York in 1926 off [Urban] Shocker.
 My first All-Star game in the summer of 1933.
 My first World Series in 1934.
 Our baseball championship in 1935.
 Leading the American League in batting in 1937.
 Voted into the Hall of Fame 1949.
 There were a few more minor thrills in leading the League in doubles, triples and stolen bases in various seasons, plus a rather rare day of hitting for the cycle.
 With kind regards, I remain
 Sincerely,
 Charles L. Gehringer

The letter was typed in script font, and above his name, the 76-year-old Gehringer had scrawled out "Charlie"—a departure from his usual "Chas."[7]

In March 1983, Charlie was featured in a *Wall Street Journal* article spotlighting senior citizens who had made a success of themselves. The theme of the piece was how older Americans conquer age by staying active. Frederick C. Klein interviewed Charlie in a hotel restaurant in Birmingham but only as they were leaving did the middle-aged man recognize Charlie, not as a businessman, but as the ballplayer he had revered as a kid 40 years earlier.

Even in his later years, Gehringer constantly received fan mail. He tried to answer as many requests as he could. He told Klein he still received about 50 letters a week, mostly from people who wanted his autograph. He responded with the shortened signature he had used all of his life: Chas. Gehringer. He said often people wrote and asked him what his greatest thrill in baseball was. "I write them and tell them about something I did in a World Series or All-Star Game because that's what they expect," he said. "But that's not the way it was. I got just as big a kick out of getting a key hit or making a nice fielding play in any game. That was my biggest thrill — until I did it again."[8]

Had Charlie written the letter to "Jack" a few years later, he likely would have included the events of June 12, 1983, among his greatest thrills. On that day, before a huge crowd at Tiger Stadium, that the uniform numbers of Gehringer (No. 2) and Hank Greenberg (No. 5) were retired. The festivities took place between games of a doubleheader with the Cleveland Indians.

What made the occasion even more special was the presence of 18 former teammates who came to congratulate the two old warriors. Elden Auker, Chief Hogsett, Flea Clifton, Marv Owen, Billy Rogell, JoJo White, and Ray Hayworth were there from the 1934–35 championship clubs, and Dick Bartell, Hal Newhouser, Barney McCosky, and Birdie Tebbetts represented the 1940 American League champions. They were all joined by other celebrated Tigers of the past, including Hall of Famer Al Kaline, whom Charlie had signed when he was general manager, and Hall of Famer George Kell, a batting champion whom Charlie traded in his desperate attempt to put some new life into an aging ballclub. Former slugging first baseman Vic Wertz and catcher Bill Freehan from the 1968 championship team were also there. Master of ceremonies was Ernie Harwell, the voice of the Tigers to a whole generation just as Harry Heilmann had been to a previous generation. To top off the day's celebration, the Tigers took two from the Indians, 4–1 and 3–1 behind the pitching of Milt Wilcox and Jack Morris.

In 1984, the Tigers won the American League championship again with a team reminiscent of the club Charlie played on 50 years earlier. Lance Parrish, the catcher, was a catalyst for the offense, just as Mickey Cochrane had been, though Parrish hit with much greater power. His 33 home runs and 98 runs batted in led the team. The double play combination of Alan Trammell at short and Lou Whitaker at second was often compared to Billy Rogell and Charlie Gehringer. The Hank Greenberg of the '84 ballclub was outfielder Kirk Gibson, who hit 27 homers and drove in 91 runs but always seemed to deliver the big hit when the Tigers needed it. Pitchers like Schoolboy Rowe, Tommy Bridges, and Elden Auker were distant memories, replaced in fans' minds by the likes of Jack Morris (19–11), Dan Petry (18–8), and Milt Wilcox (17–8). Unlike the 1934 ballclub which fell to the Cardinals in the World Series, the 1984 Tigers defeated the San Diego Padres to secure the title.

17. "They won't get me in that suit again."

As Charlie crept into old age, he continued granting occasional interviews. Reporters would go out to his acreage and be greeted by Charlie, almost always wearing dress shirt and tie. He was becoming more candid in his old age as he looked back on his career and sometimes would emphasize his points with a "Gee" or "Golly," which are as close as Charlie ever came to profanity. In a particularly revealing piece in the *Detroit News* in 1987, the 84-year-old expounded on a number of subjects.

Gehringer said the most salary he ever received was between $35,000 and $40,000 — good money in its day — when Walter Briggs was president of the club. Frank Navin was more of a penny-pincher, he said. Navin was always trying to find ways to cut salaries "if you had a bad year, like hitting .310 or so." Charlie's view about Navin's stinginess might have been tainted by the circumstance in 1924 when Gehringer was docked three days' pay for attending his father's funeral.

In Gehringer's day, there were no agents. Players went to the front office and negotiated on their own, or they just signed their contracts and returned them in the mail. Charlie recalled that Bob Fothergill, the rotund outfielder, once wore a suit to hide his fat when he went in to see Navin at contract time. But the owner was not fooled. It was winter, and Navin continually turned up the radiator until Fothergill was sweating profusely and finally signed his contract just to get out of that office.

During this interview, Gehringer said the best right-handed pitcher he ever faced was Walter Johnson — and he didn't face him until near the end of Johnson's career. "They didn't throw balls out of the game as much as they do these days. They'd get tattered and when he threw it, the ball would make a noise as it came over the plate," he said. The best left-hander was the best pitcher overall, Lefty Grove, said Charlie. Once again he recalled how Grove hit him with a pitch, raising a welt on his arm. Gehringer also repeated what he had said in the past, that Bob Feller was tough only when his curve ball was working — which was often. Without the curve ball, said Gehringer, Feller could be had. "But he'd curve you on 3-and-2," said Charlie. "That isn't in the Bible."

Gehringer declined to pick an all-time team because he said he would probably just have to change it in five years. Besides, he joked, he'd have to decide whom he would put at second base. "I mean, can you see me putting myself there? I could out-field Rogers Hornsby and Eddie Collins, but no way could I outhit them. Hornsby was awesome."[9]

CHAPTER 18

"The Good Lord needed a second baseman."

Charlie and Jo observed their 40th wedding anniversary in 1989 — a feat that many of Gehringer's old teammates would have lost bets on back in the days when his bachelorhood was legendary in Detroit and his devotion to his mother was admired by some and considered a little extreme by others. But Charlie and Jo seemed just as devoted to one another in their later years as they were back when he was an upholstery button salesman and she was a secretary. One thing for sure hadn't changed over the years: they went to mass every morning but Saturday. Charlie said, "Why don't we go on Saturdays? I don't know. Maybe that's the Jewish Sabbath and they have to have a chance."[1]

Charlie remained fairly active, nursing some arthritis but playing golf as often as he could, tending to the pheasants that populated his backyard, remaining on the Hall of Fame Veterans Committee, and signing autographs through mail he still received from fans. But age was catching up on the old guard, the men who were part of the Tiger legacy, and Charlie and Jo were often either attending funerals or sending expressions of sympathy after losing some of Charlie's oldest and dearest friends.

Hank Greenberg, the Tigers' power-hitting first baseman-turned-outfielder who later became general manager of the Cleveland Indians and Chicago White Sox, died of cancer on September 4, 1986, at the age of 75. Marv Owen, the fiery third baseman whose altercation with Joe Medwick started the fan uprising in the 1934 World Series, died on June 22, 1991, at the age of 85.[2]

On December 23, 1992, as Charlie and Jo were preparing for Christ-

18. "The Good Lord needed a second baseman."

mas at their home in Bloomfield Hills, Charlie suffered a stroke. He was taken first to a hospital and then to a nursing home to rest and begin the recovery process. But the body that had seldom failed him in his major league career and that had allowed him to have a vigorous life after baseball, finally gave out. He slipped into a coma and died on Thursday, January 21, 1993. Gehringer's death was as quiet and peaceful as he had tried to lead his life.

Friends and former teammates expressed their loss. "I guess the Good Lord needed a second baseman," said Billy Rogell, who played shortstop alongside Gehringer. "And He got the best one He could have gotten." Hal Newhouser, a youngster on the 1940 pennant winner, said, "He's the epitome of one of the great outstanding players in the history of the game." Broadcaster Ernie Harwell, who had presided over the ceremonies when the Tigers retired Charlie's uniform number 10 years earlier, said, "I just think about a very high-class guy who had the respect of everyone in his profession." Al Kaline, the youngster Gehringer signed and one of the few successes he could point to as general manager, marveled at how Gehringer's skill and the admiration he received from others never went to his head. "It was surprising to have someone as great of an athlete and as great of a ballplayer as he was to have that modesty," said Kaline, who eventually joined Charlie as a member of the Hall of Fame in 1980.

On January 25, about 200 family members, friends, and well-wishers attended a funeral mass at St. Regis Catholic Church in Birmingham with Father Dan Murphy officiating. The Rev. Chris Welsh, chaplain at William Beaumont Hospital in Royal Oak and former pastor at St. Regis, said Charlie was the greatest second baseman of all time. "But that's not why we're here. He was a good, simple, kind, generous and gallant man. He was a man who gave of himself. What made Charlie a great man is that he knew his roots." Father Welsh concluded by saying Charlie was "safe at home now."[3]

Tiger owner Mike Ilitch and former owner Tom Monaghan were in attendance as were former teammate Newhouser and three Tiger players from a different era, Bill Freehan, Mickey Lolich, and Reno Bertoia. Atlanta Braves pitcher John Smoltz, a former Tiger farmhand and Charlie's cousin sent flowers because, according to the accompanying card, "I admired him." Gehringer's body was laid to rest at Holy Sepulchre Mausoleum in Southfield.

Ten days after his death, Shirley Povich, a columnist for the *Washington Post* whose career as a sportswriter stretched all the way back to Charlie's playing days, bemoaned that his death had received little media attention outside of Detroit. "That the death of Charlie Gehringer, at 89, was given the brush-off probably speaks to the new values of the sports media. Television and the sports pages would have screamed if Michael Jordan had a slow-growth hangnail," he wrote. Povich recalled what other players had said about Charlie. Lefty Gomez had said, "All I know is that when I'm pitching, he's always on base." Wes Ferrell, who pitched to Charlie for many years, said, "He was the toughest hitter I ever faced. Sometimes he'd spot you two strikes and you couldn't get him out. He'd hit that ball and he'd beat you. Yes he would." Buddy Myer, the Washington Senator who beat out Cleveland's Joe Vosmik by a fraction of a point for the 1935 American League batting title said, "It would have been easy if Charlie Gehringer didn't take 10 points off my average with all the hits he stole from me."

Povich concluded his column, "Charlie didn't know how to strut. He was known as baseball's quiet man, content to let his bat and his glove speak for him. With both he was an artist. His kind did not come along very often. His passing should have been better noted."[4]

Perhaps the tribute that Charlie would have appreciated the most came not from a priest or a player but from a fan. Tom Stanton wrote a book about a trip he made to Cooperstown, New York, with his two sons so they could see the Hall of Fame. It brought back memories of when he and his father had made a similar trip when Stanton was a youngster. "It gives you a sense of the passing of time to stand beside your father, who is in his ninth decade, as he studies the mitt of the man he has admired since the days of Herbert Hoover," wrote Stanton. "Charlie Gehringer's life became an allegory, its lessons implicit. Be patient. Be humble. Be loyal and loving and devoted. Above all, care for your mother."[5]

One day, about a year after Charlie's death, Elden Auker, the old pitcher, received a phone call from Jo, Charlie's widow, who remained as devoted to him after his passing as when he was alive. His picture was on her bedstand, and she often picked it up and kissed it before she went to bed. Jo still went to 7 A.M. mass every morning expect Saturday just as she had done for so many years with Charlie.

Jo Gehringer wanted Auker, now 84 years old, to accompany her to

18. "The Good Lord needed a second baseman."

what had become a special place for her — the mausoleum at Holy Sepulchre Cemetery, Charlie's final resting place. As they drove onto the cemetery grounds, they likely passed the area where Harry Heilmann, one of Charlie's early teammates, was buried in Section 16.

The mausoleum was a spacious building with crypts on both sides of wide marble hallways. The place was almost always engulfed in a respectful silence, the epitome of peace and quiet that seemed fitting and proper. Most often, the only noise was the sound of footsteps on the marble floors. On this day, the place was empty and silent except for two pairs of footsteps as Jo led Auker down the long hall. They made their way to Section 18 West and stood in front of Crypt D4, the one that had a cross on it and, beneath the cross, the engraved name of Charles L. Gehringer.

Jo broke the silence. "Charlie," she said. "Elden's here. He came by to see you." Auker was startled by what was happening, yet Jo continued to speak. She told Charlie that Elden and Mildred Auker had come to visit her and were staying at the house. Then she asked Auker to speak to Charlie, to have a chat with him. For Auker, it was a moment that seemed a little awkward and at the same time seemed like the proper thing to do. "Jo's well, Charlie. I don't want you worrying about her. She misses you terribly. We all do. But she's going to be fine. We'll see to that."

At Jo's hastening, Auker continued to chat. He talked about his golf game and how as he got older, it was easier to shoot his age, and he reminisced about their days on the Tigers with Schoolboy Rowe, Tommy Bridges, Rogell, Owen, Greenberg, and of course Mickey Cochrane.

After a few minutes, Jo came forward and reverently put her hand on the crypt. Auker followed her lead and did the same. As they prepared to leave, he turned toward the crypt and said, "Take good care, Charlie."[6]

Chapter Notes

Chapter 1

1. Frederick C. Klein interviewed Gehringer for an article he wrote about active senior citizens for the *Wall Street Journal*, published March 10, 1983, under the headline "Older Americans: Actress, Ex-Senator Keep Active; So Do Nobel Doctor, Executive, Ex-Second Baseman." The author contacted Klein, now retired and living in Scottsdale, Arizona, hoping for more insights into Gehringer's character. "I remember that he was a very nice man," said Klein, but he could not recall any specifics from his luncheon with Gehringer, which took place almost 25 years earlier.
2. Richard Bak, *Cobb Would Have Caught It: The Golden Age of Baseball in Detroit* (Detroit: Wayne State University Press, 1991), 192.
3. Elden Auker with Tom Keegan, *Sleeper Cars and Flannel Uniforms: A Lifetime of Memories from Striking Out the Babe to Teeing It Up with the President* (Chicago: Triumph Books, 2006), 113.
4. Bak, *Cobb Would Have Caught It*, 358. Lerchen also testifies to Gehringer's meticulous nature, even in his playing days: "Charlie was quiet, meticulous. He shined his own shoes. Nobody touched anything of his ... Charlie was a perfectionist. Everything had to be just so — glove here, shoes there, bat over there. He was polished. He carried himself."
5. The statistics are from baseball-reference.com and Lyle Spatz, ed., *The SABR Baseball List & Record Book* (New York: Scribner, 2007).
6. William Curran, *Mitts: A Celebration of the Art of Fielding* (New York: William Morrow, 1985), 57. Curran says Gehringer made the observation in an interview with author Donald Honig.
7. Bak, *Cobb Would Have Caught It*, 205.
8. Klein, "Older Americans."

Chapter 2

1. "The Tiger Immortal Nobody Knew," *Super Sports*, October 1971, 48.
2. Fowlerville townspeople, like so many small town residents, take great pride in their community — and some take offense that Charlie Gehringer would dare to call it his hometown. A newspaperman trying to find Gehringer's birthplace drove to

Fowlerville, still with a population of about 1,000, and stopped to ask for directions from a man standing on a street corner. The man at first didn't recognize the name Gehringer but then said, "Oh, you mean the ballplayer? Did he say he comes from Fowlerville? He's just bragging. He lived in the suburbs."

3. Sheldon A. Mix, "A Visit with a Second Baseman," *Detroit News*, n.d.
4. Bak, *Cobb Would Have Caught It*, 191.
5. Ibid.
6. Veach has a couple claims to fame in addition to his lifetime statistics. In 1925, as a member of the New York Yankees, he pinch hit once for Babe Ruth. That same season, after being dealt to the pennant-winning Washington Senators, Veach hit a single with two outs in the ninth inning to break up a no-hitter by Chicago's Ted Lyons.
7. Charlie's version is recounted in Bak, *Cobb Would Have Caught It*, 191–192. Numerous other versions appear in various newspapers, but all share a common thread: Bobby Veach on a hunting trip. Veach was a Tiger outfielder for 12 years, then spent a year with the Boston Red Sox and played with Boston, Washington, and the New York Yankees in the last year of his career, 1925. He was still a Tiger when he put in the good word for Gehringer that led to his tryout. Veach had a lifetime batting average of .310.
8. Naleway played in one major league game, for the Chicago White Sox in 1924. He batted twice without a hit.
9. The minor league information was collected by a newspaper in London, Ontario, and sent to Ernest J. Lanigan, historian of the National Baseball Hall of Fame in 1952. In a letter dated November 15, 1952, the writer, name unknown, provided the information but also reported the difficulty in finding it, giving insight into the technology available in those days. He wrote, "It seems before they destroyed all these old papers, pictures were taken of a great many of them, and they can be viewed on a machine. I was allowed to use this machine and I viewed a great many sports pages, some very hard to make out."
10. Bak, *Cobb Would Have Caught It*, 192.
11. "Gehringer's Start," *New York Times*, July 9, 1942. Joe E. Brown had a lifelong love of baseball. After abandoning his hopes for a professional baseball career, he turned to acting and enjoyed a 40-year career in comic roles. Three of his movies centered around baseball: *Fireman Save My Child* (1932); *Elmer the Great* (1933); and *Alibi Ike* (1953). He helped broadcast New York Yankee games in 1953. An interesting link between Brown and the Tigers was his longtime friendship with Ty Cobb. Brown, in fact, spent about a week with Cobb when the former Tiger great was dying of cancer and starving for friendships that he had forsaken long ago. Brown's son, Joe L. Brown, picked up on his father's interest in baseball and served as general manager of the Pittsburgh Pirates for 20 years.
12. Bob Broeg, "Silent, Stylish — Keystoner Gehringer," *The Sporting News*, May 23, 1970, 24–26.

Chapter 3

1. Charles C. Alexander, *Ty Cobb* (New York: Oxford University Press, 1984), 234.

Notes — Chapter 4

2. Anecdotes about Cobb have been published in many books, magazines, and newspapers, including Bak, *Cobb Would Have Caught It*.

3. "Old Timers Recall Strange Starts," *New York World-Telegram*, October 4, 1955.

4. Gehringer got his chance just a year after another temporary illness changed the course of two careers. In 1925, Yankee first baseman Wally Pipp asked to be taken out of the lineup because of a headache. He was replaced by Lou Gehrig, who remained there for 2,130 games, and Pipp was shipped off to Cincinnati.

5. Bak, *Cobb Would Have Caught It*, 154.

6. Ibid., 195–196.

7. Alexander helped the Cardinals win the National League pennant and participated in a World Series game that has become part of baseball lore. Although Alexander had pitched the day before, manager Rogers Hornsby summoned him from the bullpen to pitch to the Yankees' Tony Lazzeri with the bases loaded and the game on the line. Alexander may have been hung over — it depends on whose version of the story you believe — but he was definitely a tired, aging pitcher brought into a tough situation. Alexander struck out Lazzeri and retired the Yankees the rest of the way to salvage a Cardinal victory. McCarthy, the Cub manager who dumped Alexander, went on to become one of baseball's greatest managers, leading the Yankees through some of their glory years in the 1930s.

8. Broeg, "Silent, Stylish — Keystoner Gehringer," 26.

9. Alexander, *Ty Cobb*, 185–189.

10. Ibid., 188. Leonard told Landis he didn't want to come to Chicago because "once in a while, they bump off people around there."

11. Moriarty would manage the Tigers for two years and then return to umpiring, the job he loved the most. Moriarty was an American League umpire for 22 years and later became a Tiger scout. When he retired for good, he had spent 50 years in baseball.

Chapter 4

1. Broeg, "Silent, Stylish — Keystoner Gehringer," 26.

2. Mix, "A Visit With a Second Baseman." *Detroit News*, n.d.

3. Wes Ferrell's career nearly paralleled Gehringer's. He came up with Cleveland in 1927 and won 193 games, pitching primarily for the Indians and the Boston Red Sox.

4. Broeg, "Silent, Stylish — Keystoner Gehringer," 25.

5. Bak, *Cobb Would Have Caught It*, 199–200.

6. J.L. Hudson also developed and manufactured the Hudson automobile. His stores were landmarks in the Detroit area, eventually merging to become the Dayton-Hudson company, the forerunner to Target stores.

7. Evans's nearly 50-year career in baseball included a stint at general manager of the Detroit Tigers (1946–51). Charlie Gehringer replaced him in that position.

8. There are several versions of how Cuyler got in Donie Bush's doghouse. In mid-season, Bush moved him from third to second in the batting order, a change Cuyler strongly objected to because he was a free swinger who didn't want the role of bunting, hitting behind runners, and generally being the set-up man for players like Paul and Lloyd Waner. In one game, Cuyler infuriated Bush when as a base runner

on first, he failed to slide into second on an infield ground ball. He tried to break up a double play by going into second standing up, but the shortstop taking the throw dropped the ball and then tagged Cuyler. Believing Cuyler would have avoided the tag if he had slid, Bush benched the future Hall of Famer.

9. Vangilder pitched in the major leagues for 11 seasons, and in seven of those, his record was within two decisions of .500. His last four seasons, two with St. Louis and two with Detroit, he was 9–11, 10–12, 11–10, and 1–0. In three other seasons, he was 1–0, 11–12, and 16–17. When he hung it up for good, his lifetime record was 99–102, a percentage of .4925.

10. "Tigers Sign Harris, Former Washington Leader, as Manager," *New York Times*, October 20, 1928.

11. Bak, *Cobb Would Have Caught It*, 197.

12. Mostil's career with the White Sox had many tragic consequences. During 1927 spring training, he tried to commit suicide. Many believed he was despondent when people discovered he was having an affair with the wife of teammate Red Faber. They remained teammates, and Faber was in the White Sox dugout in 1929 when Mostil broke his leg, ending his career.

13. Alexander looked like he had Hall of Fame potential when he broke in. After driving in 137 runs in 1929, he followed it up with 135 in 1930. Only Joe DiMaggio drove in more runs in his first two years with 125 and 167. A modern comparison would be Albert Pujols of the St. Louis Cardinals, who drove in 130 in 2001 and 127 in 2002 — great numbers, but short of Alexander's at the start of his career. Alexander's RBI totals dropped dramatically in the next three years — 87, 60, and 40 — and he was out of Major League Baseball after just five years.

Chapter 5

1. This is most often attributed to Mickey Cochrane, but variations of the same quote, changing the batting average to .350, for example, have been credited to many other ballplayers describing Gehringer.

2. Joe Falls, "Joe Falls," *Detroit Free-Press*, July 16, 1977.

3. Dan Daniels, *New York World-Telegram*, Aug. 1, 1933.

4. Falls, "Joe Falls."

5. Broeg, "Silent, Stylish — Keystoner Gehringer," 26.

6. Bak, *Cobb Would Have Caught It*, 196–197.

7. Gehringer said Lefty Gomez of the Yankees gave him the nickname of "The Mechanical Man," but it was a reference to his seemingly effortless ability to hit. Sportswriters used the nickname often in reference to his overall style of play. Doc Cramer, a contemporary ballplayer, is widely quoted as saying, "He's The Mechanical Man. All you have to do is wind him up on Opening Day and he runs on and on, doing everything right all season."

8. Bak. *Cobb Would Have Caught It*, 196–198.

9. Whitehill still had some gas left in his tank. He was 22–8 for the Senators in 1933 and 1–1 in two starts in the World Series that year. Marberry's credentials as a relief pitcher are best shown by his 1925 season with the Senators, when he appeared in 55 games — all in relief — a feat virtually unheard of in an era when starting pitchers were expected to throw complete games.

Notes — Chapter 6

10. Bak. *Cobb Would Have Caught It*, 186–187.

11. A new type of therapy called diathermy was used to treat Alexander's knee. It required heat treatments that resulted in third-degree burns on his knee and the onset of gangrene. Doctors repaired the damage so amputating the leg was not necessary, but the injury coupled with the treatment ended his baseball career. He made an attempt to come back in September but was forced to retire. His lifetime batting average was .331.

12. Bucky Harris's managerial career spanned more than 30 years, and he was universally regarded as a nice guy. While nice guys don't always finish last, as Leo Durocher is often quoted as saying, Harris was unable to move the Tigers into pennant contention. They finished fifth three times as well as 6th and 7th in his five-year tenure with the Tigers.

Chapter 6

1. Information on the Rouge plant riots was gleaned from many sources, but primarily from michiganhistoryonline.com.

2. Mike Piazza is likely to retire with a higher lifetime batting average, but many of his at-bats have come as a designated hitter.

3. Auker, *Sleeper Cars and Flannel Uniforms,* 32–33.

4. Bak. *Cobb Would Have Caught It*, 197, 227, 249.

5. Auker, *Sleeper Cars and Flannel Uniforms*, 111.

6. These were the days of Al Capone, Baby Face Nelson, and other gangsters who were constantly pursued by the Federal Bureau of Investigation. In that context, "G-men" were "government men"—good guys, in the eyes of the public. In the minds of Detroit fans, Gehringer, Goslin, and Greenberg were the "good guys" in the Tiger lineup. Sportswriters and fans often play with initials. In the 1960s, Mickey Mantle and Roger Maris of the New York Yankees were the "M&M Boys," and in the late 1990s, Craig Biggio, Jeff Bagwell, and Lance Berkman were the "Killer B's" of the Houston Astros.

7. At one time, Hubbell was property of the Tigers. He came to spring training one year and was trying to develop his screwball. Cobb, who was manager at the time, told him to quit fooling around with it. Hubbell didn't, and soon the Tigers got rid of him, and the Giants picked him up. He appeared in 253 games in his career and was elected to the Hall of Fame in 1947.

8. Baseball history is filled with examples of teams acquiring pitchers in midseason or later who provided extra strength for the pennant race. In July 1945, the Cubs picked up Yankee right-hander Hank Borowy. Eleven years later, the Dodgers acquired Sal Maglie from the scrap pile in Cleveland. More recently, in 1984 the Cubs acquired Rick Sutcliffe from Cleveland. All were instrumental in delivering championships for their new ballclubs.

9. More recent examples of "instant success" are Robert "Bo" Belinsky, a pitcher for the Los Angeles Angels, who threw a no-hitter in his rookie season, 1962, and dated Hollywood starlets while winning 10 games for the Angels. His "15 minutes of fame" ended quickly, and Belinsky won only 18 more games in an eight-year career. Mark Fidrych was a one-year sensation for the Detroit Tigers, winning 19 games in 1976 and entertaining writers and fans with antics such as talking to the ball on the

mound. In 1980, Fernando Valenzuela was rookie of the year while pitching for the Los Angeles Dodgers, leading the league in strikeouts and displaying a boyish charm that captured the nation's attention, though he could speak no English.

10. Auker, *Sleeper Cars and Flannel Uniforms*, 111.
11. Bak, *Cobb Would Have Caught It*, 257–258.
12. Dan Daniels, "From Erratic Defensive Quartet Quartet in 1933, Tiger Infield Has Developed," *New York World-Telegram*, September 1, 1934.

Chapter 7

1. Bak, *Cobb Would Have Caught It*, 232, 271.
2. John Devaney and Burt Goldblatt, *The World Series: A Complete Pictorial History* (New York: Rand McNally, 1981), 145.
3. David Pietrusza, *Judge and Jury: The Life and Times of Judge Kenesaw Mountain Landis* (South Bend, IN: Diamond Communications Press), 339–341.
4. Devaney and Goldblatt, *The World Series*, 145.
5. Dan Daniel, "Daniel's Dope." *New York World-Telegram*, October 8, 1934.
6. Bill Werber and C. Paul Rogers, *Memories of a Ballplayer* (Cleveland: Society for American Baseball Research, 2001), 154.
7. Paul Dickson, *Baseball's Greatest Quotations* (New York: HarperCollins, 1991), 161.
8. Mickey Cochrane, *Baseball: The Fan's Game* (New York: Funk & Wagnall, 1939), 183.

Chapter 8

1. Louis Kaufman, Barbara Fitzgerald, and Tom Sewell, *Moe Berg: Athlete, Scholar ... Spy* (Boston: Little, Brown, 1975), 4–13.
2. This is widely quoted, although sometimes the number of languages changes from one source to the next.
3. There are many accounts of Berg's excursion with the camera. As it turned out, his pictures were not terribly useful because Japan changed so much in the intervening years. But his deftness in handling the assignment must have pleased his superiors because he was given other assignments during World War II. He was also known for some bloopers, like wearing an easily identifiable, government-issued wristwatch on one spy mission and dropping his gun in someone's lap while on another mission.
4. Kaufman, Fitzgerald, and Sewell, *Moe Berg*, 84–85.
5. Ray made his speculations in his "Sports X-Ray" column in the *Los Angeles Times*, November 25, 1934.
6. Hank Greenberg and Ira Berkow, *Hank Greenberg: The Story of My Life* (New York: Benchmark Press, 2001), 111.

Chapter 9

1. John Devaney and Burt Goldblatt, *The World Series: A Complete Pictorial History* (Chicago: Rand McNally, 1981), 149.

2. Pietrusza. *Judge and Jury*, 345.

3. Stan Hack, the Cub third baseman stranded at third after hitting the leadoff triple in the ninth inning, returned to Detroit six years later for the All-Star Game at Briggs Stadium. Before the game, someone saw Hack, who had wonderful sense of humor, standing at the dugout gazing at the left side of the infield. "What are you doing?" the person asked. "I was just checking to see if I was still standing at third base," he said.

4. Auker, *Sleeper Cars and Flannel Uniforms*, 67.

5. *Chicago Tribune*, October 8, 1935.

6. Auker, *Sleeper Cars and Flannel Uniforms*, 68–69.

7. Bak, *Cobb Would Have Caught It*, 201.

8. *Chicago Tribune*, October 10, 1935.

9. Auker, *Sleeper Cars and Flannel Uniforms*, 112.

10. Marberry was one of the most well-respected pitchers of his time, succeeding both as a starting pitcher and a reliever, much like Hoyt Wilhelm and Dennis Eckersly generations later. But Marberry, who had made his living zeroing in on the strike zone, found it difficult from behind the plate. His weakness as an umpire was his inability to be consistent in calling balls and strikes — and he knew it. So he quit after a year and returned to his familiar position on the pitcher's mound.

Chapter 10

1. Jim Fitzgerald grew up to be a newspaper columnist with the *Cass City Chronicle*, in Cass City, Michigan. He told the story of meeting Gehringer in a column published on February 21, 1980. The encounter had occurred 44 years earlier, but Fitzgerald remembered it vividly and considered his father a hero for introducing him to Gehringer.

2. In 1926, Joe McCarthy, then a rookie big league manager with the Chicago Cubs, had a problem with his aging legendary star pitcher, Grover Cleveland Alexander, who did not adhere to training rules and was perpetually drunk. McCarthy suspended him and then sent him packing to the St. Louis Cardinals.

3. Bak, *Cobb Would Have Caught It*, 202–203.

Chapter 11

1. "Daniel's Dope." *New York World-Telegram*, November 2, 1937.

2. One writer from each American League city voted on the Most Valuable Player Award. The 1937 committee included Hy Hurwitz of the *Boston Globe*, John P. Carmichael of the *Chicago Daily News*, Gordon Cobbledick of the *Cleveland Plain Dealer*, H.G. Salinger of the *Detroit News*, Max Case of *New York Evening Journal*, James C. Isaminger of the *Philadelphia Inquirer*, Glen Wallar of the *St. Louis Globe-Democrat*, and Francis Stan of the *Washington Star*.

3. "Daniel's Dope." *New York World-Telegram*, November 13, 1937.

4. "Gehringer Gets the Duke: Could It Be Sentiment?," *New York World-Telegram*, November 2, 1937.

5. "No Job-Seekers More Deserving of Votes Than Tigers' Gehringer," *Detroit News*, November 2, 1937.

6. The beating of the auto workers had some baseball ties. Harry Bennett, an "assistant" of Henry Ford, was also a friend of Mickey Cochrane. In fact, Cochrane stayed at Bennett's Wyoming ranch while recovering from his nervous breakdown in 1936. Another thug was identified as Eddie Cicotte, who worked in the auto plant's service department after Commissioner Landis banned from him Major League Baseball because of his participation in the 1919 "Black Sox" scandal. Cicotte and seven teammates on the Chicago White Sox had been accused of conspiring to fix the World Series.

7. "Gehringer a Blue-Chip Businessman," *The Sporting News*, January 8, 1966.

8. Sheldon Mix, "A Visit with a Second Baseman," *Detroit News*, n.d.

9. Poffenberger once missed a game he was scheduled to start because he was hung over and asleep in his hotel room. On another occasion, he called room service and ordered "the breakfast of champions"—two eggs and a bottle of beer.

Chapter 12

1. Hy Goldberg, "Sports in the News," *Detroit News*, May 5, 1939.

2. Ibid.

3. Though Heilmann was one of the American League's greatest hitters, many fans who never saw him play knew him primarily as the voice of the Tigers. He was the play-by-play radio announcer from 1934 until 1950, when he was diagnosed with lung cancer. Knowing his old teammate was seriously ill, Ty Cobb started a campaign to get him elected to the Hall of Fame. In 1951, he received 67 percent of the vote, a few votes shy of the 75 percent needed. He died in July 1951. The next year, he was elected to the Hall of Fame.

4. Benton pitched for the Tigers for several years then for Cleveland and Boston, closing out his career in 1952. Perhaps his biggest claim to fame is being the answer to a trivia question: he is the only big league pitcher who faced both Babe Ruth and Mickey Mantle.

5. Dave Anderson, *Pennant Races: Baseball at Its Best* (New York: Doubleday, 1994), 111.

6. Ibid., 123.

7. Floyd Giebell was 1–1 with the Tigers in limited service in 1939. He was 2–0 in 1940, both wins coming in the last two weeks of September, first over Philadelphia then the pennant-clincher against Cleveland. In 1941, he made 17 appearances, 15 in relief, and was ineffective, giving up 45 hits and 26 walks with no decisions in 34⅓ innings. He left baseball and led a quiet, unassuming life out of the spotlight. He died in 2004 at age 94.

8. Anderson, *Pennant Races*, 126.

9. Bob Feller, *Bob Feller's Little Black Book of Baseball Wisdom* (New York: McGraw-Hill, 2001), 57.

10. Columnist Williams compared Carroll's proficiency to that of "Bonesetter" Reese, an Ohio chiropractor of a generation earlier whose patients included stars such as Babe Ruth, Grover Cleveland Alexander, and Dazzy Vance. Baseball people say an important quality in trainers is the ability for them to know their limitations. Joe McCarthy once asked a prospective trainer what he would do if he came across a ballplayer with a broken ankle. "Hell, I'd call a doctor," said the man. He was hired.

Chapter 13

1. The Reds "unretired" the number in 1942 but retired it again about a half-century later in honor of another catcher, Johnny Bench.
2. Devaney and Goldblatt, *The World Series*, 169.
3. Bak, *Cobb Would Have Caught It*, 205.
4. Ibid., 295.
5. "The Tiger Immortal Nobody Knew," *Super Sports*, October 1971, 61.
6. Ibid.
7. "Daniel's Dope," *New York World-Telegram*, September 26, 1940. Wish Egan scouted for the Tigers for 40 years and coached off and on for them. When not on a scouting venture, he was a fixture around the ballpark and was well known and well liked by Tiger personnel, writers, and visiting players. Those he signed to Tiger contracts include Hal Newhouser and Dizzy Trout.
8. Ibid.
9. Ibid.
10. *New York Times*, December 11, 1940.
11. *New York World-Telegram*, March 29, 1941.
12. Bak, *Cobb Would Have Caught It*, 205.

Chapter 14

1. *New York Times*, January 16, 1942.
2. *New York Herald Tribune*, May 3, 1942.
3. Rowe pitched sparingly for Brooklyn in 1942 and then spent five years with the Philadelphia Phillies, where he won 52 and lost 39. He retired after the 1949 season with a career mark of 158 wins and 101 losses. More than one-third of his wins came in Detroit's three championship years, 1934, 1935, and 1940. Newsom pitched nine more years and was well-traveled. He had two tenures with both the Senators and the Philadelphia A's and also pitched for Brooklyn, the St. Louis Browns, the Yankees and the Giants. At the end of his 20-year career, he had a record of 211 wins and 222 losses.
4. Gehringer's career statistics were compiled by the Society for American Baseball Research.

Chapter 15

1. *The Sporting News*, May 11, 1949.
2. The Cochrane anecdote was published in the Jax newspaper and then retold in *The Sporting News* on April 12, 1945. It might not have received too much attention because on that day President Franklin D. Roosevelt, Commander-in-Chief of the armed forces, died at Warm Springs, Georgia.
3. *Detroit News*, Nov. 22, 1945.
4. Ibid.
5. Bak, *Cobb Would Have Caught It*, 206.
6. *The Sporting News*, May 23, 1970.
7. Auker, *Sleeper Cars and Flannel Uniforms*, 109.

8. Ibid.
9. *The Sporting News*, May 11, 1949.
10. Salsinger's tribute to Gehringer appeared in his column, "The Umpire," published May 12, 1949, in the *Detroit News*.
11. *Chicago Tribune*, June 14, 1949.
12. *New York Times*, June 20, 1949.
13. *New York World-Telegram*, June 22, 1949.

Chapter 16

1. Steve O'Neill is not a Hall of Fame manager and probably never will be. But he has a record unmatched by most Hall of Fame managers. In managing for all or parts of 14 years with the Cleveland Indians, Detroit Tigers, Boston Red Sox, and Philadelphia Phillies, he never had a losing season. He retired with a record of 1,039 wins, 819 losses, and a winning percentage of .559.
2. *New York Times*, April 12, 1950.
3. Ibid. Burnett owned the Dallas Eagles from 1948–1955. He installed the first organ in the Texas League. In 1952, he signed Dave Hoskins, an African American player, leading to the integration of the Texas League. Dallas finished first in 1952, 1953, and 1955. Burnett died in 1955 at age 57.
4. *Los Angeles Times*, July 29, 1951.
5. *The Sporting News*, August 8, 1951.
6. Bak, *Cobb Would Have Caught It*, 207.
7. *The Sporting News*, October 2, 1952. Obviously, Gehringer was correct in his assessment of the young ballplayers. Kuenn won a batting title with the Tigers and had a brilliant career. Kaline and Mantle both were elected to the Hall of Fame. Many years after he left Tiger management, Gehringer looked back on signing Kaline as a highlight of his brief stay in the front office.
8. Hutchinson's managerial career included stints in Detroit, St. Louis, and Cincinnati, where his club won the National League championship in 1961. Williams's criticism of Gehringer and the Tigers appeared in a column in the *New York World-Telegram* on July 18, 1952.
9. Bak, *Cobb Would Have Caught It*, 207.
10. Ibid., 136–137.

Chapter 17

1. *The Sporting News*, January 8, 1966. Gehringer finished with 19 home runs but slipped to a .298 batting average.
2. *New York Times*, February 8, 1951.
3. *The Sporting News*, February 23, 1963.
4. *The New York Times*, November 13, 1965.
5. *The Sporting News*, May 25, 1968.
6. Bill James, *The Politics of Glory: How Baseball's Hall of Fame Really Works* (New York: Macmillan, 1994), 259.
7. The letter to "Jack" is on file in the National Baseball Hall of Fame library in Cooperstown, NY.

8. Klein's interview with Gehringer took place in early 1983. His story, also referenced in Chapter One, was published in the *Wall Street Journal* on March 10, 1983.
9. *Detroit News*, February 8, 1987.

Chapter 18

1. *Detroit News*, February 8, 1987.
2. Members of the Tiger championship teams of 1934–35 and 1940 had amazing longevity. Flea Clifton died December 22, 1997, at the age of 88. Birdie Tebbetts died March 24, 1999 at 86. Chief Hogsett died July 17, 2001; he was 97. Ray Hayworth died September 25, 2002, at age 98. Billy Rogell died August 9, 2003, also at 98. Elden Auker died August 4, 2006, at 95.
3. Widely quoted in many newspaper and wire service reports.
4. Povich's tribute was published January 31, 1993, in the *Washington Post* under the headline "Quiet Greatness Should Not Go Gently."
5. Tom Stanton, *The Road to Cooperstown: A Father, Two Sons and the Journey of a Lifetime* (New York: St. Martin's Press, 2003), 100.
6. Auker, *Sleeper Cars and Flannel Uniforms*, 107–108.

Bibliography

"Aching Dogs of Tiger Veterans Moan and Groan." *New York World-Telegram*, March 29, 1941.
Alexander, Charles C. *Ty Cobb*. London: Oxford University Press, 1984.
"All-Stars of 1933 Recall Scene of Glory." *New York Times*, July 5, 1983.
Anderson, Dave. *Pennant Races: Baseball at Its Best*. New York: Doubleday, 1994.
Auker, Elden, and Tom Keegan. *Sleeper Cars and Flannel Uniforms*. Chicago: Triumph, 2006.
Bak, Richard. *Cobb Would Have Caught It: The Golden Age of Baseball in Detroit*. Detroit: Wayne State University Press, 1991.
"Baseball is Only an Avocation to Gehringer, Former Tiger Star." *New York Times*, January 15, 1951.
"The Bobo Legend." *New York World-Telegram*, September 30, 1940.
Broeg, Bob. "Gehringer Did Everything Right." *The Sporting News*, January 28, 1978, 50.
_____. "Silent, Stylish — Keystoner Gehringer." *The Sporting News*, May 23, 1970, 24–26.
Cantor, George. *Tigers Essential: Everything You Need to Know to Be a Real Fan*. New York: Triumph, 2007.
Cochrane, Mickey. *Baseball: The Fan's Game*. New York: Funk and Wagnalls, 1939.
"Cubs Wonder If Moriarty Will Get Last Laugh." *Chicago Tribune*, October 10, 1935.
Curran, William. *Mitts: A Celebration of the Art of Fielding*. New York: William Morrow, 1985.
Daley, Arthur, "Sports of the Times: Still Listening." *New York Times*, February 8, 1951.
Daniel, Dan. "Daniel's Dope." *New York World-Telegram*, August 1, 1933.
_____. "Daniel's Dope." *New York World-Telegram*, November 2, 1937.
_____. "Daniel's Dope." *New York World-Telegram*, November 13, 1937.
_____. "Daniel's Dope." *New York World-Telegram*, August 21, 1940.
_____. "Daniel's Dope." *New York World-Telegram*, September 26, 1940.
_____. "Daniel's Dope." *New York World-Telegram*, June 22, 1949.
_____. "From Erratic Defensive Quartet in 1933, Tiger Infield Has Developed." *New York World-Telegram*, September 1, 1934.
"Deaths." *Time*, June 13, 1955.
"Detroit Divides with White Sox." *New York Times*, September 3, 1929.

BIBLIOGRAPHY

"Detroit's Fair-Haired Boy: Infielder Charlie Gehringer." *New York Times*, April 4, 1929.
"Detroit's New GM Faces Tough Task." *The Sporting News*, August 8, 1951.
Devaney, John, and Burt Goldblatt. *The World Series: A Complete Pictorial History*. New York: Rand McNally, 1981.
Dickson, Paul. *Baseball's Greatest Quotations*. New York: Edward Burlingame, 1991.
Ebling, Jack. *Tales of the Detroit Tigers*. New York: Sports Publishing, 2007.
Einstein, Charles. *The Fireside Book of Baseball*. New York: Simon and Schuster, 1956.
"Eleven Hits by Tigers Repulse Athletics." *New York Times*, July 22, 1930.
"End of Gehringer's Long Career Sighted as Tigers Use Substitute." *New York Herald Tribune*, July 6, 1941.
"Ex-Solon Pilot to Get Job." *Los Angeles Times*, October 19, 1928.
Falls, Joe. "Old Master Gehringer to Tutor McAuliffe in Second Base Play." *The Sporting News*, February 23, 1963, 37.
Fehler, Gene. *More Tales from Baseball's Golden Age*. New York: Sports Publishing, 2002.
Feller, Bob. *Bob Feller's Little Black Book of Baseball Wisdom*. New York: McGraw-Hill, 2001.
"54,151 See Diz Dean Walk First Batter." *New York Times*, April 12, 1950.
"Figures Emphasize Yanks' Superiority." *New York Times*, December 12, 1937.
Fitzgerald, Jim. "Heroes Forget." *Cass City* (MI) *Chronicle*, February 21, 1980.
"Gehringer Eyes All-Star Poll and Hopes He'll Win." *Chicago Tribune*, June 2, 1933.
"Gehringer Gives Press Slip and Marries." *New York Times*, June 20, 1949.
"Gehringer Gives Up Textbooks to Play for Tigers." *Chicago Tribune*, June 19, 1933.
"Gehringer Honored; Hits Home Run and Three Singles." *New York Times*, August 15, 1929.
"Gehringer Injured In Auto Crash; Out Several Days." *Chicago Tribune*, June 24, 1932.
"Gehringer Injured, May Quit Baseball." *New York Times*, March 6, 1940.
"Gehringer Left Off Tiger Roster." *New York Times*, January 16, 1940.
"Gehringer May Quit Game Rather Than Ride Bench." *New York Times*, July 16, 1941.
"Gehringer No Chatter-Box; Denies Hello-Good-Bye." *The Sporting News*, April 12, 1945, 11.
"Gehringer on Mend; Limps After Operation on Tendon." *New York Times*, November 13, 1965.
"Gehringer Plays 18 Holes in Rain on 65th Birthday," *The Sporting News*, May 25, 1968, 42.
"Gehringer's Homer Wins for Tigers." *New York Times*, August 5, 1930.
"Gehringer Signs Again." *New York Times*, December 19, 1940.
"Gehringer Signs Contract with Tigers for 1934." *Chicago Tribune*, October 21, 1933.
"Gehringer Succeeds Evans as Tigers' GM." *New York Mirror*, July 29, 1951.
"Gehringer, Tigers' Silent Coach, Lets His Actions Speak for Him." *New York Herald Tribune*, May 3, 1942.
"Gehringer to Quit Game Unless Pilot Job Opens." *Detroit News*, November 22, 1945.
"Gehringer to Succeed Evans as Detroit Boss." *Los Angeles Times*, July 29, 1951.
"Gehringer Will Report to Camp." *New York Times*, December 11, 1940.
"Gehringer Will Visit Japan to Serve as Batting Tutor." *The Sporting News*, January 2, 1965, 8.
Gettelson, Leonard. *World Series Records*. St. Louis: *The Sporting News*, 1976.

Bibliography

Goldberg, Hy. "Sports in the News." *Detroit News*, May 15, 1939.
Greenberg, Hank, and Ira Berkow. *Hank Greenberg: The Story of My Life*. New York: Benchmark, 2001.
Greene, Sam. "Fowlerville Farmboy Completes His Climb." *Detroit News*, February 6, 1949.
———. "Lieut. Gehringer Bids Farewell after 17 Seasons with Tigers." *The Sporting News*, January 7, 1943, 2.
"Hall of Famer Gehringer Called 'Perfect Player.'" *The Sporting News*, May 11, 1949, 2, 10.
"His Back Injured, Gehringer May Quit." *Chicago Tribune*, March 6, 1940.
"His Last Headline." *New York Times*, September 3, 1952.
Holaday, Chris, and Mark Presswood. *Baseball in Dallas*. Mount Pleasant, SC: Arcadia, 2004.
Honig, Donald. *Baseball America: The Heroes of the Game and the Times of Their Glory*. New York: Macmillan, 1985.
"Honor New Hall of Fame Ball Stars." *Chicago Tribune*, June 14, 1949.
James, Bill. *The Politics of Glory: How Baseball's Hall of Fame Really Works*. New York: Macmillan, 1994.
"Joe Falls." *Detroit Free Press*, July 16, 1977.
"Joe Medwick, Gehringer Top Major Hitters." *New York World-Telegram*, August 8, 1937.
"Just Listening." *New York Times*, July 27, 1952.
Kashatus, William. *Lou Gehrig: A Biography*. Westport, CT: Greenwood Press, 2004.
Kaufman, Louis, Barbara Fitzgerald, and Tom Sewell. *Moe Berg: Athlete, Scholar ... Spy*. Boston: Little, Brown, 1974.
Kayser, Tom, and David King. *Baseball in the Lone Star State: The Texas League's Greatest Hits*. San Antonio, TX: Trinity University Press, 2005.
Klein, Frederick C. "Actress and Ex-Senator Believe in Conquering Age by Staying Active; Father of Conglomerate, Ex-Second Baseman and Nobel Winner Agree." *Wall Street Journal*, March 10, 1983.
"The Last G-Man: Gehringer Still Follows Tigers Closely After 44 Years." *Detroit News*, February 8, 1987.
"The Legends Recall Game's Top Legend." *Chicago Tribune*, July 5, 1983.
Lieb, Fred. *The St. Louis Cardinals*. New York: Putnam, 1944.
"Looping the Loops." *The Sporting News*, October 2, 1952, 24.
"No Job-Seekers More Deserving of Votes than Tigers' Gehringer." *Detroit News*, November 2, 1937.
"Obscure Trainer One Reason Why Tigers Lead Race." *New York World-Telegram*, September 14, 1940.
Okrent, Daniel, and Steve Wulf. *Baseball Anecdotes*. New York, Harper & Row, 1985.
"Old Timers Recall Strange Starts." *New York World-Telegram*, October 4, 1955.
O'Neil, Bill. *The Texas League: 1887–1987 — A Century of Baseball*. Austin, TX: Eakin, 1987.
Pietrusza, David. *Judge and Jury: The Life and Times of Judge Kenesaw Mountain Landis*. South Bend, IN: Diamond Communications, 1998.
"Quiet Greatness Should Not Go Gently." *Washington Post*, January 31, 1993.
Rathgeber, Bob. *Cincinnati Reds Scrapbook*. Virginia Beach, VA: JCP, 1982.
Ray, Bob, "Sports X-Ray." *Los Angeles Times*, November 25, 1934.

"Red Rolfe Fired as Tiger Manager." *Los Angeles Times*, July 6, 1952.
"Red Ruffing Club's First Hurler to Win 10 Games." *New York World-Telegram*, July 31, 1940.
"Rest Puts New Life in Mechanical Man." *New York Times*, November 14, 1940.
"Riotous Tigers Gang On Goslin After Victory." *Chicago Tribune*, October 8, 1935.
Ritter, Lawrence. *The Glory of Their Times*. New York: Random House, 1966.
"The Silent Man Hardly Silent These Days." *Detroit News*, February 8, 1987.
Society for American Baseball Research. *The SABR Baseball List & Record Book*. New York: Scribner, 2007.
Spoelstra, Watson. "Gehringer a Blue-Chip Businessman." *The Sporting News*, January 8, 1966, 7–8.
Stanton, Tom. *The Road to Cooperstown: A Father, Two Sons and the Journey of a Lifetime*. New York: St. Martin's, 2003.
Stump, Al. *Cobb: A Biography*. Chapel Hill, NC: Algonquin, 1996.
"This Is Exciting." *Detroit Free Press*, June 7, 1934.
"Tiger Fans Pick All-time Team." *Albany Times Union*, September 27, 1999.
"The Tiger Immortal Nobody Knew." *Super Sports*, October 1971.
"Tiger Second Baseman Snaps Playing Record." *New York World-Telegram*, May 9, 1931.
"Tiger Set Up Stirs Unease of AL Owners." *New York World-Telegram*, July 18, 1952.
"Tigers on Top." *Los Angeles Times*, May 6, 1929.
"Tigers' Run in Ninth Tops Athletics, 6–5." *New York Times*, May 16, 1929.
"Tigers Sign Harris, Former Washington Leader, as Manager." *New York Times*, October 20, 1928.
"Tiger Star Only Modern on All-Nine." *New York World-Telegram*, May 23, 1938.
"Tigers Triumph in Ninth." *New York Times*, July 13, 1929.
"Tigers Win Twice from the Indians." *New York Times*, July 5, 1930.
Werber, Bill, and C. Paul Rogers III. *Memories of a Ballplayer*. Cleveland: Society for American Baseball Research, 2001.
Williams, Joe. "Gehringer Gets The Duke: Could It Be Sentiment?" *New York World-Telegram*, November 2, 1937.
"With 2,000 Games in Pocket, Kaline Eyeing Series Next." *The Sporting News*, May 4, 1968, 11.
"World Series." *Time*, October 14, 1935.
Vincent, Fay. *The Only Game in Town*. New York: Simon and Schuster, 2006.
"Yanks Stop Tigers Behind Pipgras." *New York Times*, July 24, 1929.

Index

Aaron, Henry 147, 166
Adams, Amos 10
Adams, Sparky 36
Alexander, Dale 40, 42, 45, 46, 47, 48, 50, 53
Alexander, Grover Cleveland 24, 106
All Star game 2, 7, 53, 65, 66, 88, 96, 104, 107, 117, 124, 125, 147, 149, 153, 171
Anderson, Alf 150
Atlanta Braves 175
Auker, Elden 8, 55, 60, 67, 68, 71, 74, 75, 76, 77, 86, 87, 89, 90, 91, 93, 96, 99, 103, 104, 105, 106, 108, 109, 116, 119, 132, 153, 172, 176, 177
Auker, Mildred 97, 177
Averill, Earl 40, 82, 107

Bak, Richard 69, 166
Baker, Del 33, 103, 118, 119, 124, 127, 128, 132, 133, 138, 142, 146, 147, 148
Baker, Frank ("Home Run") 158
Bancroft, Dave 35–36
Banks, Ernie 166
Bartell, Dick 127, 128, 135, 139, 140, 142, 172
Baseball Writers Association of America 111, 152, 170
Basler, Johnny 14
Batts, Matt 162
Bearden, Gene 162
Beatty, Jack 15
Beaumont Exporters 51
Bell, Roy ("Beau") 120
Benton, Al 128, 131, 143, 147
Berg, Morris ("Moe") 82, 83, 84, 125, 169
Bertoia, Reno 175
Black, Bud 162
Black, Joe 166
"Black Sox" scandal 28, 87
Bloodworth, Jimmy 146, 147

Blue, Lu 36, 37
Bluege, Ossie 38
Boland, Bernie 27
Bolton, Chester 85
Book Cadillac Hotel 45
Boston Braves 24, 36, 87, 134, 137
Boston Red Sox 17, 25, 26, 32, 34, 38, 40, 41, 46, 47, 49, 50, 51, 63, 68, 70, 80, 83, 89, 103, 118, 124, 127, 131, 162, 169
Boston University 60
Bradley, Alva 129, 130, 135
Braves Field 104
Bridges, Tommy 46, 47, 48, 50, 53, 55, 56, 60, 61, 67, 71, 74, 75, 76, 86, 87, 89, 91, 92, 95, 99, 101, 103, 104, 105, 106, 116, 119, 122, 127, 128, 131, 132, 133, 136, 138, 147, 163, 172, 177
Briggs, Walter ("Spike") 114, 116, 118, 124, 146, 160, 161, 166, 173
Briggs, William O. 98
Briggs Stadium 8, 98, 114, 126, 128, 131, 143, 161, 163
Brock, Lou 19
Brooklyn Dodgers 36, 72, 73, 83, 105, 136, 155, 166
Brown, Clint 82
Brown, Gates 169
Brown, Joe E. 17
Brown, Mordecai (Three Fingers") 155
Brown, Warren 170
Buffalo Bisons 128
Bugaboo bug spray 127
Burnett, Dick 158
Burns, Edward 97, 98
Burns, Jack 102
Bush, Donie 36

Cain, Bob 162
Campanella, Roy 166

195

Index

Campbell, Bruce 139, 140, 147
Capone, Al 52, 90, 125
Carlton, Tex 72, 74
Carroll, Denny 135, 136
Carroll, Ownie 37, 38, 39, 42, 45
Cascarella, Joe 82
Cash, Norm 169
Cavaretta, Phil 93, 94, 95
Chapman, Ray 51
Charlie Gehringer Day 7, 41
Chicago Cubs 24, 32, 36, 90, 91, 92, 93, 95, 96, 97, 98, 106, 127, 137, 151, 157
Chicago Tribune 53, 96, 97
Chicago White Sox 22, 23, 25, 28, 40, 41, 47, 52, 66, 83, 87, 100, 102, 108, 115, 119, 124, 128, 131, 134, 142, 166, 168, 169
Christman, Mark 120
Chrysler Corporation 114, 152
Cincinnati Reds 12, 21, 24, 28, 42, 105, 128, 136, 137, 138, 139
Cleveland Indians 23, 26, 27, 32, 35, 36, 39, 40, 47, 51, 52, 63, 66, 82, 83, 85, 86, 87, 102, 106, 115, 117, 124, 127, 128, 129, 131, 132, 133, 147, 148, 162, 166
Cleveland Plain Dealer 130
Clifton, Herman ("Flea") 62, 93, 96, 172
Cobb, Ty 2, 6, 11, 13, 14, 15, 17, 19, 20, 21, 22, 23, 25, 26, 27, 30, 33, 42, 57, 60, 62, 64, 65, 70, 98, 122, 125, 129, 154, 158, 159, 170
Cobbledick, Gordon 130
Coca Cola 25
Cochrane, Mickey 1, 7, 40, 41, 56, 57, 59, 60, 61, 62, 63, 65, 67, 68, 70, 71, 72, 75, 76, 77, 81, 85, 86, 89, 90, 92, 95, 96, 97, 98, 100, 102, 104, 105, 106, 107, 108, 109, 111, 114, 115, 116, 117, 118, 119, 122, 125, 140, 150, 153, 158, 159, 163, 169, 172, 177
Cole, Bert 13
Collins, Eddie 46, 140, 142, 148, 173
Collins, Rip 34, 72
Columbia University 83
Combs, Earle 31, 35
Comiskey Park 53, 88
Coolidge, Calvin 1, 3
Cooney, Jimmy 32
Corriden, John 93
Cotton Bowl stadium 158
Cramer, Doc 80, 147
Crawford, Sam 13, 70, 170
Cronin, Joe 65, 153, 165
Crowder, Alvin ("General") 67, 68, 73, 76, 86, 89, 93, 99, 103, 104, 106
Crowder, Enoch 68
Cuyler, Hazen ("Kiki") 36

Dallas Eagles 158
Daly, Arthur 168
Daniel, Dan 1, 43, 71, 79, 110, 111, 130, 140, 156
Dauss, George ("Hooks") 13, 22, 25
Dean, Jay Hannah ("Dizzy") 1, 72, 74, 75, 76, 79, 86, 98, 104, 107, 120, 154, 158, 159
Dean, Paul 72, 74, 75, 98
Delsing, Jim 162
Demaree, Frank 91, 93
DeMars, Billy 150
Derringer, Paul 136, 137, 138, 139
Detroit Free Press 43, 62, 65
Detroit News 43, 111, 125, 147, 150, 154, 167
Detroit Tigers 1, 6, 11, 12, 13, 14, 15, 17, 18, 20, 22, 23, 24, 25, 26, 27, 30, 32, 33, 34, 35, 36, 37, 38, 39, 40, 41, 42, 43, 45, 47, 48, 49, 51, 52, 53, 55, 56, 57, 58, 63, 64, 66, 67, 70, 71, 73, 75, 76, 80, 82, 86, 87, 88, 89, 90, 91, 92, 93, 95, 96, 97, 98, 99, 100, 102, 104, 105, 106, 107, 108, 109, 110, 114, 115, 116, 117, 118, 120, 122, 123, 127, 128, 131, 132, 133, 138, 139, 140, 141, 142, 143, 144, 146, 151, 157, 160, 161, 168
Dickey, Bill 65, 103, 105, 154
DiMaggio, Joe 103, 110, 111, 119
Dobson, Joe 131
Doby, Larry 166
Dodge, Daniel 125, 126
Dodge, Lorraine MacDonald 125, 126, 140, 141
Dolittle, Jimmy 85
Dollfuss, Engelbert 82
Donabedian, Harry 159
Dropo, Walt 162
Dugan, Joe 52
Durocher, Leo 72, 73, 75

Easterling, Paul 37
Egan, Wish 141
English, Woody 93
Ervin, Sam 6
Evans, Billy 35, 160
Evers, Johnny 141
Evers, Walter ("Hoot") 162

Faber, Urban ("Red") 40
Falls, Joe 43
Federal Bureau of Investigation (FBI) 90
Feldman, Chick 43, 45
Feller, Bob 117, 127, 129, 131, 132, 133, 134, 149, 162, 173
Ferrell, Rick 63
Ferrell, Wes 33, 176
Fischer, Carl 51, 87
Fisher, Ray 12

196

Index

Fitzgerald, Ed 160
Fitzgerald, Jim 105
Forbes Field 88
Ford, Henry 58, 73
Ford Motor Company 114
Forsyth, Ray 2, 113, 114, 151, 166, 170
Fothergill, Bob 23, 25, 32, 34, 37, 47, 122, 173
Fowler, Ralph 10
Fox, Nelson 169
Fox, Pete 51, 86, 91, 96, 106, 108, 122, 128
Foxx, Jimmy 41, 46, 65, 82, 88, 122, 153, 154
Frauhoff, Harvey 97
Freehan, Bill 169, 172, 175
French, Larry 95
Frey, Benny 12
Frick, Ford 95
Friedolph, Ann 114
Frisch, Frank 54, 65, 72, 75, 77, 141, 153
Fullis, Chick 77
Funk, Eliza ("Liz") 46

Galan, Augie 95
Gallico, Paul 79
Galloway, Chick 36
Garcia, Mike 162
Garver, Ned 162
Gashouse Gang 72, 73, 80, 90, 137, 153
Gehrig, Lou 1, 21, 24, 31, 35, 65, 70, 82, 83, 85, 103, 108, 111, 119, 124, 147, 153
Gehringer, Al 11
Gehringer, Charles: boyhood 10–12; courtship 152–153; death 175; elected to Hall of Fame 154; enters into business 114; fielding strategy 48; first Major League home run 24; as general manager 160–166; hitting strategy 32–33; last game as active player 147; marriage 155; meeting Al Capone 52; minor league career 14–18; number retired 172; personality 1–9, 43–45, 99, 110, 111, 113, 149, 150, 152; playing in pain 140, 142; possible romance 125, 126, 140; released from Tigers 145–146; in retirement 167–175; signing with Tigers 13–14; signs as coach 146; talk of retirement 127, 130, 140, 141, 142; trip to Japan 82–85; wins batting title 109; wins Most Valuable Player Award 110–113; World Series versus Cardinals 72–81; World Series versus Cubs 91–101; World Series versus Reds 136–140
Gehringer, Josephine Stillen 2, 9, 152, 153, 155, 156, 161, 167, 174, 176, 177
Gehringer, Lenard 10, 11, 13, 16
Gehringer, Therese (Theresa) 10, 11, 13, 80, 126, 151

General Motors 25, 114, 160
Georgia Tech 20
Gettysburg Address 8
Gibson, Kirk 172
Gibson, Sam 22, 23, 24, 25, 32, 33, 34
Giebell, Floyd 133, 134, 138
Giles, Warren 170
Gill, George 106, 109, 116, 120
Gilliam, Jim ("Junior") 166
Ginsberg, Joe 162
Goldberg, Hy 125, 126
Gomez, Vernon ("Lefty") 1, 52, 53, 54, 66, 80, 82, 83, 103, 176
Gordon, Joe 124
Gorsica, John 128, 136, 138, 139, 143
Goslin, Leon ("Goose") 56, 57, 63, 64, 68, 70, 74, 75, 86, 87, 89, 90, 96, 97, 99, 103, 105, 106, 115
Grabowski, Johnny 52
Graham, Frank 170
Greenberg, Hank 51, 53, 55, 56, 60, 63, 65, 70, 74, 76, 79, 80, 86, 87, 88, 89, 90, 91, 92, 96, 100, 102, 104, 105, 106, 108, 115, 116, 117, 118, 119, 120, 122, 127, 128, 131, 133, 134, 135, 136, 138, 139, 143, 144, 146, 148, 151, 154, 157, 162, 163, 171, 174, 177
Grew, Joseph Clark 84, 85
Griffith, Clark 37, 38, 39, 165
Grimm, Charlie 90, 91, 93, 95, 97, 137, 158
Grove, Robert ("Lefty") 1, 33, 34, 41, 46, 56, 68, 80, 131, 149, 153, 173

Hack, Stan 93, 95
Hadley, Bump 107
Hallahan, Bill 53, 54, 74
Hall of Fame 2, 7, 14, 16, 37, 68, 152, 154, 155, 156, 159, 170, 175
Haney, Fred 17
Harder, Mel 129, 131, 132
Hargrave, William ("Pinky") 30, 37
Harridge, Will 170
Harris, Bob 120
Harris, Dave 50
Harris, Ned 147
Harris, Stanley ("Bucky") 7, 37, 38, 39, 40, 45, 49, 53, 55, 60, 65, 86
Harper's Magazine 5
Hartnett, Charles ("Gabby") 92
Harwell, Ernie 126, 172, 175
Hatfield, Fred 162
Hayes, Frank ("Gabby") 82, 85
Hayworth, Ray 51, 62, 86, 89, 119, 172
Hegan, Jim 162
Heilmann, Harry 11, 13, 14, 20, 23, 25, 26, 34, 37, 38, 39, 40, 42, 46, 122, 126, 127, 154, 172, 177

197

Index

Hemsley, Rollie 129
Henderson, Rickey 19, 147
Herbert, Ray 162
Herman, Billy 95, 96
Herman, Floyd ("Babe") 105, 109
Hershberger, Willard 136, 137
Higgins, Mike ("Pinky") 119, 128, 131, 138, 139, 147
Hildebrand, George 40
Hitler, Adolph 82
Hogan, Shanty 36
Hogsett, Elon ("Chief") 46, 47, 48, 50, 69, 70, 76, 86, 90, 93, 99, 102, 104, 172
"Hold That Tiger" 97
Holloway, Ken 14, 22, 39
Holy Cross University 37
Hoover, Herbert 176
Hoover, J. Edgar 90
Hornsby, Rogers 36, 45, 141, 173
Houteman, Art 161, 162
Howard, Elston 166
Hoyt, Waite 31, 34, 35, 37, 45, 46, 47
Hubbell, Carl 37, 65, 66, 88, 104, 125, 153, 154
Hudson, J.L. 10
Huggins, Charles 6
Hull, Cordell 85
Humphries, Johnny 117
Hutchinson, Fred 119, 123, 128, 133, 161, 165

Ilitch, Mike 175
International League 129

Jackson, Travis 158
Jamieson, Charlie 32
Jax Air News 150
Jennings, Hughie 49, 70, 154
J.L. Hudson department store 35, 71, 151
Johnson, Ban 27, 28, 35
Johnson, Bob 106
Johnson, Ray 93
Johnson, Roy 39, 40, 42, 45, 50
Johnson, Sylvester 13
Johnson, Walter 24, 31, 34, 35, 51, 149, 173
Jones, Bobby 154
Jordan, Michael 176
Jurges, Billy 93, 95

Kaline, Al 2, 163, 164, 169, 172, 175
Kansas State University 55
Kell, George 161, 162, 172
Keltner, Ken 129
Kennedy, Vern 114, 116, 120, 132
Kerr, Paul 170
Kissele, J.M. 114
Klein, Chuck 95

Klein, Frederick C. 6, 9, 171
Klem, Bill 79
Koenig, Mark 31, 45, 46, 49
Konstanty, Jim 169
Kuenn, Harvey 163
Kress, Ralph ("Red") 120
Kryhoski, Dick 162

Laabs, Chet 120
Lajoie, Napoleon 7, 140, 142
LaMotte, Bobby 30
Landis, Kenesaw Mountain 28, 30, 35, 77, 79, 95, 97, 144, 145
Lane, Frank 165
Larsen, Don 74
Lary, Lynn 99
Lawson, Roxie 106, 108, 109, 116, 120
Lazzeri, Tony 31, 35, 103
Lee, Bill 95, 98
Lee, Thornton 131
Lemon, Bob 162
Lenhardt, Don 162
Leonard, Hubert ("Dutch") 26, 27, 28, 131
Lerchen, George 8
Lewis, Duffy 158
Lexington Hotel 52
Lipon, John 162
Lisenbee, Hod 32
Little, Royal 6
Littlefield, Dick 162
Lolich, Mickey 168, 169, 175
Lombardi, Ernie 136, 137
Los Angeles Dodgers 19
Los Angeles Times 85
Lou Gehrig's Disease 120
Lyon, Cecil Burton (Mrs.) 84
Lyons, Ted 25, 40, 41

Mack, Connie 29, 34, 46, 53, 56, 57, 59, 82, 88, 100, 122
Macy's department store 35
Madison, Dave 162
Malaney, John 170
Mantle, Mickey 163, 165
Manush, Henry ("Heinie") 23, 24, 25, 34, 36, 38, 56, 57, 65, 68
Maranville, Rabbit 154
Marberry, Fred ("Firpo") 51, 53, 63, 69, 71, 76, 86, 87, 100
Martin, Billy 43
Martin, Johnny ("Pepper") 72, 73, 76
Mays, Carl 51
Mays, Willie 166
McAuliffe, Dick 168, 169
McCallister, Jack 36
McCarthy, Joe 1, 24, 106, 129

Index

McCormick, Frank 136, 139
McCosky, Barney 119, 123, 128, 131, 132, 136, 140, 147, 172
McGraw, John 1, 53
McInnis, Stuffy 36
McKain, Archie 119
McKechnie, Bill 36, 137, 139
McLain, Dennis 168, 169
McManus, Marty 30, 31, 32, 34, 39, 40, 45, 47, 51
McNair, Eric 82
"Mechanical Man" 2, 48, 69, 100, 142
Medwick, Joe 72, 74, 76, 77, 78, 79, 174
Meusel, Bob 31, 35
Miller, Ed 82
Miller, Otto 30
Milnar, Al 131, 132
Minnesota Twins 169
Minoso, Minnie 166
Monaghan, Tom 175
Moore, Bill 19, 20
Moore, Wilcy 35
Morgan, Chet 116
Morgan, Ed 119
Moriarty, George 7, 29, 36, 37, 38, 60, 65, 93, 95, 97, 98, 117
Morris, Jack 172
Most Valuable Player Award 2, 51, 70, 89, 110, 111, 113, 117, 140
Mostil, Johnny 40
Mullen, Billy 30
Municipal Stadium 88, 116–117
Murphy, Dan 175
Myatt, Glenn 32
Myer, Buddy

Naleway, Frank 15
Navin, Frank 13, 14, 16, 26, 28, 29, 38, 59, 68, 85, 98, 99, 141, 149, 172, 173
Navin Field 13, 14, 19, 27, 38, 40, 41, 58, 71, 75, 91, 98
Netherland Plaza Hotel 138
Neun, Johnny 32, 126, 168
New York Daily News 79
New York Giants 24, 35, 36, 37, 39, 65, 73, 100, 137, 153, 166
New York Herald Tribune 146
New York Times 29, 39, 168
New York World-Telegram 71, 110, 140, 156, 165
New York Yankees 7, 13, 17, 20, 21, 22, 24, 25, 26, 32, 34, 35, 36, 37, 41, 45, 46, 47, 51, 52, 53, 59, 62, 64, 65, 66, 67, 70, 74, 80, 82, 88, 99, 103, 104, 105, 107, 108, 110, 111, 116, 119, 120, 124, 127, 130, 131, 134, 137, 139, 143, 144, 146, 147, 157, 158, 162, 165

Newark Bears 129
Newcombe, Don 166
Newhouser, Hal 119, 123, 128, 133, 136, 143, 147, 157, 161, 172, 175
Newsom, Lewis ("Bobo") 120, 121, 122, 127, 128, 131, 132, 133, 135, 136, 137, 138, 139, 143, 146
Nichols, Kid 155
Nixon, Richard 6
North Carolina State University 5

O'Farrell, Bob 36
O'Neill, Steve 148, 157
O'Rourke, Frank 21, 22, 25, 30, 31, 35
Ostermueller, Fritz 88
Ott, Mel 154
Owen, Marv 51, 61, 63, 65, 68, 70, 74, 76, 77, 156, 79, 86, 93, 96, 105, 106, 107, 108, 109, 115, 118, 119, 148, 172, 174, 177
Owens, Brick 75, 76, 98

Pacific Coast League 23, 39, 40
Paige, Leroy ("Satchel") 166
Parrish, Lance 172
Pasek, Johnny 56
Pearl Harbor 144
Peckinpaugh, Roger 36
Pennock, Herb 31, 34, 35, 62, 80, 155
Petry, Dan 172
Pesky, Johnny 162
Philadelphia Athletics 23, 27, 29, 33, 34, 36, 40, 41, 46, 47, 49, 56, 60, 68, 80, 82, 87, 89, 99, 100, 103, 122, 128, 129, 150
Philadelphia Phillies 36, 147, 169
Piet, Tony 115
Pillette, Herman 14
Pipp, Wally 21
Pittsburgh Pirates 36, 150, 153, 154, 155
Poffenberger, Cletus ("Boots") 118
Polo Grounds 65, 88, 137
Povich, Shirley 176
Powell, Jake 102
Pratt, Del 14, 17, 18, 21
Princeton University 83

Quinn, J. Robert 155

Radcliff, Rip 143
Ray, Bob 85
Reagan, Ronald 5
Reuther, Walter 113
Reynolds, Carl 63
Rhodes, Bill 15
Rice, Harry 36, 37, 38, 39, 40, 41, 45
Rickey, Branch 73, 155
Rigney, Johnny 132, 133

Index

Rigney, Topper 14
Ripple, Jimmy 139, 140
Rogell, Billy 49, 56, 60, 68, 70, 71, 74, 75, 76, 77, 86, 97, 105, 106, 122, 127, 148, 172, 175, 177
Rolfe, Red 103, 157, 161, 165
Roosevelt, Franklin 82, 107, 144, 145
Roosevelt, Theodore 9
Root, Charlie 91, 92
Rosen, Al 162
Ross, Don 116
Rowe, Lynwood ("Schoolboy") 51, 52, 55, 56, 60, 61, 63, 67, 68, 69, 70, 71, 73, 74, 75, 86, 87, 89, 91, 93, 95, 99, 101, 102, 103, 104, 105, 106, 107, 109, 116, 118, 119, 120, 133 127, 128, 131, 132, 135, 136, 138, 139, 143, 146, 147, 163, 172
Ruel, Herold ("Muddy") 51, 165
Ruffing, Red 103
Ruth, George Herman ("Babe") 1, 20, 24, 25, 26, 31, 33, 35, 50, 53, 56, 59, 65, 82, 83, 84, 87, 92, 98, 103, 116, 117, 122, 124, 153, 158, 167, 168

St. Louis Browns 21, 30, 32, 34, 36, 37, 38, 40, 41, 47, 55, 56, 68, 87, 102, 106, 120, 122, 128, 150, 157, 162
St. Louis Cardinals 24, 36, 71, 72, 73, 74, 75, 81, 90, 93, 120, 139, 153
Salsinger, H.G. 69, 154
San Diego Padres 172
San Francisco Seals 39
Scott, Pete 36
Sewell, Joe 104
Shaughnessy, Frank 170
Shocker, Urban 24, 31, 35
Shore, Dinah 97
Shotton, Burt 36
Simmons, Al 65, 100, 105, 109, 153, 154
Smith, Floyd 12
Smoltz, John 175
Solters, Moose 63
Sorrell, Vic 37, 39, 40, 42, 47, 48, 50
Speaker, Tris 26, 27, 30, 158
Spink, J. Taylor 150, 154, 163, 170
Spoelstra, Watson 150, 151, 167
The Sporting News 150, 151, 154, 163, 165, 170
Sportsman's Park 74
Stanton, Tom 176
Stewart, Lefty 30
Stewart, Marlin 162
Stone, John 38, 46, 47, 48, 50, 56
Stoner, Ulysses ("Lil") 22, 23, 34
Sullivan, Joe 87
"Sultan of Swat" 2

Summa, Homer 32
Summers, Bill 134
Swanson, Gloria 6
Sweeney, Bill 36, 37, 38

Tavener, Jack 37, 38, 39, 49
Taylor, Ben 162
Tebbetts, George ("Birdie") 119, 128, 134
Terry, Bill 73, 154
Terry, Boyd 142
Texas League 23, 37, 51, 158
Thomas, Bud 122
Thompson, Hank 166
Thompson, Junior 136
Tiger Stadium 172
Time magazine 93
Trammell, Alan 172
Traynor, Pie 154, 155
Tresh, Mike 115
Trosky, Hal 129
Trout, Paul ("Dizzy") 119, 124, 128, 133, 138, 143, 147, 157, 162
Trucks, Virgil 147, 157, 161, 162, 163
Tulsa Oilers 158
Turner, Jim 136, 138

Uhle, George 39, 40, 41, 42, 46, 47, 48, 52
United Auto Workers 114
University of Alabama 17
University of Michigan 8, 12

Vance, Charles ("Dazzy") 72, 98
Vander Meer, Johnny 117
Vangilder, Elan 36, 37, 38
Veach, Bobby 11, 12, 13, 14, 20
Vernon, Mickey 146
Virgil, Ossie 166
Vitt, Oscar 129, 130, 131, 132, 133, 135
Vosmik, Joe 176

Wade, Jake 103, 119
Walker, Bill 72, 74, 88
Walker, Fred ("Dixie") 115, 116
Walker, Gerald ("Gee") 49, 50, 68, 74, 79, 89, 103, 104, 105, 106, 108, 111, 115, 123, 163
Walker, Hub 49
Wall Street Journal 6, 171
Walters, Bucky 63, 136, 138, 139
Waner, Paul 154
Ward, Arch 53
Warneke, Lon 91, 95
Warner, Jackie 30, 39
Warstler, Hal 82
Washington Post 176
Washington Senators 7, 23, 24, 25, 28, 31,

Index

32, 34, 35, 37, 39, 41, 50, 51, 53, 55, 56, 57, 65, 67, 68, 82, 83, 87, 99, 100, 102, 106, 115, 122, 128, 146, 155
Webb, Earl 50, 103, 104
Weiland, Bob 63
Weiss, George 165
Welch, Jimmy 36
Wells, Ed 22, 25
Welsh, Chris 175
Werber, Bill 80
Wertz, Vic 162, 172
West, Fred 27
Whitaker, Fred 172
White, Hal 147
White, Joyner ("Jo-Jo") 63, 68, 74, 86, 89, 91, 92, 93, 105, 106
Whitehill, Earl 22, 25, 26, 34, 37, 39, 40, 42, 46, 47, 48, 50, 51, 53, 82, 83, 122
Wight, Bill 162
Wilcox, Milt 172
Williams, Joe 71, 111, 135, 141, 142, 165
Williams, Ted 122, 127, 161
Wills, Maury 19
Wilson, Jimmie 137, 138
Wilson, John 15
Wilson, Woodrow 144
Wingo, Al ("Red") 23, 38
Wood, Jake 168
Wood, Joe 27, 28
Woodall, Johnny 37
World Series 2, 7, 26, 36, 39, 46, 51, 59, 60, 71, 72, 73, 81, 82, 86, 90, 91, 92, 95, 97, 98, 99, 102, 106, 118, 119, 122, 134, 136, 137, 138, 139, 140, 141, 146, 147, 149, 157, 158, 168, 171
Wrigley Field 93
Wuestling, Yats 45
Wynn, Early 162

Yale University 28
"Yankee Clipper" 2, 110
Yankee Stadium 41, 67, 99, 124, 130, 169
York, Rudy 108, 109, 116, 118, 122, 128, 131, 133, 134, 136, 138, 139, 143
Youngs, Ross 35

Zeller, Jack 118, 119, 120, 124, 127, 128, 146

www.ingramcontent.com/pod-product-compliance
Ingram Content Group UK Ltd.
Pitfield, Milton Keynes, MK11 3LW, UK
UKHW042005140426
5217IPUK00015B/992